THE THIRTEEN CLUB
A JOURNEY FROM RICHES TO RAGS AND BACK

HOWARD M. LAYTON

THREE SPIRES PUBLISHING
BROOKFIELD, CT

Published by: Three Spires Publishing
Post Office Box 5267
Brookfield, CT 06804-5267 U.S.A.

Printed in the United States of America

Library of Congress Catalog Card Number 00-104134

Layton Howard M.

THE THIRTEEN CLUB:
A Journey from Riches to Rags and Back
Howard M. Layton
First Edition

ISBN 0-9676008-0-4

Book Design: Paul Perlow
Production: Kathryn-Ann O'Brien

For my children
and
my children's children.

*T*his book is a biography. The events described in its pages are as real and as accurate as collective memories and painstaking research have been able to make them. Place names are given as they were at the time of the events described. Some in Europe were changed at or after the end of World War II when territorial borders were drastically re-drawn. The people are real people and with few exceptions, their names in the text are their real names.

The author asks to be excused for, in one or two instances, writing about what he believed might have been in the minds of others.

ACKNOWLEDGMENTS

For their patience and forbearance over a long series of interviews:

Lászlo B. and Brigitte de Simon, Nokomis, Florida; Erzsébet, Nárcissza, Tamás, András and Paul Ludányi, of Connecticut and Ohio; and Paulette Layton for translating her grandmother's recollections of events.

Virág Prilelszky and her daughter Tücsi; Gyongy Prilelszky and Márika Gaal, all for their overwhelming hospitality during the author's visits to Hungary and for their eagerness to help him in every possible way.

Judith Szendefy and her mother for giving up precious vacation time together so that Judith could help as interpreter for the author.

The author also wishes to express his sincere thanks to the following, for helping him to establish the historical accuracy of the text:

Mr. Paul E. Speicher
Department of Transportation Maritime Division
Office of Ship Construction
Washington D.C.

Mr. Tibor Szilágyi,
Press Attaché
Embassy of the Republic of Hungary, Washington D.C.

Norbert Számvéber
Hungarian Military Records Center in Budapest.

Kilvinger Otto
Kaposvár newspaper SOMOGYI HIRLAP.

For their very helpful and insightful comments and their constructive criticism in reviewing the manuscript, I am grateful to Linda Abbett, Brian Jud, my daughter Christine (Muffin), editor Steve O'Brien, and my dear friends Mildred Roberts and Virginia Weston.

My special thanks also, to Kathryn-Ann O'Brien who coped so cheerfully with my sometimes misguided concepts of what the inside of a book should look like.

Last, but by no means least, I am most grateful for the patient ministrations of my mentor and editor, Professor Theodore A. Rees Cheney.

FOREWORD

Men, women and children flock to these United States for countless reasons—opportunity, freedom, escape from oppression, or just plain restlessness. Their stories, as they strive for a better life in this great country, can be especially moving. Many start truly from scratch, often having limited knowledge of the English language, and not knowing the ropes. And equally often, they start with little more than their dreams and the clothes on their backs.

"The Thirteen Club—A Journey from Riches to Rags and Back,"—is one of those stories. Early on, my wife Priscilla, and I as a college professor in Illinois, played a small role in the life of the woman who features in this account. Today, as we gather around our dinner table, we remember and reflect on her journey.

The author brings us an authentic history of a Hungarian family and an Englishman making their separate ways to these shores, ultimately meeting and building a high-tech manufacturing business together.

Entrepreneurs, whether citizens or newcomers to these United States, will find inspiration and encouragement in this true account of a handful of immigrants, and their struggles to rebuild their lives after fleeing their home and the land of their birth.

August Molnar,
President
American Hungarian Foundation
New Brunswick, NJ.

INTRODUCTION

Walter Johnson traveled a lot. As a senior facilities engineer with Western Electric Company in North Andover, Massachusetts, and already approaching retirement age, he'd eventually earned the right to take five whole weeks vacation each year. Those were the days he lived for. But he didn't journey to the remote reaches of Tibet or China, or bask on the beaches of the Caribbean or the pebbled shores of the Riviera. Those exotic destinations were not for him. Instead, with his mobile home, or with his automobile, he explored the length and breadth of these United States and Canada. Each year, he followed a different route, and even after doing that for fifteen consecutive years, it was his conviction that he hadn't even scratched the surface of the wonders that were to be seen and savored in his own beloved continent.

But Walter seldom traveled on business. He preferred to let his younger colleagues do that. Besides, he didn't think it was necessary. Western Electric's vendors would do a good job, he said, because they were all in it for the long haul, and they all knew that if they messed up, their chances of enjoying a long term relationship with his company would be in serious jeopardy. He knew he was right about that, so he didn't make inspection visits to vendors' factories if he could help it.

Except that one time. That was when I talked him into coming down to see us; to shake hands with the men and women in our company who were taking such pride in designing and building the processing equipment that was rapidly spreading itself around the North Andover factory.

On that day, sitting around the table at Chuck's Steak House in Danbury, we were relaxing after a satisfying lunch. Walter, and his colleague Marlyn Lewis, had toured our plant, seen our setup, and talked with a good assortment of our engineering staff and production workers. They'd expressed satisfaction with their visit and with the equipment designs we'd reviewed that morning. Then, at lunch, Walter told me what he'd really come for.

"All right, Howard, now that we've wrapped things up as far as the business stuff is concerned, you can quit your sales pitch—and while we work on our coffee and dessert, you can tell us a bit about your history."

"What do you mean, Walter? What would you like to know?"

"Well, you know, the company history. How you people came to be doing what you're doing in the first place. I don't want to hear about your profit and loss statements and accounting strategies—or any of the business stuff itself. I want to hear about you and Nárcissza, and the people who made the business tick.

"OK Walter, I'll give you a thumbnail sketch. We designed and built our first product in 1961. It was an ultrasonic clea—"

He cut me off. "No, no. I want to know your *history*—

where you both came from and how you got started. All that sort of thing."

"That's a long story, Walter. It really goes back—back to the time when there were no semiconductors or chips, nor any of the kinds of technical products that we're working with today. In fact," I added, "if you're really interested in what makes us tick, that would take us back as far as World War II."I looked at him questioningly across the table. "You surely don't have time to listen to all that today, do you?"

"Well, that's the interesting stuff," Walter insisted. "And we're not in a hurry—unless you are."

I studied his face, looking for an indication that he was having me on, but his thoughtful expression and deeply furrowed brow gave no such impression, so after a moment or two to figure out just where I should start, I got down to it.

"OK Walter, here goes."

A couple of hours later, on our way out to the parking lot, Walter tapped my shoulder.

"That was pretty interesting stuff, Howard. You really ought to write a book about it."

"Someday, Walter," I said. . "Someday."

That was more than twenty years ago. Walter is no longer with us, but in the years between, others who have come to check us out have listened to our story, too, and in their turn, have made similar suggestions.

So now that 'someday' has arrived, I hope you will agree with Walter Johnson—that the story I told him . . . is interesting stuff.

ONE

U p at the north end of Main Street, near where the railroad tracks cross the hardtop, a stately beige brick
building fronted by tall trees and a small, well-kept lawn, sits
back off the west side. The people of Danbury know it as the
home of the Elks, an organization that for more than a century
has worked to help the youth and the war veterans of their
city. To this end the Elks Lodge of Danbury, Connecticut,
plays host to a continuum of business and private social
functions, charity dinners and lunches, birthday parties, and
private and business anniversaries. Tonight on this crisp
November evening in 1997 it is host to one such event.
Within its walls, in the banquet hall on the ground floor, the
men and women of a small, high-tech manufacturing company called Interlab, are celebrating a thirteen-year span in
business. Tonight is the third of such celebrations, so tonight
is the thirty-ninth anniversary of their company's founding.

We approach this night of revelry at the Elk's Lodge as if
it were the opening scene of a motion picture.

◈

The night cold and crisp. The camera tracks down Main Street from way up at the north end. The view is straight ahead and the glare of oncoming headlights blurs the screen sporadically. The sound of small-town evening traffic comes and goes. We cross the intersection at North Street and make our way down toward Franklin. Soon, thin lines of light, reflected from embedded railroad tracks, ripple down the screen as we approach and pass over them. Not far ahead, the red glow of taillights recedes and merges with brighter street lighting in the distance. We pass in front of the Elks Lodge. The view swings to the right as we turn into the driveway at the south side of the building. We catch a glimpse of the front lawn and the flagpole as we come alongside the south wall. In a moment the camera pans to the right, toward an open window on the ground floor. The lens zooms in for a close-up as we intrude, and the scene in the banquet hall fills our screen. In a moment we are in their midst, and we join their celebration.

Everyone is there: our families and friends, our vendors and customers, and most of those who've served our small enterprise through good times and bad, through triumphs and disasters. Tonight they are all there. They are enjoying the evening as they laugh and talk and clink their glasses or lose themselves in dance.

Over at the bar-hutch at the back of the hall, that slim fair-haired young man is John Prittie. Well, actually, he's not all that young. His boyish, smooth-skinned face belies his near forty years. He is, in fact, the 'old man' of the sales team. His companion—the well-set, sandy haired chap with the ruddy complexion—that's Bob Sendewicz who heads electrical engineering. Picking up their beers, they turn and stroll over to the table near the side wall, where they join more engineers.

There's Bill Fenton who runs development, talking about his hobbies with computer guru Mike Lee. Right now, they're deep into model clock-making, but that soon turns to boats and home-built airplanes as chief engineer Ken Krizan and Tücsi, the tall, attractive young woman who runs sales administration, join them. Despite the fact that they work together all week, they seem to be enjoying each other's company.

At the next table there's Chuck Wrinn of the Housatonic Industrial Development Corp. Chuck, who in earlier days orchestrated the financing for the purchase of the company's factory, is talking with Bob Macklin of Ridgefield's Village Bank. Bob, a quiet and unassuming man, has watched the growth of the company from its early days and has been an unwavering supporter through all its financial ups and downs. On the opposite side of the room, we see more of the company's employees, past and present, engrossed in conversation; those who've gone before, catching up with others who are with the company today. Production supervisor Glenn Dages and his lovely wife Ellen have just joined two of Interlab's former sales engineers, John Tanner and Matt Gallagher. Matt's tall and elegant wife Gwen sits with them. They're all teasing John about the time he drove Interlab's exhibition van under an overpass, which, as he had abruptly discovered, proved a few inches too low for the purpose.

The camera pans to the dancers. Near the middle of the floor, my wife Nárcissza and I are dancing to the music of the 'Merry Widow' waltz. Vice-Presidents Tamás (Tom) and Patyi (Paul) Ludanyi share the floor with us, gyrating enthusiastically. They, Nárcissza's right and left hand in business, are also her brothers. With their spouses, Renate and Teresa, both graceful and accomplished dancers, they are reveling in the timeless beauty of this old-fashioned waltz. As there are only a few on the floor for this one, we take advantage of the extra room for movement. Longer steps, bolder turns, around and around, faster and faster—we're whirling around the floor as fast as we can.

As the exuberance of the occasion swells to its peak, the scene begins to fade. The music and the dancing gradually dissolve into a new scene. We are transitioned back through the years and across the seas to the cratered fields of Europe where our story begins. It is 1944 and against a background of rolling hills and vineyards, a small child stands under the open sky, watching in wonder as the bombs fall close around her.

She heard the droning long before they arrived. She was used to it. At first it was so faint it could hardly be heard above the rustling of the leaves in the coppice bordering the vineyards where she and her brothers and Édesanya came every year to spend their summers. Then, as she turned her eyes toward the northern sky she saw them—formations of lumbering war birds returning from their bombing missions in eastern Germany. In the early morning they had come, these mighty fleets of American bombers, their noise thunderous as they passed overhead, climbing toward the Alpine peaks on their way to their targets. Then between mid-day and mid afternoon, they would return, and once out of the areas of heavy ground fire and clear of the mountains, they would gradually descend along the same route over Southern Hungary again, on their way to their home bases, far to the south.

Today, as often happened, her mother Erzsébet (Elizabeth) had gone with her four sons and their maid to buy groceries

in the village near Bagola. The round trip to the village center, two kilometers distant, took most of the day, so they'd set
off in the morning, taking a picnic lunch with them. When
they finished their shopping, they would find an unoccupied
bench in the small park nearby. There, they'd rest themselves
and eat their sandwiches. After lunch they would make their
way back home at a leisurely pace, arriving at the vineyards
again near mid-afternoon. Patyi (Paul), the youngest, rode
serenely in a large well-sprung baby carriage, seeming to
absorb every new sight and sound. Always on his best behavior during these shopping expeditions, he evidently wanted
everyone to know how much he was enjoying himself.

His older brothers Tamás, András, and Tony, looked forward to these outings too. They'd feast their eyes on all the
good things on display in the grocery store and the bakery,
and were sometimes able to prevail on their mother to buy
sweets for them. There wasn't much to be had in wartime
Hungarian villages, but they could usually count on finding
their favorite licorice candy shoestrings (medvecukor). When
that wasn't available, colored rock candy filled the bill. Not
as tasty, but it did last longer.

Tony, but three years old, couldn't always complete the
round-trip on foot, but not wishing to be thought of as a
mere infant and as helpless as his baby brother, he'd plod on
stoically until he could plod no more. Most often, by the time
the family arrived back at the vineyard, and were making
their way up the path to their home again, Tony would be
asleep in the baby carriage alongside his baby brother.

So Nárcissza was alone on this August day. The air fresh
and the sun shining as it was today, she was free to play and
enjoy a few hours in the vineyards all by herself. When it
rained she'd use the opportunity to explore the closets,

nooks and crannies of the huge white stucco mansion which had become her family's summer home. Known affectionately as the 'Garden of Eden' it sat proudly atop a rolling hill, a vantagepoint that offered a panoramic view of the surrounding grape-growing countryside.

A large derelict ballroom with parquet floors, a huge fireplace and two old, out-of-tune grand pianos occupied more than half of the upper floor of the mansion. Through a double door at one end of the ballroom, a second room, almost as large, and now bare of furnishings, had once been a flourishing restaurant. The wooden verandah surrounding the house at that level had been similarly neglected. When she and her brothers played out there, they had to stay close to the wall of the house to avoid falling through spaces where the floorboards were loose or missing.

The ground floor, by contrast, had been completely refurbished and redecorated. Nárcissza and her family had two large bedrooms there, and a spacious living and dining area. At the other end of the building there were the caretaker's living quarters, with a cavernous basement below, serving as a wine cellar. With its land and vineyards, and with the old mansion on it, the place was a country paradise. Her father, Colonel Antal Ludányi, had purchased it at a very modest price—a considerable privilege since in those times there was little opportunity for the general public to purchase land at any price. But Colonel Ludányi was a Vitéz. Through acts of heroism as a lieutenant in the first World War, he'd earned the coveted title of Knight of the Order of Vitéz, an honor bestowed by the Regent on citizens, civilian or military, for outstanding service to their country. With that title came certain privileges. The opportunity to purchase land for personal use at an affordable price was one of them.

These occasions when she could sometimes be alone at their summer home were a special treat for Nárcissza, for although she loved her parents and her brothers very much, she found peace and joy in occasional solitude. Erzsébet understood her daughter who sometimes seemed too old for her ten years, and when Nárcissza would occasionally ask to be excused from the family's comings and goings, she didn't raise objections.

But this day was not like other days, for Nárcissza began to hear gunfire from the direction of Nagykanizsa, the town to the north, where an artillery division was stationed. She found this unusual because Hungarians didn't really regard the Americans as an enemy and did not defend themselves against their aircraft as they came over. They were simply considered to be enemies of the Germans. But the previous week there'd been some 'carpet' bombing nearby—perhaps not in the spirit of aggression, but more likely because the American fliers had some bombs left over that they had to get rid of. They had nonetheless done a fair amount of damage and the present gunfire was probably a Hungarian reaction to the attack on their villages. As the formations came near and the droning rose to a crescendo, one of the behemoths burst into flames and, falling away to one side of the formation, came hurtling toward the ground in a heart-stopping spiral. Nárcissza was petrified and fascinated at the same time. She couldn't take her eyes from the vivid scene before her. She was sure the plane would land right on top of her, right there where she stood under the pine tree, but she could not move.

In less than a minute, as the bomber came closer to the ground, she saw that her eyes had deceived her, for it fell among the trees several hundred meters away. She shud-

dered as she heard the noise of its impact and felt the rever-
berations in the air and under her feet. Then she saw a little speck in the sky, circling the other bombers. It looked
just like a mosquito attacking a flight of eagles, but very
soon another of the bombers spurted flame and began to
descend more steeply than its neighbors. Black smoke
trailed from its wings as it continued its flight toward to its
base somewhere beyond the southern border. As it passed
overhead, parachutes came billowing from its belly one after
another, but the airplane kept on flying.

The little speck continued its relentless attack on the
bombers, circling and picking them off one at a time, and
before the last of the several flotillas had passed overhead,
two more bombers had fallen out of the sky, disgorging their
aircrews, parachuting them to safety. Nárcissza stood there,
transfixed, and continued to watch. In the end, when they'd
gone, she saw the little fighter plane on its way down and
coming near, with the engine coughing and one wing on
fire, and somehow it was glorious. The whole display had
seemed to her like a modern version of David and
Goliath—this little airplane and the small under-equipped
Hungarian artillery battery had taken on the disdainful and
all-powerful enemy and had badly bruised him.

She stood there sobbing, overcome by the example she'd
seen of willpower and boundless courage prevailing against
crushing odds, and she knew in her child's heart that what
she had witnessed and experienced on this August afternoon in 1944 would stay with her always and would become
a part of who she was and who she would become.

TWO

The front moved closer to Budapest by the day. The colonel's wife Erzsébet and their children were already at their home in Kaposvár where, at the end of August, they'd returned from their summer home at the vineyards near Bagola. She'd brought some of their horses and a couple of wagons with them. Erzsébet had received a warning from her husband that upon their return to Kaposvár, she should make preparations for departure at what might be very short notice. They should plan to take everything of value with them. Meanwhile they should carry on as usual and await further word from him.

At first they'd been told that when the time came for them to leave, they would all proceed to Zala, the regiment's base, where a larger evacuation of families of the military was being organized. Later, Antal had advised them against this, since in his view, Zala was likely to fall to the Russians within a month of the fall of Kaposvár. Instead, he would arrange for them to go to Csallóköz, an area to the northwest of Budapest which was of less immediate importance to the Russians. There, they would be safe until their evacuation across the border into Germany could be arranged. Antal was profoundly relieved when on November 20th during a brief lull in the fighting, he was given a short leave of absence to carry out his plan and take his wife and children and a number of other families to Csallóköz himself. Upon reaching the area, they would proceed to the small village of Bacsfa on the Danube shore, where they would stay with relatives.

In the intervening weeks Erzsébet busied herself packing. Although she treasured her beautiful porcelain and china sets and cut-glass bowls and glassware, she knew they wouldn't survive the kind of traveling conditions they would have to contend with. As she stacked these things in the display cabinets she ran her fingers over the two old Chinese platters that, her grandmother had told her, a wealthy acquaintance had offered to buy for their weight in gold. But there was no time or opportunity now to dwell on what might have been.

The sorting and stacking done, she closed the glass doors and turned to give her attention to things of more practical value—comforters, sheets, blankets, and cooking ware; things such as her beautiful Damask tablecloths. There were sets of these, some for six places with matching napkins, and some for twelve. These would take up very little room, but would fetch a good price whenever they'd need money for food or shelter. Then, sandwiched between clothes and blankets, she packed all her silver and jewels and others thing of value that she could barter for food, or sell later if she had to. Finally she packed the small collapsible cot for Patyi.

When her husband learned that Erzsébet had packed the cot, he objected, declaring that it would take up too much valuable space. Much to his surprise, however, his usually quiet and compliant wife responded defiantly and with hands on her small hips she glared up at Antal's stern face. "Well then, I'm not going," she said vehemently. "I need a clean place for this little child, so no matter where we go, I can set up a bed for him."Indignant, she continued. "Other people are carting trunks of porcelain that it wouldn't even occur to me to bring with us, but this bed will fold and with its thin mattress it will take up very little space. Without this, I'm not going." The colonel looked down at his wife's determined face and smiled indulgently. They took the bed.

By this time, some of the Ludányis' relatives and other officers and their families had assembled in or close to Antal's home in Kaposvár. The town itself was swarming with new arrivals who, as the result of the Rumanian turnabout and the Russian advance, were fleeing west by the thousands. Antal knew he'd have his hands full. When he'd arrived there on the morning of the 20th, he'd found that two rooms of his home were already occupied by a captain Nonay and his wife and son. This officer had been injured in the first world war so had not been on front line duty. Then an aunt and cousin had arrived and it had been necessary to find accommodation for them, too. Altogether there was much confusion. All schools had closed several weeks before. The buildings were needed for the accommodation of women and children fleeing from the east. Canon fire could already be heard in the distance. It was clear to Antal that he'd have to get them out of there without delay. In fact, he decided, they must leave that very day,

When they were all lined up and ready for departure, he found he would be taking a total of five families. There were the Krizanics—a woman whose daughter's husband was Ludányi's regiment doctor, who had, in fact, delivered Tony a few years earlier. The seven-months pregnant wife of a

Major Szabados had also joined them. Next, they had been joined by the wife of Ludányi's adjutant, Captain Létay, their two-year-old son, and her mother and grandmother. Finally, Kosa, a warrant officer in his mid-sixties, and his wife and nineteen-year-old daughter, joined the party, too. By the afternoon, they were ready for departure.

Nárcissza joined those who'd been assigned to the ambulance, and Erzsébet and her sons rode with Antal in his military car, with their truck following behind. The Ludányis two horse-drawn wagons would follow separately and would join them a few days later.

One small delay. When all were aboard, Erzsébet realized that she'd forgotten to bring her smoothing iron and she somehow felt it important to have that item with her. She called her daughter and bade her return to the house to get it. Nárcissza ran back to the house and quickly searched through the kitchen and the laundry room, but the iron was not in any of its usual places. On impulse, she ran to the nursery and found it on a side table. Picking it up, she moved slowly around the familiar room, allowing her fingers to touch the well-worn chairs and table she'd lived with every day; the small bed frames, now stripped of sheets and blankets; the children's clothes closets with their brightly painted doors; the toys they'd treasured, now scattered across the floor.

She stood in the middle of the room, her eyes moving once more over each piece of the beloved furniture, as if to imprint on her mind all of the shapes; the rich dark colors and the furniture polish odors around her. On her way out through the dining room she paused by the old commode that had belonged to her great-grandmother—the place where she'd kept her books year in and year out. She ran her fingers over its smooth polished surface, and as she did so, it came to her that she would not see it again. There would be no return. While others had talked optimistically about being away for a few weeks—or at the most five or six months—she knew at that moment that it would not be so. She lingered a moment longer, saying a silent good-bye. Then she ran out of the room, through the hall and into the street, not looking back. She climbed back into her place in the ambulance, and the motley assortment of vehicles began to move. Soon Kaposvár and her home were out of sight.

By nightfall, they'd reached the town of Sümeg and, with the proviso that they'd leave by noon of the next day, they had gained permission to spend the night in one of the school dormitories. They slept on blankets, or on whatever they'd managed to bring with them that would suit the purpose. Their departure from Kaposvár had been none too soon, for in the morning they received word that the city had already fallen. It was now essential that they continue their journey with all possible speed.

Surprisingly, there was talk among the women about who should go on to the north and who should go to the regiment's base in Zala. The discussion appeared to center on the acceptability of the mode of transportation. The high-born ladies, each convinced that she should accompany the Colonel in his military automobile, seemed offended by the prospect of riding in one of the trucks. The impracticability of their desires, and the necessity that the small children ride with Erzsébet so that they could sleep and be properly cared for, seemed to have escaped their notice. Even to the youthful Nárcissza it was a source of discomfort that these sophisticated ladies should so quickly lose their social graces and behave so strangely and selfishly.

Nothing to be done. The colonel, bemused by the com-

ments and the huffiness, said simply that those who wished
to continue with the group should make haste and get
aboard, and those who wished to stay should await the
transportation that would eventually come to take them
where they wished to go. With two thirds of the original
number, Colonel Ludányi set out on the journey north to
Bacsfa, and by a late hour of that night they arrived at their
destination. With a promise that he would be in touch again
soon, the colonel then left to rejoin his regiment at the front.

Rooms had been prepared for the Ludányis at the home
of their relatives, cousins once removed. Nárcissza and her
brothers settled themselves in, and set about the business of
getting to know their counterparts in their new-found family.
Of the three children they met, Imre, a boy some six months
younger than Narcissza, really intrigued her. He was, she
decided, the very first child of her age she'd met who actually knew more than she. When she thought about it, she
realized that she'd never consciously compared herself with
anyone else as far as brains were concerned. But now that
she found herself acknowledging that someone else was
smarter than she, she concluded that Imre must be a genius.

For one thing, he told her he'd fallen down a whole flight
of stairs and landed on a concrete floor at the bottom. The
fall had fractured his skull, and that, she supposed, must
have had something to do with his strangeness. Imre told
her that he was a special angel sent down from God, and in
a way she began to believe him. So they became fast friends
who regularly fought like cats and dogs but entertained each
other throughout the several weeks of their stay in Bacsfa.

At night, darkness enveloped them. They didn't have electric light because they had to save on petroleum, so she and
Imre told stories in front of the fire. On one of these nights,

Imre told her about the invention he'd thought of that used rubies to create a killer beam. With intensity he told her that this beam (actually invented in later years as the laser), would stretch across the borders of Hungary and anyone who dared step over it would be eliminated. At other times they'd play chess, and Imre mostly won because, among other things, he insisted that she could not take his queen with her pawn. "It's in accordance with the rules," he told her, and she lacked the experience to argue that it was otherwise.

When one of her father's officers, an invalid from the front, arrived in Bacsfa, Imre eventually had to abandon his privately contrived rules. The officer liked to play chess, too, and quickly pointed out to Imre that his rules differed from everyone else's. Unfortunately for Imre, exposure of his unconventional manipulations happened to coincide with Tamás's breezy entrance at the critical moment. Tamás, the eldest of Nárcissza's brothers, bent on urging everyone to listen to the story he had to tell, rushed over to the chess playing group, but when he saw the spirited banter in progress, he decided to join in and save his thrilling story for later. Profound thinking for a nine-year-old.

Imre conceded as graciously as he could manage, offering the explanation that he'd been taught to play chess by his family's butler and had assumed that what he'd learned was the way everyone else played. When all those present seemed satisfied that Imre had been adequately brought down to size, Tamás sensed that the time was right to tell his story. He told them he'd been out walking and talking with the sergeant in charge of the horses. When they'd sat on one of the stable benches for a rest, the sergeant had said, "Well, I suppose I'd better make sure my pistol is clean and ready for action." With that, he'd pulled the weapon out of its holster and fired it into the snow bank. Tamás, who had never in his nine years seen a pistol fired, except at the firing range, had been thrilled and awed by the event, especially since the horses made a fuss about it, too. They'd bucked and reared, and several minutes had passed before all was quiet again.

Tamás looked around at the faces of his listeners. Satisfied that they were duly impressed, he withdrew to his allotted corner of that one room where the Ludányis spent their nights. Soon Imre and the officer left for their own quarters, and the Ludányi family—father, mother, their maid Margit and the five children—settled themselves for the night.

In the following days, the Ludányi children, seeming to sense that these might be the last days they would spend in their homeland, welcomed every opportunity to make the most of every day. They played the days away with their cousins. When they weren't off somewhere with their new-found friends, they reveled in the frequent family sleigh rides in the crisp winter snow. The horse-drawn sleighs were roomy enough for them to travel in comfort, all wrapped up in blankets. Before they set out, the blankets would be warmed with heated building bricks to keep them as warm as possible during the long cross-country outings. Traveling this way, their feet and bodies tingling, and their cheeks reddened by the clear winter air, they were content to go on and on, suspended between a yesterday that was no more, and a tomorrow that they could not begin to imagine.

THREE

Soviet forces were already approaching the region of the Budapest outer defense positions but had halted their advance to allow time for reinforcements to be brought up from the south for the final push into the city. To take advantage of the short pause in the fighting during this phase, Colonel Ludányi was ordered to proceed to Zala to assemble reinforcements from his reserve regiment. His instructions were to bring them to the front to strengthen the defense positions and replace those who'd been killed or wounded. His plan was to take his assistant adjutant, Odor Laszlo, and chief radio operator Illes Ernö with him. On their way, they would drop Antal at Bacsfa so he could spend a day with his family, and complete arrangements for them to join a caravan of more than two hundred other military families escaping into Germany. His chauffeur, Sergeant Venczel, would drive the others on to Zala to assemble the reserve contingency, and pick up the colonel on the way back.

At mid-day on Christmas Eve, the party pulled in to the entrance to his family's temporary home. Erzsébet, preparing food in the kitchen, was the first to hear the crunching of their tires on the driveway. She rushed to open the door, but the children raced past her, bounding through the doorway to swarm all over their warrior father. He reached out and lifted Erzsébet off her feet and held her in a tight embrace. She put her arm around her husband's waist and led him inside.

She stood back from him, studying his face, noting the deeply etched lines and the shadows beneath his eyes. Pointing to a comfortable armchair she said firmly, "Édes, you must rest and I will make soup for you." Later, when he'd taken his fill of the delicious soup, he began to talk about his concerns for his family's safety. He didn't get very far before his eyes closed and deep exhaustion overtook him. Erzsébet cradled his head in her arms as he slipped into irresistible oblivion.

The three other members of his party returned the following afternoon, but to Antal's dismay their mission had failed. Because of a communications glitch, the base commander hadn't received advance notice of their mission and had been unable to assemble any reinforcements within the few hours of their stay. Realistically, there was no time now to remedy the situation. It was simply too late.

Antal, anxious to reach the front before the expected new Russian offensive began, set off for Budapest with his men. Again, they were too late. During their brief absence, the Russians had completely surrounded Budapest itself and neither Antal nor his companions were able to find a way through the Russian lines to participate in the final defense of the city. They tried unsuccessfully to make their way through the woods to bypass the Russian forces. After several failed attempts, he reported their predicament to the nearest military headquarters. The commander there instructed him to abandon his efforts and join a group in Szenc where he would take charge of the military evacuation party now being assembled, and which his own family had by this time joined. Antal concluded that although he'd continued to fight when the new fascist regime under Szallasi had taken over the government, his refusal to swear loyalty to the new leader had called into question his reliability. The new pro-German top brass had probably decided that, under the circumstances, Ludányi's new assignment was a prudent one.

Led by Colonel Ludányi, the evacuation party of about five hundred and sixty souls departed the city of Szenc the last week in March. Bound for Bavaria, they headed first to Pozsony (Bratislava), then turned west toward Austria. Four days later they crossed the border, leaving their homeland behind. They were only just in time. By April 4th the whole of Hungary was under Russian domination.

The caravan included some two hundred horse-drawn wagons and a number of coaches that would each seat three or four people. In addition, because of the fuel shortage, a pair of farm horses towed the colonel's car. Apart from the women and children, the party included the military contingent, the colonel's adjutant, the medical officer and two or three junior officers. A number of non-commissioned officers and enlisted men tended the horses and operated the horse-drawn kitchen canteen. Simple cooked meals were prepared on the move so that they were available to everyone by the time of the midday break. The only other food available for the party was whatever they had each brought with them.

Some had sufficient provisions at first to enable them to satisfy their appetites with a modest breakfast and an evening meal and so avoid the somewhat primitive fare the military provided at mid-day. After a few days, however, when supplies began to run low, increasing numbers of the travelers were turning to the military kitchen for sustenance.

On some days, Koleszár András, a cheerful priest in his sixties who called himself Andor, held services in the woods. He held Mass for those of the Catholic faith and for any others who chose to attend. A lady named Berecz, a Sunday school teacher of Lutheran faith, led religious gatherings for Protestants. In addition to his sole suitcase and his three overcoats, all of which he wore at the same time, Andor had brought a barrel of wine with him. Each day, when he'd imbibed a sufficient quantity of his wine, he would tell stories to all who'd care to listen. They were stories of a kind that gave good cheer and helped weary travelers forget their plight for a brief while. At other times Andor sat at the back of his wagon next to his barrel, drinking what he deemed necessary to maintain his own good cheer.

Duci and Dália, the colonel's riding horses, were now assigned to towing loads. They were not, of course, required to pull wagons as heavy as those that their more robust companions were called upon to cope with every day and often at night as well, but they nevertheless filled their unaccustomed roles quite well. Although Duci, inclined to be temperamental, would often refuse to tackle the steeper hills—at times holding up the entire caravan—patient coaxing, combined with the more stoic example set by her partner Dália, usually resulted in her eventual cooperation.

Mostly, when there were woods nearby, the travelers took their blankets and tarpaulins and spent their nights among the trees. At other times they found places to pull the vehicles off the roads and park them out of the way of other road users. On such occasions, the majority slept in their wagons and trucks. Erzsébet stayed in her seat in the car, with the smaller children around her and Patyi on her lap. Tom slept in the front with his father, and Nárcissza, her mattress wedged between the luggage rails on the roof of the car, settled herself serenely, and savored the cold night air. If she just looked straight up, so that she couldn't see the tops of the trees on each side, the stars and limitless constellations would envelop her and she was able to drift on imaginary rides among them before she went to sleep. On those clear, crisp nights she was no longer fleeing a relentless enemy or struggling to survive; she was riding through the midnight firmament, invincible and untouched by the uncertainties of the day.

When morning came, uncertainty returned; lack of sufficient food no longer their only problem. On the second day of their journey toward the Austro-Bavarian border, low-flying Russian aircraft attacked the caravan. Wave after wave of machine-gun fire raked their columns. They pulled off the road as fast as they were able. Although they suffered no human casualties on this occasion, the gunfire wounded two of the most able horses, and they had to be shot. They did provide much-needed food for the travelers, but their loss took its toll on the overall pace of their progress.

Late in the second week, paramilitary Bavarian police, indifferent to their plight and their evident fatigue, barred their way. No more room in their district for refugees, they told them. There was nothing they could do but turn around and look elsewhere. They retraced their steps, re-crossing the border and set up camp for the night on the Austrian side.

In the morning Ludányi led his party across the border again at a different location, but before the end of the day, officials who made it clear that there would be no asylum in Bavaria for Hungarian refugees, again stopped them. The villagers refused them water to quench their thirst and to wash their young ones. They locked their water pumps and barred their doors. They were themselves short of food and essentials for living and were in no mood to play hosts to any more of the hordes fleeing the Russian advance.

The women foraged for whatever they could find in the fields. Erzsébet, already slim and petite, began to lose weight, not only through hunger, but because of her preoccupation with the plight of her younger children. They needed milk and eggs and protein and there was not enough of any of these to be had. The military kitchen fare simply did not provide either the quality or the quantity of food needed by small growing children.

With her husband occupied with his duties during the day and the early evening, Erzsébet had to deal with this problem without his help. She became creative in preparing sourgrass and a variety of wild roots in various ways. Since her evenings were occupied with preparing meals and helping their maid with the washing and drying of her children's clothes, she chose the early morning hours to look for food.

Before the long line of vehicles started on the new day's trek, she left Nárcissza and the maid to look after the younger ones, and set off into the woods to forage for sour grass and edible roots. Antal insisted that one of the soldiers go with her, for she could not walk safely in the woods alone. On some days she'd be fortunate in her mission, the thick woods yielding an abundance of pine nuts, sorrel, mushrooms and sour grass, but often, the nearest cluster of trees that she would have time to reach, would offer her only the most meager handful of anything edible.

She learned to make the most of whatever she could find. She discovered that by mixing the items from her daily foraging with some of the grains and foods that she could get from the military kitchen, she could create an acceptable and presentable variety of dishes to serve to her family.

But it was not enough. She could feel her own strength failing, and as the days went by she saw that both Patyi and Tony, habitually energetic and interested in everything about this special adventure, were now becoming pale and listless. She was desperate and afraid. Each morning when she set off into the nearby countryside and had found a place that seemed promising for her purpose, she bade her bodyguard soldier to remain at a respectful distance as she knelt on the damp grass at the foot of the tallest tree she could find. Then, raising her head so that she could see patches of sunlight through the leaves and the branches at the top, she clasped her hands together and in a small but fervent voice she prayed, "Dear God, please help me see my children through this terrible time. Please give them strength."

On some days there would be no woods close to where they had stopped to rest, but always there was a place—a bush in a hedge dividing the fields, or a few trees in a meadow close to where they happened to be. She would pick the tallest tree or bush she could find and choose the place where she would kneel so that when she raised her eyes she could see the leaves meeting and intermingling with the sky. That somehow seemed right to her—Heaven and Earth coming together, a comforting place for her purpose.

Eventually her prayers were answered, but in a sad and unexpected way. The human members of the party were not alone in their suffering, for many of the horses, too, began to lose their strength as food became scarce. Although most were farm animals accustomed to hauling ploughs and other machinery of the land, their present loads were yet heavier and the hauling of much longer duration than even the most exacting farming schedules. Gradually, the combination of hunger and fatigue took its toll. Those horses that were ailing and no longer able to pull their loads were carefully watched. They were not allowed to die. When their last days were upon them, they were shot to provide food so that hungry men, women and children could live.

Before the journey had ended, six of the horses in the caravan had given their lives in this manner, but they had not died in vain. The protein-rich horsemeat served to supplement the other dwindling food supplies at a crucial time, and for many of the undernourished travelers, especially the children who would otherwise have succumbed before journey's end, the horsemeat made just enough difference. Even then, the shortage of food coupled with a lack of adequate medical supplies eventually took its toll of humans, too. Although the Ludányi children survived, three of the other little ones in the group did not.

After several more days and three more failed attempts to set up camp somewhere near their originally intended destination in Bavaria, Ludányi and his officers determined that, for a time at least, they would have to find accommodation on the Austrian side of the border. When they came to a sizable village, the officers sought out the mayor and requested permission for the group to stay at the farms in the vicinity. At first, permission was refused, but then the group's doctor, a Hungarian-born German from a German settlement in Hungary, told the mayor that the party was a special SS section of Hungarians with certain privileges. The mayor, very much in awe and fear of the Nazis, thereupon changed his mind and promptly issued papers authorizing the group to obtain accommodations at the various farmhouses in the neighborhood.

Colonel Ludányi and his family were fortunate in that

they were allotted a large room which had its own cooking stove, whereas most of the other families shared kitchen facilities. The disadvantage, however, was that the Ludányi's room was next to a pungent pigsty. But it could be worse, far worse. They had a place to sleep and keep warm, a place to rest themselves awhile and wash their bodies and their filthy clothes; a place that would give them time to think about tomorrow. It could be worse.

By this time, everyone was convinced that the war must soon be over, but opinions varied on just when that would be. In this rural area, far from the centers of activity, very little disturbed the everyday tranquility. They did not hear the roar of big guns or the general noise of war. They heard nothing. But their respite was short lived. A couple of days after their arrival, as the Ludányis were seated around the table in their quarters eating their lunch, one of the colonel's junior officers appeared at the door. Four Russians, whose guns were now aimed directly at the occupants of the room, surrounded him. The young officer spoke, "Colonel, I have to report to you that I'm under arrest," which was, of course, obvious. The colonel did not speak. Pale but in control of himself he rose slowly and began to unbuckle his gun belt. The lieutenant, alarmed by this action said, "Colonel, put your hands up so they will know that you have no bad intentions." Ludányi, without pausing in his action, replied, "That is the one thing that I shall never do in my life." He then handed his gun belt to the Russians.

The Americans, it transpired, had just released his captors from prison. They were hungry and thirsty and they wanted tobacco; they were not intent on killing anyone. They were about a hundred in number and they deemed it their job to round up the Hungarian soldiers and take them to the

Americans, so Colonel Ludányi and his officers and men were taken away.

When the door closed behind the departing colonel and his captors, their landlord, the old farmer, realized that the war must be over. He began to sob, wringing his hands as he paced slowly up and down the farmhouse room. In a while, he stopped his pacing and turned his gaze to the portrait of Hitler hanging on the wall. He reached out and snatched it off its hook and, continuing his pacing, he began to mutter. Like most of his countrymen, he had known nothing of the concentration camps and the atrocities that his Feuhrer had perpetrated. He had believed that Hitler would make his nation great—a world power. He crushed the portrait with his fist and, turning mindlessly this way and that, finally slammed it to the concrete floor. He was staring at it, still sobbing, as it shattered into a thousand pieces.

Erdöss, a young lieutenant, had not been in the vicinity at the time of the raid. He had learned a little of what had happened and had stayed out of sight until the coast was clear. That night he and his batman, Joseph, made their way to the Ludányis' quarters to see what they could do to help. It was not easy to stay out of sight for by this time a number of former Russian and Serb prisoners were roaming around the farmhouses, getting drunk and looting. When Erdöss and Joseph got to the farmhouse where the Ludányis were quartered they found that the doors had all been locked and the windows shuttered. Since the building was built like a fort, access was not easy, but Erdöss was a newspaper reporter who had managed to escape through the lines at the Siege of Stalingrad and he had some experience in solving such problems. He and Joseph moved around the outer wall as quietly as possible until they found an area that was out of the direct line of sight of the other farmhouses. They scanned the rooftop for a means of access to the building and discerned the outline of a small dormer window halfway up the sloping roof.

They climbed one of the iron drainpipes, hoping that their weight would not be too much. The pipe held fast. One at a time they hauled themselves over the eaves and onto the slate-tiled rooftop. Moving carefully to avoid sending any loose slates clattering to the ground, they inched their way to the dormer. Luckily the dormer window was slightly ajar—enough so that Erdöss could reach in to release the retaining bar and thus swing the window wide open. But the clear opening, now inviting their entry, was not really designed for that purpose. Even for the slim and athletic Erdöss it was a tight squeeze, but for the more rotund Joseph it proved a truly daunting obstacle. Erdöss was already inside and making his way down the attic stairs when Joseph's hissing stage-whisper compelled him to retrace his steps and go to his batman's aid. Joseph was stuck. His upper body was projecting through the dormer window opening, but his middle was firmly wedged in the window frame.

Erdöss grasped his batman under his armpits and hauled, easing the man's torso from right to left and from left to right as he did so. In this manner the rest of Joseph's body, somewhat bruised, was coaxed farther and farther through the opening. Finally, with one last heroic heave, Erdöss deposited the disheveled Joseph in a crumpled heap upon the attic floor.

Fearing that their less than stealthy entry must have been heard by the occupants of the room below, Erdöss called Erzsébet's name to avoid alarming her. Erzsébet heard, but she did not recognize his voice. As he entered the living room, he found himself looking down the muzzle of a military pistol. Erzsébet's small finger was on the trigger and her eyes told him that he had better just stand still and say nothing during those first seconds before recognition came to her. When it did, she slid, trembling, into the nearest chair, dropping the pistol on the floor beside her.

"I could have shot you," she said. Her tone was a reprimand. "Why did you have to come in like that?"

Erdöss spread his hands. "My lady, I apologize, but there was no other way."

Seeing his discomfort and aware that there was truth in what he was telling her, she relented. "You look terrible, both of you," she said. "Come over here and rest while I get you something."

A little later when the men had refreshed themselves and were seated around the table, Erzsébet gave her visitors a full account of her husband's capture. Erdöss listened to her words with growing concern.

"We must go after them and find a way to rescue your husband," he said.

"But lieutenant, no one has any idea where he was taken."

"Well, we'll check with some of the others and see what we can discover." With a parting attempt to assure Erzsébet that the Americans would not harm her husband, Erdöss and Joseph took their leave.

With the men gone, the women and children were left with little protection other than the locks and bolts on the solidly built farmhouse doors. At night, wherever the Russians were able to gain access to the interior of the farmhouses, they raped the women and stole whatever valuables they came across. In the daytime the roaming groups of ex-prisoners raided the central food stores, and when they'd taken all that they wished, they urinated and defecated on what remained.

In Colonel Ludányi's absence the women of the camp looked to Erzsébet for guidance. They needed food and didn't know what to do about the contaminated stores. Erzsébet's response to their urgent questioning was immediate and unequivocal. "We must save the food. Children have to be fed and we don't know when we shall be able to get more supplies." There were cries of protest from some of the women. "How can we possibly think of eating such stuff—we shall all be sick."

"Better risk getting a little sick than risk starving to death," Erzsébet responded sharply. "You must scoop out the worst patches where you find excrement, and get rid of as little as you can where you see urine stains. We must save the rest— wash whatever it is possible to wash and use our best judgment about the remainder."

They forthwith set about their salvaging work, eventually recovering sufficient food to meet the immediate needs of their children and ease their own hunger while they were exploring other possibilities.

By evening, Erzsébet was confronted with yet another problem. She realized that although the Russians had taken her husband's gun belt, they still had one remaining gun. She decided that she had to get rid of it before it got into the wrong hands. She took Nárcissza with her to one of the outhouses and dropped the gun into the toilet, but just as they were about to retrace their steps, they heard the sound of heavy footsteps approaching the wooden enclosure. Erzsébet froze. "Oh my goodness, they're coming in here. Ciszka, what are we going to do?"

"Shush, Édes. Unlatch the door. If they open it we'll take them by surprise and rush out." Seeing her mother's hesitation, Nárcissza reached over and slid the bolt back as quietly as she could. There were voices now, quite close at hand. A couple of Serbs were singing raucously and it was evident that they were drunk. But they did not attempt to enter the outhouse. From what Nárcissza could determine, they'd settled themselves on the ground nearby. What to do? Erzsébet was uncertain about what to expect from an encounter with the Serbs, but given their drunken condition, the chances of surviving that situation unscathed, seemed quite good.

In a while the singing deteriorated into a slurred droning and eventually petered out altogether. Mother and daughter decided that if they were going to avoid spending the night in their present unattractive surroundings, they'd better make a dash for it. They eased the outhouse door open as quietly as they could and stepped outside. They need not have worried. The Serbs were quite oblivious to their presence. They were out cold.

The day after the arrest of the colonel, the Serbs and Croats came to the Ludányi's quarters. They were looking for items of value. They, too, had been prisoners of war. One of them demanded that Nárcissza give him her typewriter. When she protested that she didn't have one, the Serb grabbed her, and from what she could determine from his gestures, he was threatening to kill her. From the isolated shouts and comments of other members of the group, she was able to understand that their leader had seen her using carbon paper for her drawings and also to make copies of her notebook entries. He was thereby convinced that she was hiding a typewriter. Much anguish and arguing followed before the blustering looter was persuaded that there was no typewriter to be had.

The group left, but not for long. Soon they were at the door again, this time looking for transportation. A French prisoner from a neighboring farmhouse had told them that Colonel Ludányi had a military car, and they had come to take it. This time there was no denial. The raiders were shown the whereabouts of the car, but when they found it, they discovered that its gasoline tank was empty. Undiscouraged, they decided that they would use horses to pull it. They wanted the Ludányi's horses and they bullied other refugees into telling them where they were kept. The group then made their way to the stables, with Nárcissza and her mother close behind. They made straight for Duci and Dália, but this was too much for Nárcissza to bear. She screamed as the raiders made an attempt to harness her beloved animals. She clung to their necks and would not let go. She yelled at the men defiantly, "No, you will never take these horses from me. I will never let go. I will hang on to them no matter what you do." In a moment, taking the cue from his sister, Tamás joined her protest, screaming as loud as he could.

Taken aback by this spirited outburst, the leader paused to assess the situation. Meanwhile, Erzsébet began talking urgently in German. "It would be stupid to take those two horses," she stated vehemently. "They are riding horses and are not as strong as the others." Her words eventually got the attention of a prisoner from one of the neighboring farms who'd joined the party. "There are farm horses in these same stables," she told him. "They are far more capable of pulling the car than any riding horse."

The Serb, unconvinced, regarded Erzsébet skeptically as her frantic assertion was communicated to him, but in light of the commotion and the continuing fiery defiance of the Ludányi girl, he decided to look for himself.

"Show me."

Erzsébet didn't understand his words but their meaning was clear enough. She pointed to a neighboring section of the long barn. "They're in there," she said.

The group moved off in the direction she'd indicated. As they rounded the partition and approached the stalls beyond, the Serb's experienced eye was already appraising the heavily muscled animals stabled there. They drew near for a closer examination. No one spoke for several tense moments. Then the Serb looked up at Erzsébet. He nodded slowly, acknowledging that she had not misled him. Duci and Dália were spared.

FOUR

O n their arrival at the American army headquarters, Colonel Ludányi and his fellow Hungarian captives learned that Germany had surrendered and that, indeed, the war in Europe was over. Nevertheless, they were detained three days for questioning, living on one potato a day per man. On the fourth day, the colonel and his officers and men were released and escorted back to the Hungarian camp, weary and weakened, but otherwise unharmed. Shortly thereafter, an occupying contingent of the American army arrived at the camp. It was an occasion for celebration. The tired and hungry refugees received them with joy and gratitude. Their long and desperate flight was over.

But it was evident even to the eleven-year-old Nárcissza that for a few of the women in their party the arrival of the Americans seemed to be offering more than freedom. They were finding that the occasion provided an acceptable way to solve the food problem too. With husbands absent, food could be obtained from the Americans in exchange for more intimate expressions of gratitude. Here and there in the early morning hours when she was fetching water or outside on other chores, she was able to observe a door quietly opening and the stealthy departure of a figure in uniform. It was a time when she was able to see people more clearly than ever before for what they were and what they truly believed in—a time when nothing was hidden.

The majority, she realized, had not been changed by the extreme adversities suffered in the course of their escape. They did not covet the property of others nor did they engage in behavior that would have been unacceptable to them in better times. But there were a few who had different standards. They ate, drank, laughed and joked more freely with their rescuers—and took them to their beds.

The morning after their arrival, the American major in charge of the local occupying contingent came to confer with Colonel Ludányi about future planning. It was in his mind that the colonel, as the senior officer in the camps, should be their spokesman and should serve as their liaison with the American occupying forces regarding the administration of all the camps in the neighborhood, and the future disposition of their inmates. Antal was nonplused by the proposal. He tried to make the American understand that he, Ludányi, was a representative of the armed forces of the erstwhile enemy. With gestures and a few words in German, he did his best to let the major know that the many Poles, Czechs and other allied occupants of the various refugee camps in the neighborhood would not take kindly to the appointment of one of the enemy's officers as their leader. He made the rounds with the major, all the while attempting to convey his misgivings to that officer and hoping they would encounter someone who could speak English well enough to explain the situation. Eventually the difficulty was solved when a Polish officer translated for Colonel Ludányi and was able to make his position clear.

The major, visibly disappointed with this turn of events, said so in no uncertain terms. Colonel Ludányi had impressed him favorably at the earlier interrogation. Apart from noting his senior rank, the major had taken a liking to this tall, slim and serious officer, and he'd marked the colonel for liaison work. But he was obliged to concede that perhaps it would not be prudent to give Ludányi this particular job. Reluctantly, he appointed another officer to the position, and Antal was able to turn his attention once more to the needs of his own group.

And so they settled and strengthened themselves. The children were fed and washed and clothed. Their cheeks slowly regained their color and their parents hoped again. It was a respite. Tomorrow began to look a little more promising. In spite of the pig odor, the Ludányis were content with their large room. There was a place for all of them—father, mother, the five children and their maid. Each had a corner, a space they could call their own.

They began to plan for the future. Some of the refugees were attending organized seances to see whether they could get a little guidance on what to do and where to go, and whether it would be safe for them to return to their homeland. The Ludányi's maid, Margit, was among those officiating at the seances, and on one occasion Erzsébet asked her when she, Erzsébet, and her family, would be getting home. Margit replied that she preferred not to reveal what the table had told her. Erzsébet was vexed. "Well then," she asked, "will it take another year?" Margit was still evasive but when Erzsébet persisted, she told her mistress that it would take more than a year. "Tell me when it will be," Erzsébet demanded, but at that point Margit, by refusing to say more, had for all practical purposes answered the question.

Eventually, the refugees were divided into three groups. The soldiers who had been attached to the caravan to tend the horses and operate the mobile kitchen made up the first group. They had chosen to return to Hungary, and by September they were on their way. They all promised to write and let everyone in the camp know when they had reached their destination. But time passed and no letters came—save one. That letter came from the wife of one of the Ludányis' friends, a lieutenant colonel, whose son had been with the group and had joined those who had already returned to Hungary. The letter, unsigned, included the statement, "Due to your medical condition, Erzsébet, I don't think you should come home until your doctor advises that it is safe for you to travel." The Ludányi's knew that their friends were aware of Erzsébet's excellent health, so there was no mistaking the warning they'd received. They would not return to their homeland.

By the time the second group had left in November, only a few families remained. Aside from the Ludányis, the Bereczs, who after eighteen years of marriage had been blessed with the birth of their first child, had joined them. There was Hasszán, a Bosnian who claimed that he was a 'Bég'—a Turkish aristocrat. Hasszán, nearly sixty years old, had fled Hungary with his pregnant twenty eight year-old wife. Rumor had it that he'd been involved in some sort of espionage and had no illusions about what would happen to him were he to return to Hungary. Andor, the old Catholic priest, stayed, too, eventually ending his days in a Belgian monastery. The medical officer who had come with the group, stayed so that he could search for his wife who'd fled Hungary before him. He knew only that she was somewhere in Germany, but he intended to find her.

There were a few others: a young subaltern, a family called Ost who had five children; a Count Gyulay and his wife and daughter; and finally a couple of old peasants whose horses had survived the hardships of the flight from Hungary. These latter eventually made their way back home by themselves, taking their horses with them.

It was quiet now at the farms. The Ludányi children were thoughtful and subdued— as if they sensed the closeness of yet another turning point in their lives. On the evening following the departure of the second group, they retired early to their corners as their parents finished clearing away the supper things and sat at the table to consider the future. The usually naked light bulb, directly over the tabletop, was shaded now. Its light, confined to a single pool, illuminated only the faded beige-and-brown tablecloth and Antal's and Erzsébet's faces. The rest of the room lay deep in shadow. Nárcissza lay quietly, her child's mind drifting in and out of sleep as the intermittent drone of her parents' voices came to her ears.

Antal was talking. "Erzsikém (my Elizabeth), I'm finished as a military man. That's obvious, isn't it? If we were to return to Hungary it's certain that the Russians would execute me, or at the very least condemn me to a life in prison. And outside of Hungary there can be nothing for me to do militarily." As he sat quietly at the table with his intense gaze focused on his wife's dear face, he began to tell her what he felt he needed to do.

"Erzsébet, I have to learn to do something else. Right now, like so many other career soldiers, I have no skills of use in the world outside, and if I just go after a laboring job in reconstruction or factory work, I will always be a laborer or an unskilled worker. I have to start again and learn a trade," he said. "If I don't do that now, it will be more difficult as time goes on. We will have no chance to give the children the opportunities they need."

Erzsébet reached across the table and took his hands in hers. "I can work, too, you know. The people around here want to pay me to do needlework for them," she said. . "We will be all right, Tonikám (my Tony). You will always take care of us one way or another."

"But that won't just happen all by itself. I shall have to do something to make it happen," he said. "I have been thinking, Édes. Right now, carpentry or furniture-making seem to me to make the most sense. I could use those skills here or anywhere we might go. Woodworking skills are needed in every country—and it's satisfying work. At the end of the day you have something to show for your labors, and I think I could be good at it."

Erzsébet answered her husband. "You will always do good work in whatever field you choose, édes uram (dear husband); you must do work that will satisfy you—work that you believe in." Their voices low, they continued with their planning long after Nárcissza had ceased to hear them.

A fresh morning breeze lifted his spirits as he walked down to the nearby village of Hochburg. Hardly two miles from the group of farms known as Parsdorf, where he and his family were quartered, Hochburg had seemed to Antal as good a place as any to begin his search for work. He bought a local newspaper at the general store, but he didn't find any advertisements of the type he was looking for. He asked the proprietor of the store whether he knew of a woodworking company or even a building contractor where he might get a job as a carpenter's helper. When that inquiry did not result in any promising possibilities, Antal tried his luck at the automobile repair place located at one end of the short stretch of paved roadway known as Main Street. Seeing no one near the pumps outside, nor in the little cubicle that he took to be the office, he walked over to a corrugated iron shed that he assumed was a repair shop and glanced inside. In a few moments a tousled blond head of hair slid out from under a pickup truck and a young oil-smudged face turned to look up at him.

"What can I do for you?"

Antal crouched down to get closer. He told the young mechanic of his quest, but the boy shook his head even before he'd finished talking. "You're not going to find anything like that around here," he said. "With all the men gone we need lots of workers, but not for the skilled trades. There's not enough work for craftsmen as it is—unless you want to be a plumber or a mason."

Antal got a similar response at the local café where he discussed his purpose with a sprightly woman behind the counter who introduced herself as Gerty. "You will have to go to a bigger town for that," she told him. "You'll have to go to the town of Burghausen or to Braunau, but even there I wouldn't bet on your chances of getting anything but laboring work." He thanked the woman and went on his way. By the end of the day he'd decided that in spite of what he had been told, he would have to try his luck in town. He told Erzsébet that he would go to Burghausen the following day.

In the morning as he was about to leave, Erzsébet called to him from the yard outside. She told him she'd been talking with their neighbors about his search for a woodworking job, and she'd heard that a wagonmaker named Greiner had a place in the small district of Alheim, less than two kilometers distant.

A wagon maker? Antal thought a bit about that. Yes, he mused, wagon making could be considered a skilled trade. You had to make wheels and hubs, axles and shafts to build a wagon. You had to do carriage work and iron forging, too. If one learned to do those things, the same skills would be valuable in other woodworking trades, too.

He changed his plan. In less that an hour, with the aid of the somewhat sketchy directions his wife had given him, he found himself at a roadside gate leading to a small farm. A signpost close to the gate announced that this was the place of Otto Greiner, wagonmaker. He made his way up a deeply rutted path that led from the gate to a white painted farmhouse building. He saw that the house backed onto the edge of a coppice. The long wooden shed attached to the right side of the main building was, he supposed, the wagon making place. He walked around to the end of the shed and stood for a while outside its iron-studded wooden doors, both of which were now wide open. Two new-looking wagons were parked on a hard dirt area outside. They seemed well built, he noted. Moving closer to the open doors, he stood watching a sinewy man of medium height as he worked at a wheel-balancing jig inside. The man's thick but deceptively sensitive fingers were busy making a series of tiny adjustments to clamps around the periphery of a wheel, presumably so that it would run true.

At the far end of the workshop Antal could see a younger man working with leather harness straps, treating them with some sort of oily substance which, he supposed, was intended to prevent them from cracking or drying out. Closer at hand the framework of a wagon's lower body was in course of construction, at that moment raised up on wooden trestles, having its axle leaf-spring anchors bolted to its underside. Antal found himself very much intrigued with the procedures he was watching. It was all so interesting and he marveled that the making of such a seemingly simple vehicle required so much attention to detail. A good trade, he decided. People would need horse-drawn wagons for a long time to come. Although in the years between the wars, the automobile industry had expanded in his homeland and had appeared to be replacing the horse-drawn wagon, he had noted that the change really seemed confined to the larger cities. Out in the country he'd seen very little change. If anything, there were more wagons now than ever. And, he supposed, things would be the same in Argentina or Australia or wherever they might go. Horse drawn wagons would always be needed.

Pausing for a brief rest, the wagon maker straightened his back. As he did so, he became aware of Antal watching him. He pushed a matte of silver-gray hair from his eyes and wiped the half-rolled sleeve of his brown flannel shirt across his glistening face. "Grüss Gott," he said. "What can I do for you?"

"You are doing fine work sir," Antal told him. "I would like to learn those skills. As a matter of fact, I would like to know whether you might have a job for me."

The craftsman shook his head. "Sorry, I can't afford to hire anyone right now," he said. He studied the serious face before him for a moment or two, then he held out a large callused hand in greeting. "I am Otto Greiner," he said. "It is possible that I shall need some help in a few months. Come inside and I'll show you around."

Antal followed the man into his workshop and listened intently while Greiner told him about wood and iron working equipment, and wagon building methods. He imagined himself spending his working days in this setting, surrounded by the paraphernalia of the wagon-making trade, with the pungent odors of wood stain and resin, of shavings and sawdust in his nostrils from morning till night, and it came to him that the work of a wagon maker would be all right for him. It would suit him well and he would be good at it.

"I would like to make a proposal to you, Herr Greiner," he said when their tour of the workshops had ended. "I would like to work for you through the winter until the spring. You would not have to pay me anything, but in return for being as much help as I can be, I would like you to teach me the craft of wagon making."

The grizzled artisan stared at Antal for a few moments, sizing him up and assessing his sincerity. Then he put out his large hand again. "Very well," he said, "that seems a fair arrangement. I will do it, but first we will try it for a month to find out whether you are suited to this kind of work. If, by the end of that time, either of us is not satisfied with the arrangement, we shall shake hands again and part. On that understanding, you may start as soon as you wish."

Antal applied himself to his newfound work with a zeal born of his conviction that the choice he'd made for his post-war trade was good and practical. While he would really have preferred to work directly with horses, he consoled himself with the thought that through his wagon building work, he would at least remain associated with the world of horses, albeit indirectly. Then, too, the skills he would acquire in wood and iron working would better equip him to support his family in the very uncertain times ahead.

Throughout the winter of 1945-1946 he dedicated himself to his purpose. He learned how to use the lathe and turn the wooden wheel spokes. He worked with the planes and chisels and the cab-forming tools; with the joining and iron-banding jigs. And he learned the fine finishing and cabinetwork for which some of the better wagon makers were famous.

The months flew by and springtime came sooner than he would have wished, but his dedication to his training over the winter months had not been in vain. Early one evening as he finished clearing up after the day's work, his tutor came to him. Nodding toward a bench near one of the work-tables, he spoke quietly.

"Sit please," he said. When they had both taken their seats, Otto pulled a leather pouch from his shirt pocket and stuffed a charred briar pipe with black tobacco. Holding the pipe in his hand without lighting it, he continued, "Antal, my friend, your training is over. You know as much about wagon mak-ing now as I do. It is not right that I should let you work any longer without paying you. From now on you will be paid a proper wage for your work." It was Antal's first post-war job.

But the euphoria that his new status had brought to Antal was short lived. Back with his family in their room near the pigsty he learned that the old farmer had become tired of accommodating his uninvited guests. He had tolerated the situation because the colonel had kept him supplied with tobacco from the substantial supply he had brought with him from Hungary, but now the tobacco container was empty. The farmer had nothing more to gain by letting them stay any longer. He urged them to move on—and one evening, to make his point, he tore out the single light bulb fitting that hung from the ceiling above the dining table and left them in darkness.

On countless occasions, Erzsébet had in vain urged her husband to be less generous with the tobacco, for she knew the farmer would have been satisfied with much less than

Antal had given him. But they knew now that they would have to move without delay. They talked long into the night about their options. They needed to sleep, yet they knew that sleep would not come until they'd managed to find a workable solution to their problem. Who would provide shelter for people who had very little to offer in return, except a willingness to work? And even if they found domestic employment for the two of them, where would they find an employer willing or able to accommodate a family of seven?

Their plight seemed hopeless. From time to time one or the other would make coffee so that they might warm themselves and continue to think productively, but in the end, fatigue, both emotional and physical, compelled them to rest. Antal and Erzsébet, still fully clothed, lay down and slept.

The small hours gave way to the chill of early morning. All too soon the first rays of the new day were spreading across the pitted ceiling. Antal stirred and opened his eyes, staring at the white plaster above him as if coming out of a trance. Suddenly he was fully awake and sitting bolt upright. "Of course," he said out loud. "Of course!" He turned to his wife, nudging her urgently. "Erzsikém, Erzsikém, I have it. I have an idea!"

In the summer, a certain Countess Castell and her daughter, on learning that some fine horses were stabled in the neighborhood, had come to look at them. At the time, Antal had explained that most of the horses did not really belong to him; they were the property of the Hungarian military so he could not sell them. Nevertheless, a lengthy conversation had ensued and a friendship had begun.

"Do come and see us soon," the countess had said as they were leaving. "We shall be looking forward to your visit."

But now, Antal recalled something else she had said in the course of their discussions. She had mentioned that a number of refugees were living and working on her estate, and that had proved a win-win situation. In helping them, she had also helped herself. There were flower and vegetable gardens to be tended, horses to be groomed and cared for, and several buildings to be maintained. There was a sawmill on the property, and some of the refugees were busy with that activity, too.

Antal decided that since the countess' estate was only four miles to the north of where they now lay next to the pigsty, this would be as good a time as any to take up her invitation.

Two days later, they were taking a glass of schnapps in the drawing room at the Castell mansion. The countess, on hearing of the Ludanyi's circumstances, responded warmly.

"We have a lot more room here, so you're welcome to come and stay with us," she said. Then, to dispel any impression of charity in her suggestion, she turned to Antal and added, "Please don't hesitate. There will be work you can do to pay for your family's accommodation, and you will have plenty of time off to look for paid employment."

Just after breakfast time on the following Saturday, one of the Castell wagons pulled up alongside the pigsty next to the Ludanyi's quarters. When, in response to a gentle tapping sound, Erzsébet opened the door, a lanky, freckle-faced youth greeted her. Doffing his cap, he said, "Hope I'm not too early ma'am. I've been sent to fetch you all."

Antal was not immediately able to put his new skills to work to earn a living, for there were no jobs to be had in the craft he had learned. He had, however, heard about a need for workers at the American food distribution center where the Marshall Plan, an American lend-lease arrangement created to provide war-ravaged countries with food and with badly needed products until they could help themselves, was in operation. In due course he got himself a job at one of the silos, working as a technician on the repair and maintenance of the machines and mechanical equipment. It was heavy physical work, but it gave him back his dignity and, increasingly, his physical strength. His mood and his outlook for the future became more optimistic. He worked diligently and stoically at the silos for about a year until it was determined that there was no longer a need for the plan. The center was closed and the work force disbanded.

On learning of this, the countess asked Antal if he would care to help in the estate sawmill where building boards and roofing frames were manufactured. He was more than glad to accept her offer. It would be paid employment and he'd learn interesting new aspects of the woodworking trade. But a few months later he suffered a setback. While working at one of the electric saws, a board had flown off the machine and struck him hard in the stomach. The blow had left him with injuries from which he did not fully recover. Because of this he was unable to resume his work at the mill.

Again, the countess came to the rescue. One day when he was sufficiently recovered, she asked him to have coffee with her.

"I wonder whether you would care to help me with the garden," she ventured. "Hans is a gem, but the poor fellow badly needs help. I think he's afraid that I'll replace him and he's breaking his back trying to prove to me that he can still handle everything himself. He needs someone to work with him and help him with the endless projects begging attention in the huge vegetable garden and elsewhere on the estate."

"I shall gladly do whatever I can, Countess. But I don't know whether, in my present condition, I could give Hans the kind of help he'd need."

"Don't worry, colonel, Hans likes you and I'm sure he will manage to work things out so that you will not be overtaxed. He's very strong and can still handle the heavy work, but he just doesn't have time to get to everything else these days."

It was settled. In the garden, Antal did what the chief gardener told him to do and although his boss felt obliged to call him 'Colonel,' and would frequently ask him whether he would mind doing this or that rather than give him orders, the two worked well together. Nor did the chief gardener object or show resentment when from time to time the countess, strolling in the garden, would disturb them at their work and ask Antal to join her for a cup of coffee and a chat. The strange menage seemed to work quite well. Antal was a happy man again. There was far to go and the future was still uncertain, but he was confident now, that he and his family would find a better life together than they could have hoped to find again in his ravished homeland.

The children were settling down, too. In the early spring of '46, after having missed nearly two complete years of schooling, Nárcissza and Tamás were able to take up their education again.

A local organization had established a school to help displaced persons acquire a better understanding of the German language. It was a start, and the two siblings, happy to grasp the opportunity, were enrolled. They attended until the end of the school year in June, but the combination of post-war chaos and hopeless overcrowding, together with the recognition that the school was only a stop-gap facility, made it difficult for even the most diligent children to settle down and study. Brother and sister were indeed able to learn a little German during that time, but conditions were not conducive to learning much else.

Their early discontent with the limited program, and their strong desire to resume a formal education did not go unnoticed, however, and Nárcissza's oft-repeated comments to her family and friends about the matter eventually reached the ears of a sympathetic neighbor. At the Castell estate, the Ludányi family occupied one large room on the second floor of a building known as the Hunting Lodge, one of three buildings originally set aside for employees, but now also providing shelter for several refugees. They had a toilet to themselves, a sort of semi-outhouse, and they shared a communal kitchen with another refugee family, the Bereczs. Helga, a seventeen-year-old student attending a Bavarian gymnasium, lived directly below the Ludányis on the first floor. On learning of the Ludányi girl's plight, and wishing to be helpful, Helga said she would try to arrange an interview for Nárcissza with the principal of the gymnasium she was attending. The principal, on hearing that Nárcissza had achieved excellent grades in her previous schooling, and unaware that she had not had the opportunity to attend more than the first four weeks of the fifth grade, agreed to Nárcissza's enrollment.

Located across the border in Bavaria in the town of Burghausen, the gymnasium was about six kilometers away from the Castell estate. Nárcissza would have to walk that distance twice each day, but she welcomed the opportunity. In October she received her border permit. The following day, she donned her blue and white dress and sat patiently while her mother brushed and combed her hair carefully, and wove it into neat braids. She set off across the bridge over the river that marked the border between the two countries and in just over an hour and a half she entered the gates of the gymnasium and reported for registration.

In most of continental Europe, the standard educational curriculum called for a minimum of eight years of schooling. Those who were interested in learning a trade would enter an apprenticeship in the calling of their choice. Those interested in commerce would, at the end of the first four years, transfer to a commercial high-school and spend the next four years studying subjects applicable to a career in commerce. For a professional business education such as that applicable to a career as an accountant, a further four years of study for an 'upper commercial' education was required.

Those interested in a classical education and an academic career would, for a further eight years, attend a 'gymnasium'— the continental European version of a school for preparing for university. They would immerse themselves in physics, chemistry, biology, geography, etc. They would study mathematics through to calculus and learn a minimum of three languages in preparation for entry to university.

The principal's assistant at the Bavarian Gymnasium examined the report card that Nárcissza had brought with her. She noted that it had been issued by the last school Nárcissza had attended in Hungary, and that it bore the stamp of a gymnasium. From this she concluded that the girl had completed the first year of gymnasium and was ready for the second year. In fact, Nárcissza had completed only one month of first year gymnasium before the school in Kaposvár had been obliged to close its doors—and that had been nearly two years ago. By contrast the students in the class she was now assigned to had already had a year of English, whereas she had had but three lessons in that language and was as yet able to speak only a few words of German.

Not an encouraging situation. She struggled valiantly to decipher the words in the notebooks in front of her, and whenever she had a chance, she asked other girls for help. For the first day or two, the tests were easy and she managed to scrape her way through, but on the third day, the test was a German composition about a farmyard which, for Nárcissza, was more than confusing. She knew her farmyards and could just about make herself understood in German, but her knowledge of German grammar was virtually nonexistent.

As the corrected report cards were handed out, the teacher in charge of the class read out the results of the tests one at a time, announcing the name of the applicable student in each case. She made no attempt to spare the feelings of those who had not done well. A grade of five for one student, three for another; six for that one and two for the next, until all reports had been reviewed—save one. Nárcissza held up her hand to let the teacher know she had not received her report card.

The teacher then turned to the class and called for attention. "Ah yes," she said, "I have one very interesting composition here." She read Nárcissza's test paper aloud to the class. As the students heard the first examples of the bizarre grammatical errors in Nárcissza's composition, they began to titter.

The teacher continued reading, and as the amusement grew, the giggling grew louder. Soon, the class was in an uproar as more than fifty students abandoned themselves to the pleasure of rolling in their seats and laughing uncontrollably at what they had heard.

Slowly, as the climax of the occasion passed, and as heads began to turn to look at the hapless author, they saw the girl in the sixth row sitting quietly with her head up, gazing straight ahead, and with arms folded across her lap. They saw the hurt on the pale face and they grew silent.

The teacher did not appear to notice the change of mood. At the end of the period, she turned her attention once more to the girl sitting by herself in the sixth row, and in a matter-of-fact voice, spoke to her from her podium. "You know, Ludányi, the gymnasium is not really the place for you. Why don't you try to get into sixth grade in a regular grade-school—a volkschule?" she advised, and with that she dismissed the class. Nárcissza didn't understand all of the things the teacher had said but she knew she had been publicly dismissed—thrown out. She gathered her things, her valuable notebooks and pencils and her father's satchel, and set out on her long journey home.

What could she tell her parents and brothers—and her friends? What could she do? She thought about this as she trudged down the gentle slope through the picturesque border-town of Burghausen and crossed the bridge over the blue-green waters of the Salzach to the Austrian side. She didn't take the winding road up the steep hillside to the Castell Estate. Instead, she climbed the almost vertical foot-path that went straight up the hillside, where a lookout bench was placed about halfway up for pedestrians to rest on the way. She would throw herself off the cliff right there at the lookout, she decided.

When she reached the bench, she went over to the railings at the roadside and looked down. She could see the road below where one of the hairpin bends came almost directly below the lookout. She kicked some stones over and watched them bounce off the rocks and eventually land in the dust at the side of the road below. She imagined herself falling in the same manner, twisting and turning and finally, her mangled and bloody form spread out for the passers-by to see and wonder at. Her troubles would be over and there would be no explaining to do to her friends and parents and her brothers. She would be free and they would mourn their loss.

As she came out of her reverie, a sudden fury overcame her. She picked up her satchel, loaded with all her precious and hard-to-come-by books and pencils, and with a defiant cry, lifted it over the guardrail and threw it with all her strength to the rocks below. She watched as the satchel fell and bounced off the hillside protrusions, finally scattering its contents across the roadside below. She stared for a short time at the place where her belongings had fallen, and having vented her anger in this manner, she began to feel a little better. She went over to the bench to sit for just a minute to calm herself and to gather her strength for the final act, but the minute became two minutes, and the two minutes became three. Slowly a plan was taking shape in her mind, a plan so audacious that it simply had to work. The more she thought about it, the more convinced she became that she would have to put it to the test. And to do that, she would have to postpone her suicide.

She retraced her steps to the bridge far below, working out the details of her plan as she went. By the time she'd made her way down to the bridge, and from there up the winding road to the place where her satchel and papers lay, she was satisfied that she had thought of everything. She arrived home later than usual but no one suspected that anything was amiss, and she did not tell them that anything was.

The following morning Nárcissza went to school as usual and sat in her usual seat, six rows back on the left. The students crowded around her, all of them talking at the same time. She somehow managed to ask them odd questions, from which they deduced that she did not understand that she had been thrown out. She pretended not to notice the puzzled expressions on some of their faces as they continued to talk. She pretended not to understand anything that referred to her dismissal. The girls did not press the matter further. They were ashamed of their behavior of the day before, and for reasons that they might not have been able to explain, they were glad she had returned. The teacher who had dismissed her was puzzled, too, but instead of asking Nárcissza why she had come, she decided to let the matter lie for the moment to give herself time to consider what she should do next.

Fortunately for Nárcissza there was a mathematics exam that day and because, apart for some differences in signs, math is the same in any language, Nárcissza's grade turned out to be the best in her class.

Teacher and students alike settled down to the idea that Nárcissza would stay. They decided that, after all, she did belong, and they began to help her. The teacher who had earlier dismissed her, now gave her special lessons once a week and told her how much German and how much English she should be writing each day. Her parents never knew what she had been through. Not then, not ever. Her plan had worked.

FIVE
LONDON

J ust off the junction where Tottenham Court Road goes
north from the east-end of Oxford Street, there's an
insignificant turn-off called Hanway Street. The mainstream
of London traffic passes it by as if it were an aberration in
the city's layout. The urgent pedestrian flow does not divide
as it presses past its entrance, but there was a time when
Hanway Street corner was a landmark for many discriminat-
ing shoppers and business people. They would have known
it not by its own name, but rather as the location of Imhof's
showrooms where the finest in high-fidelity audio equipment and modern industrial instrument cases were dis-
played and sold.

The managing director, Godfrey (Goff) Imhof—his fresh,
ruddy complexion testifying to his love of the outdoors, and
his broad shouldered frame and sand-colored hair completing the impression of a healthy, athletic sportsman—ran his
company as a benevolent dictatorship. His eyes, one clear
blue, and the other pale yellow, were especially arresting.
Both were piercing and intelligent. One of his favorite sports

was racing-car rally driving. When not participating himself, he would stand alongside the rally trail dressed in his Harris tweeds and watch the contestants as they, ploughing through deep mud or slush, would attempt to negotiate a sharp bend or a steep hill. Seeing a spill or an open car turn upside down, a broad smile would light up his face, and the keen eyes would twinkle.

"Steady there, boys."

On the second floor of that same building, Imhof also ran a successful mobile radio-telephone distributorship, with the whole of Greater London and surrounding counties as its market. Pye Telecommunications, Ltd. in Cambridge manufactured the equipment itself. The Imhof distributorship not only sold the product to businesses and taxicab fleets, to fire fighting and police departments, and whatever other potential users of mobile radio-telephones could be found, the division also surveyed promising sites for fixed transmitter antennae. It obtained the necessary authorizations for installing radio masts at the tops of hills or on the roofs of tall buildings. In little more than two years, Imhof's Radio-Telephone Division had become the star performer of all mobile radio sales groups in the country, eclipsing even the prestigious Marconi Company in the number of units put into the field.

As manager of that division, I was proud of what we had achieved. But on this particular evening in the late summer of 1953, a passer-by, glancing up at the second floor window overlooking Tottenham Court Road, would have seen that it was open and that the lights were still burning. And if perchance he had stopped and listened for a moment, he would have heard voices raised in anger. At the conference, drawing to a close in that second floor office, the bluff and normally good-humored Goff Imhof had just learned that his company's highly successful radio-telephone distributorship for the Pye Company was to be terminated. That meant, among other things, that as manager of that challenging activity, my job would also come to an end.

I had come to the job straight out of the movie business. As an under-employed actor I was looking for a way to bridge a financial gap while the prevailing slump in the motion picture industry ran its course. I had been apprehensive about my initial interview with Imhof, but it had gone better than I had expected. He had put me at ease while I told him all about what I had been up to since I had left the service, and about my stage and film career. I thought he was letting me off lightly, but I had been mistaken. If I were to be called back for a second interview, he warned, the Pye executives would want to know chapter and verse about my technical background. My stage and movie experience would no doubt be an asset in relation to my sales work, but the Pye people would not be impressed by any of that. They would zero in on the technical stuff, and Godfrey didn't want to be found wanting in his selection process.

I well remember Godfrey's parting shot as I left his office. "Next time we see you, Howard, I hope you will have decided who you are and what your career in going to be—actor or engineer." I walked down Tottenham Court Road in a troubled frame of mind and boarded the Underground train for home. I mulled over his words. He was right, of course. I was at a crossroads. I was still struggling for an identity, for a focus for my life, and it had showed. Godfrey Imhof's words had struck home. I settled myself in a corner seat. It was not rush hour, so there was no crowding and my thoughts drifted with the rattling and rhythm of the train. I reflected on my interview. How was it, Imhof had asked, that I had decided to leave the service and launch myself into a stage career, when I had never been on the professional stage before. "If it meant so much to you, why weren't you doing it before the war?" he had asked.

"Well I think that was an accident of circumstance," I had replied.

"How do you mean?"

"Parents naturally do all they can to encourage their children in activities where they show the most interest, and while that's as it should be, it sometimes results in the masking of a true ambition by a secondary one. I had always shown interest in mechanical toys and Meccano sets, so that's what I got as Christmas and birthday gifts. It was, however, our occasional visits to school plays and to the theater that really enthralled me. I didn't reveal it to anyone because my brother and I already had our problems and got into fights at school because of our nice clothes and short pants.

Raising us all by herself, Mother did the very best for us that she knew how, but she didn't realize that children need to be dressed like their peers and boys need to be dressed like other boys. I didn't want to make matters worse, so I didn't do any play-acting or get involved in school productions because in those days it was considered a sissy thing for boys to do. Play-acting was for girls, so I suppressed my true interest in that sort of thing and concentrated on all the things that boys were supposed to be interested in. When I wasn't out hiking or biking or playing football with my friends, I played with Meccano sets and trains and buried my true interest."

"And when did you first get interested in the electrical world?"

"That was one Christmastime when I was ten years old and we were living at Cope Street in Coventry. Mother asked me what sort of present I specially wanted and I told her I would like an old wireless set I had seen in a pawnbroker's shop."

The train rattled on as I drifted and let that scene of long ago come back to me. The shops around the corner in Cox Street and up around Jordan Well were all brightly lit. It was early evening and there was a light snowfall. I was looking at all the wondrous things in the pawnbroker's window, up past Lenton's sweet shop and the bakery. Violins, drums, an old cylinder-type gramophone, a man's tuxedo and top hat, and several fancy dresses and jewelry. The proprietor saw me looking at these things and invited me inside. "Come and see some of the other things we've got, m'lad," he said.

I went inside and gazed up and down at all the shelves, loaded with fascinating things that had once had other owners; had once been part of someone else's life and ambitions; had seen others' hopes and sorrows, laughter, and tears. There were shoes and sewing machines, golf clubs, roller skates, silverware and china, and alongside the counter, a crib and a rocking horse. And there, right up on one of the top shelves—what was that? A wireless set? Yes, it was a wireless set, a table model in a small dusty walnut cabinet and there were earphones lying on top of it.

"Please, what's that?" I pointed and asked the good-natured man.

"Oh that. Well, that's a Cossor Melody Maker. It's a wireless set and that's what it's called. It seems to be in good condition, but I haven't been able to make it work, so it's going pretty cheap. I'll get it down and you can have a look at it if you like."

"Oh no, sir, don't do that. I was just curious that's all." I thanked him and took my leave. When I got back home I asked my mother whether it would be possible for me to have the Cossor Melody Maker for my Christmas present. I told her that it wouldn't cost much because there was something the matter with it and it didn't work.

My mother was puzzled that a non-working wireless set would interest me, but on Christmas day it was there at the foot of our tree with all the other wonderful surprises. For weeks I played with it and pretended it was working, until I was able to save up enough pocket money to buy a high-tension battery to power it. Then I connected it up and hooked up an aerial that I had tacked on the window frame. I wiped as much dust as I could from around the valves and other parts inside, and switched it on. Not a sound. I kept on experimenting with it day after day when I got home from school, but there was never a sound. Then one day my father came up from London to see us. He hadn't come very often since mother and he were divorced two years previously, and when he did come he usually didn't stay very long. But this time my father spent the whole weekend in Coventry and he was with us most of that time. When he saw me playing with the Cossor Melody-Maker and realized that I was not able to make it work, he began to get interested.

"Howard, my boy, how would you like me to help you make this thing work?" He instructed me to clear the kitchen table and spread newspapers across the whole of its surface. Then, striding purposefully on his artificial legs—he had lost his real ones in World War I—he went out to his car to get his toolbox. When he returned, we placed my Cossor Melody-Maker on the newspapers and opened its top. We sat at the table and began the diagnosis.

My brother Archie was sitting by the kitchen range with my mother, both of them looking on, as my father opened the small cabinet. He invited me to help him with the investigation as, one by one, he began disconnecting all the wires. It was a 'bread-board' assembly—that is, all the parts were screwed down to a thick plywood base. Following his instructions I helped him unscrew and remove every piece so that in the end the case was empty except for the small loudspeaker bolted to the back of the wooden front panel. He had brought in some rags and old toothbrushes from his car and began to clean each part. He scraped all the connections and terminals with his pocket knife until they were shiny, then he rubbed each of the copper wire ends with a piece of Emery cloth until there was not a trace of tarnish left on them.

When every piece was perfectly clean he took a small multi-meter from his tool kit and checked each component to assure himself that it was in working order. When that was done he guided me as I replaced each part. He made sure that it was as securely screwed down to the plywood base as it had been before we took it apart. Then he reconnected all the wiring, carefully tightening each terminal with a pair of blunt-nosed pliers.

More than two hours had passed when my father hooked up the batteries and the aerial and sat back. "Now," he said, "is the moment of truth." He told me to put the headphones on, then he motioned to me to turn on the front panel switch. What happened then seemed like magic. Right away I heard a gentle hissing in the headphones. I reached for the tuning knob and as I began to turn it I heard music. People were singing a hymn on the BBC Sunday morning service.

When I had got over my initial surprise and delight, and Archie and Mother had taken turns at listening to the service, my father surprised me again. "I suspect the head phones came with the set because something had already gone wrong with the loudspeaker before the set itself failed, so let's take a look." He unbolted the speaker and carefully examined the moving armature. He saw that it had become detached from its anchorage to the cone of the speaker and he proceeded to re-tighten the tiny nuts on its threaded stem. He replaced the unit in the cabinet, re-connected the wiring and switched the set on again. No further need for headphones now; the sound of the church organ filled the room.

Deeply impressed with the events of that day, I eventually decided that it would not be difficult to build a wireless set from scratch. I began to buy parts with my pocket money. Resistors and condensers could be had at junk hobby stores for very little money. Tuning coils could be wound by hand. My friend Ken Griffith's father had a multi-meter and when I had enough parts together, Ken gladly invited me over to his house so that I could check them all for continuity and insulation. In a few weeks I had built a small, one-valve wireless set. It was mounted on a plywood base, smaller than that of the Cossor Melody-Maker. It didn't have a cabinet and with only one valve, would not drive a loudspeaker. Hooked up to a pair of headphones though, it was just as good, and was able to receive almost as many stations as the Cossor. I took it to school and swapped it for a good sized Meccano set. My immediate success with that trading venture prompted me to build and swap more wireless sets for Meccano so that I was able to construct large bridges and tall windmills and steam-driven engines; huge cranes and trucks and power generating stations. In the course of the following year I amassed the largest collection of Meccano parts of any boy in Wheatley Street school or in my whole neighborhood.

As time went by I began to construct three-valve sets as well as the one-valve kind and I began to put some of them in neat plywood cases so that I had a set available to sell or to trade for whatever I needed. Bicycle parts, a Terry three-spring saddle, a remote-controlled model airplane and a complete set of the Encyclopedia Britannica were all acquired by trading my simple wireless sets for them. Aside from this, the money I got from some of my trades paid for such things as Christmas and birthday gifts for my mother and my brother.

When eventually my school days were over it seemed natural enough that I would apply for a job with a company where there were opportunities to work with mechanical or electrical products. And if there was any doubt about where that would be, it was settled when, in the summer 1932, we moved to the Coventry suburb of Stoke. Quiet and conservative, Emscote Road was located but three hundred yards from the entrance gates of the General Electric Company's Stoke factory and offices. It seemed heaven sent. I was given a tour of the whole campus during the first week and when I was shown around the Research and Development Labs I was lucky enough to meet a jovial, pipe-smoking scientist who took me under his wing right away. Bo Dutton, a red-haired giant of a man, was always punctual, so I knew exactly when he would be making his great strides up Telephone Road between the factory buildings on his way to work. I would be there at the entrance gates promptly at seven fifteen, intercepting Bo and staying with him for the length of that long Road.

For ten minutes every day, alternately walking and half running to keep up with his long strides, I peppered him with my questions about everything from superhets to sidebands, screened grids to skin effect; from voice coils to Varistors, and from cathode followers to the new television receivers which were just now coming into production at that factory. I planned my lists of questions in the evenings so I'd be able to make the most of my short morning sessions with Bo, and in that way I gained a better understanding of many of the electrical theories and practices previously obscure to me. At the Technical College I learned as much as I could from the professors and from books, but that was not the same. That was reading and studying and being told what was what, but Bo was different. Bo painted vivid pictures in my mind. When he talked as we hurried along, his explanations seemed to come alive and I could actually see the answers as if I were watching practical demonstrations in his lab. It was my ten-minute sessions with Bo that kept me fascinated with the world of engineering and opened my mind to its possibilities. And it was Bo who got me through my examinations and convinced me that engineering was the career I was cut out for.

The years slip by and suddenly I'm nineteen years old. I have a girl who, in later years, I shall remember as my first true love. Then it happens. We are at the Coventry Opera House watching 'Arsenic and Old Lace' and I'm entranced. The following evening I return to the theater alone and see the play for a second time. In the course of the next ten days, I see it yet again. It is life. It is everything. I am totally captivated. I feel myself up there on the stage, identifying with the male lead and playing his part, and I tell myself that whatever happens I must do this. I must become an actor. The following Monday I make an appointment with the director at his headquarters in Hertford Street, and in a day or two I am there, sitting across from him in his office.

He is friendly but firm. "I wish I could help you Howard, but we are a production company and we have no opportunity to work with people who have no experience. If you get yourself at least a year or so of acting school, it's possible that we could sometimes try you out in bit parts. But it's a long hard road and even if you're dedicated, it's not a promising way to make a living. If you do decide to get some formal training, come back and see us some time in the future and we'll have another talk."

That settles that. I come to my senses and chide myself for not realizing that there would be financial problems. How could I possibly go off to some acting school when a good part of my present wage was needed to help with household expenses at home? Out of the question. I thank the production director for seeing me and tell him that I hope to be back one day. That day never comes of course, and within a year we are planning to go to war.

Reality returns as the train pulls into Finchley Road station. Not much farther to go now. I had better stop dreaming and think about my next interview.

Although I had an electrical and radio engineering background, I didn't know much about mobile radio except the kind we used in airplanes, and I would not have time to bone up on the subject in any depth. I did, however, know the difference between the methods used to carry sound waves on the backs of radio waves, from the sending aerial to the receiving aerial. The popular choices were frequency modulation and amplitude modulation, and I knew the operating capabilities for which each of these techniques was best known. Basically, amplitude modulation (AM) had the better range, but the frequency method (FM) was freer from static and other electrical noise.

Godfrey Imhof, who had seemed satisfied with my general demeanor and the way I approached the interview, had warned me that the differences in the types of modulation used were the primary factors that distinguished one brand of mobile radio equipment from another. I should bear this in mind if I were to be invited to an interview with the Pye executives. I learned that the interviewers would be John Stanley, Vice President and son of the Chairman of the Pye Company, and Harry Woolgar, Director of Sales. They would certainly quiz me on this subject and I had better be sensitive to the fact that the Pye equipment was amplitude modulated. I should beware of overstating its shortcomings. I was still planning my strategy for dealing with this tricky little subject when the conductor announced that we had arrived at St John's Wood station, my destination.

Less than a week later, Harry Woolgar, a seasoned and world-wise sales executive, is leaning against the mahogany liquor cabinet in Godfrey Imhof's office. Godfrey, with the air of the impartial observer, sits comfortably behind his desk. The much-discussed interview is in progress and John Stanley is running the show. He is pacing slowly back and forth on the Persian rug. A lock of straight blond hair hangs over his young and intense face. He is studying the intricate patterns on the rug as he asks:

"Mr. Layton—Howard isn't it—may I call you Howard? How would you describe Amplitude Modulation as applied to broadcasting?"

"It carries the program material or sound waves by varying the amplitude of the carrier radio wave," I reply. "And in public broadcasting, it's able to travel over long distances and cover large geographical areas." I glance at John Stanley to see whether I can get some hint of his reaction to my answer, but he continues pacing, his eyes on the carpet.

"How does it do that?"

"Do what?"

"Go long distances."

"Oh. By bouncing off buildings and ionized layers in the upper atmosphere. That way the radio waves can hop, skip and jump over large distances—sometimes all over the world—before they are dissipated."

"And how would you describe frequency modulation?"

"Frequency modulation continually adjusts the frequency of the carrier radio wave to convey the program material, instead of changing its amplitude. The amplitude stays constant."

Still no reaction from John Stanley. His pacing is beginning to unnerve me.

"What would you say is the chief feature of frequency modulation?" he says to the carpet.

I give him the answer that I had rehearsed in front of the mirror the night before. "Frequency modulation behaves a bit more like a beam of light. That is, it's substantially a line-of-sight method. The waves can travel good distances but they don't bounce off buildings or atmospheric layers very well. They tend to get absorbed, or simply go right through the atmospheric layers, so their range of operation is typically limited to between ten and twenty miles depending on how high the base-station antenna is located above the surrounding terrain."

John Stanley looks up from the carpet for the first time. "Hmm," he says with his intense gaze fixed on the office window, "And does frequency modulation have any special advantages to make up for its more limited range?"

Better watch it now. Safer to keep my answers fairly objective for the sake of credibility.

"What FM lacks in operating range it makes up for in its freedom from background noise and static," I reply. I am sweating now.

"Which do you think is the better method for mobile radio equipment?" The question is fired at me almost as an accusation.

I throw caution to the winds. "Depends on who is doing the selling," I shoot back.

A pause. Godfrey Imhof's eyes twinkle. He looks first at John Stanley, then at Harry Woolgar. "Any more questions gentlemen?" he asks.

For the first time in the interview, John Stanley looks directly at me. "As soon as you've settled in, we'll want to see you for an in-depth briefing on the product line."

It was over. John Stanley and Harry Woolgar departed for Cambridge and it was up to me now to get on with the job and see whether I would be able to make the switch from frustrated thespian to applications engineer without falling on my face. But I was by no means alone. 'Tup' Theakston, a veteran technical salesman, was already deeply involved in making the rounds of the taxicab companies and learning how to drink as they could drink—vodka and tomato juice by the tumbler. As far as I knew, Tup had missed out on the departmental management position because of his limited technical training. Even so, his ability to erect aerial masts was very impressive, and he was an effective salesman.

Then there was Helen Barr, slim, attractive, efficient secretary, whose organizing abilities, I soon discovered, were responsible for much of our successful sales promotion work. Our base transmitter dispatcher, Bobbie Bowery, and red-headed Vera, who worked on proposals, made up the rest of the crew. It was a congenial and productive team, and little by little with dogged perseverance, we began to develop our share of the mobile radio market. We held informative lectures at the headquarters of various prospective customers and began to foster a broader awareness of the practical value of the mobile radiotelephone.

My first real triumph concerned an opportunity to equip more than sixty South-London taxicabs with radio-tele-phones. I was invited to the fleet's headquarters for final negotiations and, if possible, to collect an order and a down-payment check. In the course of my presentation to the whole group a month previously, I had learned that there were special rites of passage that one had to observe to 'qual-ify' as a vendor to this particular company, and one's success would depend quite heavily on one's compliance with those rites. I was not quite sure what to expect when I drove up to the parking area at the front of the Waterloo building but whatever it was, I told myself, I was up to it.

The 'office' with its cobblestone-paved floor and high glass ceilings was actually a courtyard in front of the main building. It was like a miniature railroad station, but the chief, Fred Cobb, quickly made me feel at home. I found him sitting at the end of a large wooden table with his great bulk flowing over the arms of a high-backed basket chair. Waving at me with a tankard in his hand, and freely spilling an alco-holic brew of some sort over the table, he indicated that I should be seated next to him and relax. Then he placed a glass beer tankard in front of me.

Instead of producing a bottle of good English Ale, however, a bottle of Plymouth Gin appeared as if from nowhere and my host proceeded to fill my tankard. He stopped at about the one-third mark, then, mistaking my dumbstruck silence and my open-mouthed stare as signs of approval, he continued to pour. I found my voice a bit later than the half-full moment and asked if I might have a little tonic water. He didn't have any of that, but instead brought forth a container of Noilly

Prat vermouth and sloshed a generous helping into my tankard.

There were no negotiations. After ensuring that I was making some progress with my drink, Fred heaved himself up out of his chair, picked up some documents from the table beside him, and ambled toward the two large doors leading to the main building. At the door, he turned. "The men liked your presentation last month," he said. Then he disappeared into the main building, leaving me to contemplate my tankard of gin.

I was tempted to go after him—to ask about the status of the order—but something told me that that would be the wrong thing to do. I somehow knew that to conclude our negotiations in the desired manner, I was expected to finish my drink. I pondered my options. I did my best to calculate the amount of gin I had to consume. A pint-sized tankard holds a pint. That's sixteen ounces. At two-thirds full, that would amount to between ten and twelve ounces of liquor. Five or six two-ounce shots! Even the thought of it churned my stomach. Surreptitiously I glanced around trying to locate a drain or waste container where I could dump the contents of the tankard, but there was nothing to be seen. Besides, I had an uneasy feeling that I was being watched through one of the many front windows of the main building.

Again I considered barging through the double doors and tackling Fred about the order, and again some sixth sense told me that that would be a mistake. It was becoming increasingly clear to me that there was not going to be a way out. I would have to drink the stuff.

In the course of my wartime service with the RAF there had been occasions when a few double gins would not have fazed me. But that was many years ago and I was totally out of practice. Nowadays, a couple of glasses of wine were my usual quota and even that much alcohol was not entirely without its after-effects the following morning. I didn't know exactly how this present binge would affect me, but I decided that it would be best to prepare for the worst. I opened my briefcase to find something to write on, and as I was taking out my notebook, I saw the sandwich that I'd bought for lunch the day before and hadn't had occasion to need. It was a valuable find. Some food in my stomach would help to absorb the alcohol. I was thankful for small mercies. I pulled the sandwich out of my case and set it on the table beside me. I wrote a couple of notes, stuffed them into my jacket pocket and put the notebook back in my briefcase. Then I began to eat and drink.

Believing that nothing could be gained by protracting the process, I took gulps of my drink and bites of my sandwich alternately and fairly continuously. It was shortly after I'd consumed the last bite of the sandwich and reduced the contents of my tankard to about the quarter level that my head began to throb and my vision began to blur. The world began to turn in front of my eyes. I seemed to be on the merry-go-round at the Coventry Fairgrounds, finding it difficult to stay on my horse. If I concentrated really hard, I could focus my eyes just for a moment or two, then I would lose it and the world would spin again. Something told me that I had better not waste time. I made a grab for the tankard, felt its rim bang on my teeth as I swung it up to my mouth a little too energetically, and was vaguely aware of some trickling over my chin as I proceeded to drain it.

The timing seemed too precise to be coincidental. I had no sooner plonked the empty tankard back on the table, than Fred Cobb's bulk appeared in the double doorway. He ambled over to where I was sitting and stuffed some papers into my hand.

"Sorry it took so long," he said. "I think you'll find that in order."

I looked down with the feeling that the hand that was holding the papers didn't belong to me. I did my best to focus on the wording. By concentrating as hard as I could, I managed to ascertain that I was holding a purchase order and a check in my hand. I looked up and opened my mouth to thank my benefactor, but he was already disappearing through the double doors. I wasn't about to make any attempt to follow him. Difficult enough to make my way to the entrance of the courtyard without alerting any prying eyes to my precarious condition. I fumbled with my brief-case, stuffed the papers in, and by a prodigious effort of will, hauled myself up to a standing position.

Proceeding in what I hoped was a substantially straight line, I made my way carefully to the entrance and turned the corner into the street. As my head began to throb in earnest and my vision became even more blurred, I knew I was running out of time to complete my plan. I passed my car, parked against the curb not far from the gates I had just come through, and made my way to the end of the street. There, I turned the corner and, leaning against a lamppost for support, I hailed a taxi.

Once inside the cab, I told the driver that I wasn't feeling well and that I would like to get to a public phone before going on to Imhof's Showrooms. We found a phone-booth within a minute or two but when I attempted to get out of the cab to make my call, I found it quite beyond my capabilities.

I fumbled for the two pieces of notepaper in my pocket, extracted some generous fare money from my wallet, and gave the papers and the money to the driver. "Please make the call for me," I said, "and read the message to Godfrey Imhof." Then I passed out.

When I opened my eyes again, I was lying on the couch in Goff Imhof's office. Evidently the taxi driver and Goff had done well by me. As I learned later, the driver had dutifully called Goff, and had then driven to the Imhof showrooms and parked at the back door in Hanway Street where Goff was waiting to meet him. Goff, with the driver's help, had then smuggled me up in the rear elevator to his office where I would have a chance to recover from the worst effects of my over-indulgence. Two cups of strong black coffee served to bring me back to some semblance of wakefulness. As I came to, I was greeted by the sight of Goff grinning at me broadly from behind his desk. As soon as I felt able to move, I reached for my briefcase and fumbled around for the hard-won purchase order and check. When I found them I handed them to Goff.

"I hope there are easier ways to get orders," I said. Then I fell back again into a deep and blissful slumber.

Success followed success and I became so involved with the daily challenges of the job that my determination to return to acting in a few months, steadily weakened. The months turned into years, and at some point along the way I acknowledged to myself that the point-of-no-return had already slipped away. Yet I was still very restless. Fascinating as mobile radio might be I could not see myself making a career of it, and in any case I didn't feel I was making enough money. Even after my crowning achievement in wresting the prestigious Automobile Association account away from

Marconi, I was still finding it difficult to support my wife and child in the pretty little piece of suburbia that was our home.

Twelve Aston Avenue in Kenton, the attractive semi-detached where Laura and I lived, was all that we needed, but its upkeep accounted for a larger proportion of my income than we'd originally expected. In addition, Laura had felt it essential that we send Peta to boarding school to broaden her horizons and her academic prospects, and this added expense strained our financial resources.

In the end we decided that we'd have a better chance of balancing our budget if we abandoned the tranquillity of outer suburbia and moved to a flat closer to my place of work. We put our house on the market fully furnished and went flat-hunting closer to town.

St. John's Wood in northwest London is a lively and attractive community, well within the compass of the London Underground railway commuting network and boasting its own underground station. It was there that in the course of one of our Sunday afternoon prospecting tours, we stumbled upon a new block of flats in which three or four units were still available.

Kingsmill, a small but well-appointed apartment building, encompassed about forty flats in all. The spacious layout of the flats suited us well, and the location, less than five minutes walk from the Underground, could hardly have been more convenient. We found an agency office right on the ground floor of the building and were fortunate enough to get a tour of the available apartments on our first visit. Number fifteen on the second floor appeared to offer the space and layout we were looking for. A large living room with plenty of windows faced southeast, and a sizable bedroom with an adjacent bathroom and kitchen and dining area, were all directly reachable from the entrance hall.

We wanted to get an idea of what the place would look like when furnished, so we asked the agent whether she knew of a furnished unit with a similar layout that we could look at, preferably one with Danish-modern furnishings. Yes—she knew of such a unit. A Swedish couple on the ground floor had a flat with the same layout and the agent was sure they'd be glad to show it to us. She picked up the telephone, found the couple in, and got us invited downstairs. By the end of the afternoon we'd signed up. Laura was ecstatic. All our present furniture would go with the house and she would have the immense pleasure of furnishing the flat from scratch.

But bricks and mortar do not a home make, and soon after we'd settled into our new quarters I realized that very little of my own restlessness had subsided with the relocation. It was Saturday morning. The September sun cast faint window-frame shadows across the mushroom-toned wall-to-wall carpet, leaving the rest of the living room almost completely gray. A subdued setting, just right for brooding. Laura had already gone out shopping to Bowman's. When we had first agreed on the desired color and pattern for the settee we'd bought, Laura had had difficulty committing herself to the actual shade. When Bowman's delivered and installed it in our flat, she was quite sure they'd made a mistake. It couldn't be the shade she'd ordered, she said, and it just didn't go with the carpet or the Sapele mahogany-and-rosewood sideboard. They would just have to change it, and Laura had gone off to see about that.

Alone in the flat, I began to review the patchwork quilt that was my life, and I thought about the events of recent years since my resignation from the service. Stage and film work had been exciting and enjoyable. I had performed before Queen Mary and had actually shaken hands with her. I had filled in for Robert Taylor for a couple of months, when he found he couldn't do two movies at the same time. In the process I had come close to drowning myself in the Wash in East Anglia and narrowly escaped piling up an expensive sports car as I raced around the mountain roads of north Wales. Oh yes, it had been exciting enough, but it had got me precisely nowhere.

Perhaps if I had been single and fancy-free I might have put up with the slings and arrows of that roller-coaster existence long enough to establish myself. But I had not had that luxury. One needed to start young in the acting business, and at twenty nine, my first agent had complained that I'd left it rather late. I had reminded her that there'd been a war on, but her response had not been sympathetic. "You should have got out at the end of the war instead of signing on again," she said. "I guess you just couldn't make up your mind what you wanted to do with your life." And of course she had been right. The war had interrupted my career and left me, like so many others, unsettled and, in a way, lost.

The switch to sales engineering and my job at Imhof's had probably been a good move in the circumstances. The long-term possibilities and the attainable heights in the business world were perhaps not as lofty or appealing as a career in stage and film work might have been, but the course would be less precarious and more financially rewarding on the way up. Yes, for a married man with responsibilities, it had been a move in the right direction. Not by any means a final move, but probably the right one. When Laura returned and told me of her successful discussions with Bowmans, I was in a more cheerful mood.

The Imhof RadioTelephone division continued to prosper.

We equipped the fleets of the Automobile Association and a multitude of police, fire, ambulance and taxicab services, and introduced this new communications tool to a growing number of London area businesses. Based upon our projections and estimates of the potential market for the product, we were formulating plans for a considerable expansion.

Now suddenly, that September evening conference in Godfey Imhof's office had changed everything. Goff, the accomplished businessman, was negotiating a handsome compensation for the loss of the Pye distributorship, but for me there was no other activity in the company that would be right for my kind of qualifications. I was a trained radio and electrical engineer and the other departments of Imhof's were strictly retail. They did not require, and would not make optimum use of, my sort of background.

But Goff thought otherwise. He offered me the management of his company's new high-fidelity department. He assured me that the task of growing it to the size that he intended for it, eventually eclipsing all other such outlets in London, would be fulfilling and financially rewarding for me. I was by no means convinced, but I listened attentively to the details of his offer. Sensing my doubts, he rounded off his presentation with a statement which, although proffered with the best of intentions and good humor, filled me with dismay. "Howard," he quipped, "so long as you don't steal the petty cash, you have a job here for life."

At Imhof's for life? Spend the rest of my days selling high-fidelity equipment to finicky, nit-picking retail consumers across London, when there was a big exciting world out there to be explored? Use all those years of engineering training to sell the merits of a Wharfdale speaker or a Leak amplifier to temperamental music buffs or tone-deaf dentists, while the world out there was overflowing with opportunities to market sophisticated machinery and instrumentation to industries all over the country, or even the whole wide world?

If Goff had just offered me the job instead of making it seem like a life sentence, it might have been different. Viewed as an interim occupation, to work at diligently until something more in line with my background could be found, it could be seen as a kind and generous offer. It was not too much to expect that a person suddenly losing the job of his or her choosing would be glad of any reasonable means of filling in, until suitable replacement employment could be found. But Goff had not put it that way. In his concern to assure me of his high opinion of my capabilities and of his desire that I continue as an Imhof employee, he'd scared me into the realization that I would have to leave—and soon.

I thanked Goff for his offer and for his faith in me. Then I told him that I would have to leave. He was visibly disappointed but he understood. He gave me the job anyway, and said that whenever I needed time off to attend a job interview I should just fit it into my work schedule and make sure that another member of the staff was suitably briefed to cover my absence. His generosity paid off, for almost a year elapsed before I closed my office door at Imhof's for the last time.

SIX

Antal, anxious to find some way to make his daughter's daily twelve-kilometer round trip a little easier for her, gave Nárcissza permission to use his bicycle. Designed for carrying a 70 kilogram machine gun and equipped with tires that had seen far better days, it was his army bicycle which, because of knee injuries that he'd sustained in World War I, he seldom rode. Although daunted by the prospect of pushing the machine up the winding road on the Austrian side, Nárcissza didn't wish to seem unappreciative of her father's thoughtfulness, so she made what use of it she could.

The brakes were satisfactory, so she could get up speed and save a lot of time on the downhill segments of the journey. But the uphill push on the way home tired her more than if she had walked all the way. Her dilemma was eventually solved when the now treadless tires began to suffer more frequent punctures than there was time for anyone to deal with. As the winter snow spread itself across the countryside, Nárcissza bundled herself up in her mother's winter coat. Wearing her father's cut down military trousers and a pair of his army boots stuffed with newspapers to take up the extra space, she resumed her trudging again, up and down the hills and across the valley to school.

Slowly, she began to solve the mysteries of German grammar and as a result, her tests in all subjects steadily improved. Her grades at the end of her first year at the gymnasium were not outstanding, but were rated above average, and in mathematics she was ahead of everyone.

The tuition, however, was not free. There were fees to pay, modest enough by the standards of the time, but for Nárcissza, a considerable sum. She was obliged to find unusual and creative ways to raise the money. She started by smuggling postage stamps across the border and she also carried letters back and forth for relatives and friends. She didn't know why they elected to use this method of communication but it was all gainful employment, and the small sums paid for her services contributed usefully to her central purpose. As she gathered experience in exploiting the money-earning scope of her daily border crossings, she found other avenues of income. She smuggled special paper for rolling cigarettes. Although still readily obtainable in Austria, the commodity was almost non-existent in Germany. This particular smuggling activity, which she fondly referred to as her 'paper route,' ultimately became one of her best sources of income.

In time, she found yet another source of income to add to her portfolio. An elderly Scottish lady, Ida Macdonald, who had long served as governess for the countess' children and had also taught French and English to local students, took it upon herself to tutor Nárcissza in the English language. Progress was rapid. At the end of two years the family doctor, who lived about a mile away from the gymnasium she was attending, invited Nárcissza to give English lessons to his daughter. The job, lasting through the winter months, was a welcome source of additional income for her, but since during the worst of the weather it was not practical to make the journey home on her tutoring days, she stayed overnight at the doctor's house.

There were no spare bedrooms, so she shared the attic with the doctor's maid. The roof was uninsulated and one could sometimes catch a glimpse of moonlight between the roof tiles. When it snowed, the flakes would drift through the cracks and form a coating on the eiderdown comforter that covered her bed. Warm and snug in her cocoon, Nárcissza welcomed these nights. Sometimes she would take a nightlight—a sort of shielded candle—to bed with her and read under the covers for a while before going to sleep. Then, after a long night of breathing fresh cold air, she would awaken with reddened cheeks and a special eagerness to greet the new day.

Oh, how she wished they could all stay in Austria and make a home of their own; settle down and live their lives without having to wait for the phone call that would uproot them again; without having to wonder where they would be in one, or three, or six months time. By this time they'd formed attachments and were all busily engaged in getting on with their lives and putting the sadness and upheavals of earlier times behind them.

Nárcissza had grown to love her life at the Castell's and her schooling at the gymnasium. She wanted to finish her time there and go on to university, then make a career in some important scientific field. Deep down, she wanted to do all those things without ever having to move again. On many occasions her parents, too, would talk into the night about their future, examining possibilities for making a life for themselves and their children without having to journey to some unknown shore far across the ocean and learn the ways and mores of a totally strange society. In many ways, the people in Austria were much like themselves. True, the language was different, but they were beginning to deal with that difference and were feeling more and more at home at the Castell estate as they did so.

They knew that in North and South America, or in any of the far countries, they would have far more than language barriers to contend with. But the more they talked, the more Antal and Erzsébet realized that the changes and challenges they were trying to avoid would not hamper their children. They would adapt to new places and people in their stride and, sorry as they might be to leave their now familiar surroundings and newfound friends, they would quickly find new ones as children do. They would seek out and grasp the opportunities that would await them in the New World, opportunities that refugees would not find in the shattered remains of their own continent.

They would have to go. The slow, methodical bureaucracy of the various displaced persons organizations would one day get around to their particular case and find a future home for them, and they would have to be ready for that day. In the interim they would have to remind themselves constantly that they were refugees in transit, and in so reminding themselves, they would be better prepared when the day would come for them to move on.

That day came early in 1949. Antal had named several different countries in his family's emigration application papers and had made Argentina their first choice. The consul notified them that the opportunity for transfer to

Argentina had arrived. The paperwork for transfer of refugees required that they move to an official transit camp at a town called Wegscheid near Linz. A few days after hearing from the consul, they were saying their tearful good-byes to their friends and neighbors and boarding the transfer wagon. The long, slow train journey that followed, did little to lift their spirits. By the time they arrived at their destination they were tired, hungry—and too late. The commandant informed them that the quota for Argentina had been filled. They would now have to wait for the next opportunity to emigrate to some other country on their list of preferences.

Wegscheid, a seemingly endless stretch of long wooden buildings on both sides of the road, gave the appearance of an American army barracks. On one side, some two thousand Christians were housed in a section designed for half that number, and on the other side were about five thousand Jews. There were no furnishings; the refugees used whatever blankets, sleeping bags, boxes, trunks or suitcases they'd brought with them. Those who hadn't been able to bring anything to sleep on were allotted straw or straw sacks. Wood burning stoves provided heat and the means to cook food for those who chose not to eat at the central mess. Toilets were in two sections of a single central building. One row of about thirty toilets served for the men, and on the other side of a partition which did not even come close to the ceiling, a similar row of toilets was provided for the women. There were no separations between the individual toilets in the rows, so there was no privacy. Men sat in a row in their section and women sat in a row in theirs. For washing, pails and basins could be filled at one of several outside faucets, then heated on the inside woodstoves if desired.

Across the road, the Jews seemed somewhat better off,

probably because the Americans felt that they had suffered enough. They had better food and better facilities and were provided with pillows and blankets.

Again, the Ludányi family occupied one fairly large concrete-floored room. Although poorly insulated, this was not of importance as far as the outside walls were concerned, for they had arrived in April, and spring came early in that part of Europe. But the insulation of the walls between their room and those of their neighbors was quite another matter. One could not help overhearing the conversations in the rooms on either side. On one side a Jewish man of about fifty years shared a room with his beautiful German wife, considerably taller than he, and perhaps twenty-five years his junior. They talked a great deal during the evenings and made a variety of other sounds during the night. Sometimes, during the late evenings when the neighbors' conversations were in progress, Nárcissza's parents, embarrassed by the subject matter, would attempt to prevent their children from deciphering it by engaging in loud and animated discussions of one sort or another.

When, in spite of this, Nárcissza managed to hear and understand some parts of the conversations, her parents looked at each other horrified as she translated the subject matter to them and asked them to explain to her the meanings of the discussions. They didn't say much, nor did they rebuke her for listening. They simply didn't want her to become too interested or attach too much importance to what she'd heard. Nárcissza concluded that this must be the time when people made love, but she was never able to hear anything zesty. Tamás, who slept next to the wall, was able to compensate for this. Sometimes as they lay in bed he would relay information to her, item by item, about all the intriguing sounds he heard: the moans and the sharp intakes of breath; the rhythmic creaks of complaining frameworks; trampoline sounds, undulating in intensity, but all the while building and building to crescendos that sometimes shook the wall where Tamás had his ear. Then there were sounds of gasping and long drawn-out cries. Tamás knew from what he'd heard on previous occasions that pretty soon after that, all would be quiet.

After awaiting developments for about two months, they learned that the commandant of another camp at nearby Asten, was on the lookout for an English speaking interpreter. He had learned of Nárcissza's presence at Wegscheid and had arranged for the family's transfer to his location. Asten, a much larger camp, accommodated more than five thousand refugees in much less crowded conditions. The Ludányis were allotted two small rooms this time, and the floors were wood rather than concrete. The roads between the barracks were hard top rather than dirt and the outside toilets with separating partitions offered more privacy. There was a building called the entertainment center where meetings and stage performances were held, and there were sports fields for soccer and other games. It was at least a step in the right direction, but when the commandant, a Scotsman, saw Nárcissza, he was visibly dismayed. He spoke complainingly to the Hungarian who had transferred the family and had brought Nárcissza to see him. "How am I going to tell people that I have a secretary when she is just a kid with pigtails?" Narcissza didn't get that job, but all was not lost. Since at fifteen, she was the only young person around who could speak English, another job was invented in which she was able to serve as translator for the International Scouts.

Some six weeks had passed when they got further news from the camp office about where they might eventually go.

"The United States was on your list of preferred destinations. Somebody wants to talk to you about that."

They were advised that the Catholic Church Refugee Organization wanted them to go to Linz for an interview, and that Nárcissza, whose English was better than her father's, should call to make the arrangements. A day or two later, when Antal journeyed by trolley bus to Linz, the lady interviewer at the Catholic church offices explained that a job opening existed in Virginia in the USA. There, a landowner by the name of Carter, was interested in sponsoring a family who would work on his farm and tend his horses and train them. The lady reviewed the Ludányi's application forms and asked some questions. She explained the basis of the offer, the food and accommodations, and the wages that went with the job. Antal signed a contract.

To Antal it seemed like a heaven-sent opportunity to make a new start in life, a way to provide for his family and do the kind of work he would enjoy—working with horses. Within a few days the Ludányis received another call, this time from the American consulate. They were scheduled for an interview as soon as they could arrange for medical clearance. They were able to take care of this requirement right there at the camp hospital where they were checked for freedom from tuberculosis and venereal diseases. The interview took place at the camp, too, in the course of a routine visit by the consulate representative.

Finally, the displaced persons office informed Antal that with all other formalities out of the way, it would now be necessary for him to journey to Linz again for interrogation by the United States Intelligence Agency. The US was not eager to invite Nazis into the country, so Antal's political affiliation had to be established. When he had seated himself in the interrogation room, the interviewer posed the first standard question and waited for the routine answer. It was understood among Hungarian senior officers that at interviews with representatives of the Allies they would not state that they had fought in the war. They might say that they had taught at the academy or served at training camps or in supply services, or in a host of other occupations, but it was considered against their best interests to confess to direct involvement in the fighting. Many years later Antal learned that most officers had based their answers on this policy and the Intelligence Agency expected it, but he knew nothing of this at the time. The interviewer regarded Antal across the table as he posed the question: "What did you do, Mr. Ludányi?"

Antal replied, "I was a colonel in the Hungarian army and I fought the Russians at the front as long as they let me. I was never a Nazi but I fought the Russians to the end."

The interviewer continued with the questioning. At the conclusion of the meeting he rose and shook Antal's hand., "You'll have no trouble, Colonel," he said.

Less than a week later, the Ludányis were advised that their application for emigration to the United States had been approved and that they should stand by for transfer instructions. Within a month they were on their way.

A direct journey to Bremen, their designated port of departure, was not possible at the time because many of the war-damaged bridges and tracks en route had not yet been repaired. First they journeyed to Salzburg and remained there at another camp for several days, and from there they were taken to a former German military barracks in Bremen to await their boarding instructions. On the twelfth of August, one thousand and fifty-three refugees, the Ludányis among them, left the barracks, and after a train journey of some two and a half hours, they arrived at the dockside for embarkation.

The United States Naval Ship, General R.M. Blatchford, was not particularly large by modern standards or even by standards of the time, but with a displacement of some fifteen thousand tons and a troop carrying capacity of more than three thousand souls, she was certainly an impressive sight. But the Ludányi children who had not seen an ocean-going liner before, did not have much opportunity to stand there on the dock and gaze up in wonder at her vast profile or at the tier upon tier of decks and portholes spread along her considerable length. They were herded with such urgency along the concrete dock and up the gangway to the gaping entrance to the ship's interior that they had difficulty in keeping together as a family. Once inside, they were immediately separated.

The older boys, Tom and Andrew, were placed with their father and sent in one direction, and the small children, Tony and Paul, in another. Nárcissza was herded off with some other young women, and Erzsébet was left searching frantically for her young ones. The errors were eventually rectified, and Tony and Paul were reunited with their mother. By the time the great ship had left the Bremen docks behind and made its way to the open sea, the scattered family members were able to settle down with a comforting knowledge of each other's whereabouts. They had learned that mealtimes in the dining hall would give them opportunities to gather together and exchange news about their adventures and about events and people in their various and separate living quarters. The children adapted quickly to life aboard ship. They made friends and told stories about where they had been and where they were going, and about the wonderful adventures that were awaiting them in that larger-than-life land called America.

By the third day at sea their spirits were dampened by sickness in the family. András had come down with strep throat and had become so ill that he had to be isolated in the ship's hospital. For several days no one was permitted to see him. When, eventually, he began to respond to treatment, his recovery was hampered by sea sickness. The seas were swelling noticeably as the ship reached mid-ocean. Skies to the west were darkening by the hour. By morning of the fifth day they were in the midst of a vigorous storm which threw towering breakers at the bow and rolled the ship as if it were a hollow toy. The severity of the storm and its effect on the ship's passengers was later reflected in the evening attendance in the dining room. Of the entire passenger complement for that sitting, only nine souls were to be seen that night. Six of them were Ludányis.

By morning, the brooding skies were behind them and the seas were becoming calm again. Despite the storm, András was making progress with his recovery. The air was fresh and electric with talk and conjecture about the fast approaching end to their journey. As they awoke on the morning of the seventh day they were aware of a total lack of the rolling motion that had been part of their waking lives for the last week. Children were shouting and urging their siblings and parents to come up on deck. They were in the still waters of the Hudson River moving slowly past the Statue of Liberty on their left and the tip of Manhattan Island on their right. Diminutive tugboats were drawing them toward the midtown docks. They stood at the rails, quiet and fascinated as the General Blatchford slid slowly and silently into its designated berth. Ship's crew and dockhands manipulated winches and hawsers at bow and stern until all motion ceased. The most fateful voyage of their lives had reached its end. A bustling Monday morning greeted them, and a warm sun shone down to welcome them to the land where they would set about rebuilding their lives.

SEVEN

My third unsuccessful job interview revealed to me where my future would lie, but the manner in which it did so was quite unexpected. The job itself seemed to have a lot to offer. The Philips Company in London needed an applications engineer to negotiate contracts in respect of a range of electrical components and systems. The post would involve extensive travel over the length and breadth of the country. I sent in my resumé and, in due course, the company replied, inviting me to attend an interview.

Philips occupied an impressive building in the eastern part of London and when I approached the front office, the receptionist greeted me as if I were some sort of celebrity.

"If you will follow me to the conference room, Dr. Partridge will join you in a few moments. Meanwhile," she said, "I'll bring you some tea."

The room into which I was ushered looked more like a reading room in an exclusive West End club than any industrial reception room I'd encountered. Dark mahogany paneling and ceiling-high bookshelves covered all four walls. A long marble-topped coffee table sat centrally on a dark-toned Persian carpet ringed by several overstuffed leather chairs. Tea and biscuits appeared shortly after I had seated myself. Then I was left alone.

After about half an hour, a tall, lean and conservatively dressed man strode briskly into the room and announced that he was Dr. Partridge and that he was sorry he'd been detained and had kept me waiting. As I rose to greet him, he indicated that he wished me to stay in my seat, but remained standing himself. Then without further small talk he proceeded with the interview.

When he had satisfied himself that I was comfortably settled, Dr. Partridge looked down at me through his thick horn-rimmed glasses. His head was tipped back slightly, enabling him to look straight down his aquiline nose directly into my eyes.

"I take it that you are familiah with our product line Mr. Layton," he said.

"Enough so that I don't think I shall have much trouble learning whatever else I would need to know," I replied.

"Splendid. So tell me about yawself and yaw background."

I gave Dr. Partridge an outline of my prewar electrical engineering training at the Coventry Technical College and a brief mention of my industrial experience at the General Electric Company. Then I followed with a review of my communications and radar training at the Royal Air Force College in Cranwell, and concluded with a thumbnail sketch of my sales engineering work at Imhof's.

Dr. Partridge walked slowly back and forth, pursing his lips and occasionally nodding his head as I talked. When I'd finished, he stopped in front of my chair and, looking down at me again along the length of his aristocratic nose, he spoke in a manner that could only be described as condescending.

"Hmm. Well, I'm afraid your background is not quite what we are looking for. I will concede howevah, that you seem to be familiah with electriciteh."

On the way back to Imhof's in the Underground, as I reflected on my interview with the Philips scientist, I concluded that this was the way things were going to be in postwar Britain, just as they had been before. I would forever encounter the old-school disdain for those who had hoisted themselves up by their own bootstraps, who had not been to Oxford or Cambridge, nor had the benefit of a start at Eton or Harrow. I realized that wartime service had changed me and I no longer had the patience to grapple with this asinine type of discrimination. Before the day was through, I made my decision. In the evening at dinner, I told my wife that I wanted to leave the land of my birth and seek my fortune elsewhere.

"But where would we go?" she asked, not unreasonably.

"Anywhere," I replied.

"What do you mean, anywhere?"

"I mean we should go wherever a promising opportunity happens to lead us— Australia, Canada, South Africa. Even the USA if that's the way things happen to work out."

Laura was quiet for a bit, then she got to thinking about the practical implications of what I'd said.

"What about our flat and all that furniture?" she asked.

"Well, the fact that we've fixed it up so nicely will ensure that we get a good price for it," I replied.

She pondered that some more. Then she said, "You're complaining all the time about the lack of sunshine in this country, and how it affects your mood. Maybe the thing to do is go somewhere where there's more sunshine."

I thought about that for a while. It was true that after spending some four and a half years in the sunny climes of the Middle Eastern war zones, my return to the frequently dull and sunless days of my homeland had had a profound influence on my disposition and on the perceived quality of my life. Perhaps if my war service had not taken me overseas I might never have become aware of the importance of sunshine to my sense of well being, but it served no purpose to think about that now. Laura's comment made a lot of sense. It we were going to move, we might as well go somewhere where there was lots of sun.

Within the next week or so I made the rounds of the big travel agencies on Regent Street and Haymarket. As part of the information packages I collected, I made sure to obtain data on the weather patterns and hours of sunshine to be expected in the various countries of interest. To my surprise I discovered that all the countries I had considered as likely places to go, enjoyed considerably more hours of sunshine per annum than dear old England. That meant that our options were open, and with this realization I wrote for listings of the job opportunities in each of the countries on my original short list. In due course I had correspondence going with companies in Australia, Canada, New Zealand and even South America. Then, just as things were coming to a head in my negotiations with an electrical instrument manufacturer in Canada, an opportunity cropped up from a totally unexpected source.

In the course of my work at Imhof's hi-fi division I had become friendly with the sales manager of one of our high-fidelity equipment suppliers. When I had told Victor Weake about my plan to emigrate he had mentioned that during a recent round of golf, he'd met an interesting chap who had said something about wanting to start an export business and needing a business partner. Victor didn't know what sort of partner was needed or whether it would involve investment of capital which I did not have, but he thought it would be a good idea for me to meet the man he had talked with. The conversation had slipped from my mind, but then one evening Victor telephoned me.

"Remember the chap I told you about who's looking for a business partner? "

"Yes, I remember."

"Well, he wants to see you. His name is John Ould and when I told him about your success at Imhof's, he seemed very interested."

No sooner had I digested that bit of information than John Ould called me at home and introduced himself. Toward the end of our discussion, he said he would like to meet me.

"Would you care to drop by my office for a chat?" he asked.

We made an appointment for the following Monday.

Berkeley Square is an attractive corner of the West End, but certainly not representative of modern business environments. Its old-world charm and leafy quiet did not seem in keeping with the brisk and businesslike setting I had expected to find. I made my way up the short flight of steps at the front of the terraced building. At John Ould's office on the first floor the door was opened by an amiable-looking man of about forty years or so, a little taller than I--probably about six feet—and slightly more heavily built. Thinning blond hair receded from a wide forehead. He introduced himself as John Ould and regarded me with kindly but sad eyes explaining that he had opened the door himself because he had not yet had the time to hire a secretary or other office help.

The offices of John Ould Limited seemed as subdued as their surroundings but from what I was able to see, they were well furnished and comfortable.

"Do come in and make yourself at home," he said, and soon we were engaged in a relaxed exchange. After apologizing for the fact that there was no one around to serve us tea, John came quickly to the point.

"Victor has told me enough about your technical background and experience, to give me all the information I need for the present as far as your qualifications are concerned, so perhaps you could fill me in a bit about your personal life." He smiled. "Only as personal as you want to be, of course. After that I'll provide you with as much information as I can about my own situation and plans."

He glanced at me for approval, and when I nodded, he added, "I'm looking forward to hearing your story."

I really didn't know where to begin. "What sort of things would you like to know?" I asked.

"Oh, just a bit about what you've done before and what sort of education you've had. Don't be nervous about telling me--I just want to get to know you a bit as a person. Then you can quiz me in turn and ask as many questions as you like."

That seemed fair, so I cast about in my mind for a place to start.

"I suppose you could say I come from a typical middle class background. I was brought up in Coventry and went to school there. My parents were divorced when I was eight years old and I don't remember the years before that when my father was at home. He worked as an aircraft inspector for the government and I only saw him when he paid us an occasional visit. I remember when I was fifteen years old, my father, in one of his generous moments, offered to send me to Oxford. I had finished at the Central Advanced School and had just signed up for the Engineering College Program at the General Electric Company when my father raised the matter with my mother.

My mother didn't go for my father's suggestion at all. She put the question to me in a way that made it difficult for me to give her anything but the answer she wanted.

'Howard,' she said, 'your father is talking about sending you to Oxford, but you don't want that, do you? You don't want to be at some boarding school away from home; you'd much rather be at home with us, wouldn't you?'

I didn't feel that I could hurt her and tell her that it was an opportunity I had longed for, so I told her that I wouldn't enjoy being away from home. My mother took that as a definite answer and told my father that I wouldn't want that—I would not want to be away from home. So it didn't happen. Instead, I went to the Coventry Technical College for three years as part of the GEC educational program, and that's where I got my initial electrical engineering training."

John motioned me to continue.

"What happened after that?" he asked.

"Well, about three years later, as soon as I'd finished at Coventry Tech., they put me in charge of a special assembly shop, making industrial power amplifying equipment for export, and about a year after that we were at war. I remember it was Sunday, September third, and I was sitting on the roof of the factory, working on the camouflage painting. All through the summer, most of the young men in the factory had been taking turns at painting in their spare time because by late spring everyone knew that war was inevitable and that we had better get ready for it.

My friend, Doug Phillips, called up to me from the road below. He told me that Prime Minister Neville Chamberlain was on the radio and he yelled for me to come down and listen. I scrambled down the ladder and joined the crowd around the radio. I can still hear that solemn and troubled voice: '. . . I have to tell you that this country is now at war with Germany.'

John nodded that he remembered that day.

'Whoopee!' Yes, that was our reaction. We just didn't know any better. All we saw was a chance for adventure. That same afternoon, I packed up my painting stuff and rushed off to the recruiting office with Doug to enlist in the Royal Air Force. A few weeks later we got our orders to report to the induction center at Cardington, to be kitted out and categorized for training. I badly wanted the pilot training course, but in the beginning that was mostly reserved for regulars and those who'd joined the RAF Reserve during the previous year or so when the recruitment campaign had started. In the end I was listed for navigator-bomb-aimer training and promised that I would be placed on the waiting list for a pilot's course when my turn would come."

"Did you fly over Germany? "

"No. After a year or so of flying training, I was posted to the Middle East and spent four and a half years there, first based in Aden and doing raids on airfields in Abyssinia, and on some of the coastal towns that the Italians were occupying in the Red Sea area, then later against Rommel's forces in the Western Desert. When we weren't on operational flying, instead of going drinking with the boys, I spent most of my time in my tent, reading and studying. Whenever we got a chance to visit Alexandria or Cairo, I bought books on technical subjects and on languages, too. I taught myself French and a little Italian and was able to make use of it whenever we had time off to go into the cities.

I remember how accomplished I felt when I bought my first novel printed in French and read it from cover to cover. It was Les Miserables and I kept the copy as a souvenir. But it was only after my return to England in January 1945 that I got a chance to do any more formal schooling. I went to the RAF College at Cranwell for a fifteen-month full-time radio-engineering course and then served as Signals Officer at the Eastern Fighter Sector until the end of the war. After it all ended, I signed on for a permanent commission, but I just couldn't settle down to the routines and 'red tape' of peace-time service.

In the end I resigned and set about studying for a career on the stage. I'd always been convinced that my real calling was the stage. It seemed to me that if I didn't get started on it while I was still young enough, I would always wonder what it would have been like, and why I had not had the gumption to go for it while I had the chance. I knew I would blame myself later in life if I didn't. I got myself accepted by the J. Arthur Rank School at the Connaught Theater in Worthing on the south coast and followed that with some successful years in Repertory Theater in England and Scotland. At first, because I was considered good looking and a ladies' man, they cast me mostly in romantic roles. In practice, however, I found I did best when I played the part of a cad or a ne'er-do-well—or even a buffoon. I enjoyed my most outstanding success in the role of Charles Stanton, the cheat and suave seducer, in J. B. Priestley's 'Dangerous Corner.' But I'm rattling on a bit and I'm sure you don't want to hear my whole life story."

"No, please go on. I think it's a good idea for us to learn as much as possible about each other if we're going to be partners. Besides, I reserved the morning for this purpose—and I would imagine you did, too."

"Well, later I restored a little of my faith in the better side of my character by playing in a romantic role at the Richmond Theater in London—a special performance for Queen Elizabeth's grandmother, Queen Mary. We played to a packed house—a wonderful mixture of members of London's high society and of ordinary working people. The play, 'Romance,' one of Queen Mary's favorites, had been selected at her request. It seemed to have pleased everyone, for at the final curtain, we were given a standing ovation. Looking up at Queen Mary's box from my position in the curtain call lineup, I could see that she was applauding, too.

After the curtain had come down for the last time, that truly regal lady let it be known that she wished to meet the whole cast, and one at a time, we were escorted to her box. Before entering, we were given brief instructions on how best to conduct ourselves. If she offered her gloved hand, one would not shake it. One would place one's own hand under hers to raise it slightly, while bending as if to raise it to one's lips. One wouldn't quite get that far, one's lips would not actually touch her hand—it would simply be a symbolic gesture.

The ladies of the cast were advised that they would gently take her hand, if offered, and simply curtsy. One was asked to remember that if the Queen engaged one in conversation, one should avoid prolonging it. At eighty-five years of age, long discussions could tire her. Better to answer whatever specific question she might ask, but resist any temptation to enlarge on it, and simply refer to her as 'Ma-am,' rather than 'Your Majesty.'

As we were to be presented to Queen Mary in alphabetical order, my turn came about half way through the list. When, at last, I stepped inside the red velvet drapes hanging at the entrance to her box, I found myself truly awed by her tall, statuesque appearance. A champagne-colored hat in the form of a silken turban accentuated her height.

Despite her most imposing presence, she was quick to put me at ease. She extended her hand as I had been advised that she might, and I bowed and lifted it a little in the manner I'd been instructed. Without waiting for me to speak, she began commenting on my performance in the play. I was so preoccupied with my concern to behave appropriately and avoid falling over my own feet, that I didn't register exactly what she said. But I do know that in her rich and incisive voice, she was telling me how much she'd enjoyed the play—and specifically my part in it. She made me feel that I had done a wonderful job of acting, though, in fact my part had been quite small.

'Thank you very much, ma-am,' I said. Then with a final bow, I backed carefully away from her august presence, and eased myself through the thick velvet drapes into the friendly embrace of the shadows beyond. A day to remember."

John seemed absorbed in my reminiscences, so I continued.

"After that, I worked in small parts in movies, and even took over a role for Robert Taylor for two full months when he was making the film 'Conspirator.' He was called back to Hollywood quite suddenly. A conflicting schedule left him with insufficient time to do anything except the close-ups and a few of the medium shots, for his present film. To cope with that situation, the casting director called me in to the Elstree Studios to check out my profile against Taylor's. They made us stand back-to-back to compare our builds and height. When they were satisfied with that, they set to work with the make-up, and in the end only his co-star, Elizabeth Taylor, could to tell us apart. Maybe that wasn't too surprising since the rest of the cast was mostly British and they hadn't met Robert Taylor before either. But I'm carrying on a bit and I'm sure you don't want to know the ins and outs of movie making."

"Perhaps the technical side wouldn't mean much to me," John replied. "But I'd certainly like to hear a bit about your experiences."

"Well, after Taylor left, I did everything else: the long shots, most of the medium shots, and even some of the near close-ups that he'd simply not had time for. It was an exciting time. I almost got myself drowned in the duck-shooting sequence. We were out there, walking the Flats—the vast stretches of sea-level flat land and mud banks on the East Anglian coast. That's an area of the Fen district near the Wash, ideal for duck-shooting forays. One afternoon near sundown, when the camera sequence had been completed and the crew had left, I stayed behind with two other actors. We thought we might do a little private duck shooting ourselves. We became so engrossed with this, that we didn't notice the onset of twilight, nor did we notice the increasing depth of the water we were wading through, as the tide steadily advanced, preparatory to submerging the entire area. Then, suddenly, one of our trio did notice.

'Hey, which way do we have to go to get out of here?' he called.

We looked around, a full 360 degrees. The gentle rise of the shoreline could no longer be seen. Whichever direction we looked, we could see only water, with long ridges of mud banks projecting here and there above the surface. In the distance, we could see one or two lights ahead of us, and one or two behind. We couldn't tell whether they were on shore, or whether their light came from ships or lighthouses.

In the end, we simply took a vote on which direction to proceed. We walked for what seemed a very long time, with the depth of the water lapping at our shins hardly changing. From this we concluded that we must be walking more or less parallel to the shore, but approaching it at a shallow angle, just sufficient to offset the effect of the rising tide. By mid evening, we discovered that our guesswork had been fairly accurate. We came ashore, wet and weary, some two miles from the point on the coastline where we'd set out that morning.

With our feet on dry land again, we talked of our experience of that day as if it had been a great adventure, but you won't be too surprised when I tell you that I haven't been duck-shooting since.

A couple of weeks later, I came close to piling up an expensive sports car in the Welsh mountains, but by the time I'd finished that assignment, the whole movie industry was in a slump and even the stars were having a difficult time finding work. That's when I applied for the job at Imhof's. I think you know the rest."

John was smiling. "What a colorful background. It's no wonder you did so well in your sales job. You probably could not have had a better training for sales work than you got as an actor." He laughed. "I'm glad you told me your story—very glad. I feel I'm beginning to understand what makes you tick." Then he rose and added, "But let's break now for an early lunch at my club. I'll tell you my own story while we're there."

An hour or so later, we were sipping our coffee after a satisfying lunch of lentil soup, pork pie and salad. John leaned back in his chair and fixed me with a steady gaze. "I am a concert pianist," he said. He noted my surprise and paused for a moment to give me time to digest that information. Then he added, "But I have long felt that I'm not temperamentally suited for the life of a professional pianist and that I would feel more at home in the business world, preferably import-export." I couldn't understand why he would wish to give up such a fulfilling occupation just to switch to a career in business, but then, I reflected, while my reasons had been different, I'd done just about the same thing myself a few years previously. I made no comment, so he continued:

"Last year I inherited a goodly sum of money from my father and that windfall has given me the opportunity to make the switch to something I'd prefer to do."

"But why import-export?" I asked.

"Because it seemed to me a stimulating type of activity without requiring much in the way of a specialized education," John replied. "Also, I know the United States reasonably well, especially the East Coast, so I thought that would be a good place to start. My present objective is to open an office in New York as soon as practicable." Then he smiled that kindly hurt smile and added, "I have a girl over there, too, so an office in New York would give me more opportunity to visit her and persuade her to marry me."

It all sounded very exciting and I began to get enthusiastic about the idea of joining him. But if John was planning to open a New York office, he would probably expect me to handle the home base at Berkeley Square and that didn't seem to be in line with my own objectives. I thought I had better explore that further.

"John, what exactly is your interest in me?" I asked.

"Well, from what I've learned, you have a strong technical

background, so I thought we could work with products compatible with that background and experience."

I was flattered by the thought that he was considering shaping his enterprise around my particular expertise, but I could also see the drawbacks as well as the advantages. If we were able to secure export agencies with some reliable British manufacturers, technical expertise would be required to sell them in the USA, so John would need to get some technical training himself and that would take time. Still, to get the ball rolling while he set about educating himself in the required technology, he could, of course, take me with him to New York. That course of action would suit me very well. I decided to pursue this avenue.

"John, to sell electrical and electronic products, you would need to acquire enough technical knowledge to be able to thoroughly understand their capabilities and sales features. That would take some time and if you don't mind my asking, I'm wondering how you'd deal with that and how you'd plan to get some sales going in the interim."

John looked at me, not quite comprehending. Then he laughed, "No, no," he said. "You misunderstand me. I don't plan to do the selling. That would be your job. I have it in mind that I shall run the London office and you will take care of the New York end."

It took me a minute or two to absorb that pronouncement.

"Do you have an office there yet—a base of operations?" I asked.

"No, nothing. I would leave it to you to set that up. I'd give you a budget of course, and you would work with that."

My stomach churned a bit. This was going to be something more of a challenge than I'd been aiming for.

John Ould turned his kindly eyes directly upon me and

smiled. "Why don't you go home and discuss the idea with your wife? If you both decide that this kind of adventure appeals to you, we can meet again and make arrangements to get the show on the road."

"When would you want me to start if we came to an agreement?" I asked.

"Well, just as soon as you could cut loose from your present job." He paused. "We should probably spend about three months fixing up some agencies, then I think it would be a good idea to get you over to the States as soon as possible."

I took my leave. Plenty to think about—both exhilarating and scary at the same time. But it would get me to foreign shores, and that's where I wanted to be, wasn't it? Better find out what Laura would have to say.

Back home in St. John's Wood, I immediately telephoned the Tourist Department of the American Embassy to update myself on the climate in the United States.

"How much sun do you have?" I asked the travel representative.

"Well, the sun is always shining somewhere in America. It's a big country. What part are you interested in? "

"Oh, yes, of course." I'd forgotten how big the United States really is." Let's talk about the climate in the New York area."

By the time I put the phone down I'd discovered that New York enjoyed considerably more hours of sunshine per annum than any part of the British Isles. With this encouraging information to hand I joined Laura at the dinner table and briefed her on my interview with John Ould.

We talked long into the night. To my surprise I found Laura quite taken with the idea of setting up in New York.

She seemed confident that we would make a go of it, and quite fascinated with the idea of moving to another big city area. She did insist, however, that for the present, our nine-year-old daughter, Peta, would remain at the boarding school in Kent, where she'd been enrolled the previous year. Laura's thought was that at holiday times we would simply arrange for her to fly to New York to join us.

By morning, we'd made our decision and were already planning the sale of our flat.

On the way to the boat

EIGHT

S he was falling, falling, faster and faster. The rocks below were spinning around so fast that she couldn't focus her eyes on the panorama rushing up to meet her. Then she realized that it was she who was turning, not the rocks, and she arched her back in an instinctive effort to arrest her rotation. It seemed to work, for now, no longer turning, she could see her satchel lying there at the side of the road with all her school books scattered around it. She would land directly on top of it and she prepared herself for the impact. But then at the last moment there was a loud whistling sound and she screamed. She awoke as the shrieking of the train's whistle continued. Curled up in the corner of her seat, and bathed in perspiration, she lay limp with Erzsébet cradling her head as the train lurched and rattled its way south through the summer night. They were on their way to Richmond, Virginia, and to their future home.

Earlier in the day after disembarkation, they had been met by representatives of the Catholic Church and shepherded through customs and immigration. Later, they were taken to Grand Central Station where, after waiting until late evening, they'd been put aboard the night train to Richmond. From there they were to be taken by road to their future home and place of employment, the Carter estate and farms. It was a destination they would never reach.

On arrival at Richmond station the following morning, they were transported with their suitcases and bundles to a nearby hotel where two rooms were reserved for them for an overnight stay. They were far from luxurious accommodations but after the privations they'd suffered over these last several months, they provided a much-needed lift to their morale. Comfortable beds with plenty of room to spread themselves, the choice of hot bath or shower, clean towels and private toilets complete with soft toilet paper; dressing tables with large mirrors. And downstairs, food awaiting them, already paid for. By late morning they'd refreshed themselves in body and spirit. They were clean, rested, and full. Then they were given the news that would once again sorely test their stoicism.

The young priest who'd brought them to the hotel the previous day came to see them. Clearly ill at ease and having difficulty in choosing his words, he eventually managed to explain that somehow the vacancy at the Carter estate had already been filled, and that they no longer had a place for the Ludányis at that estate. He did his best to assure them that the displaced persons committee in his diocese was already working on the problem and that he expected to have a place for them by the following morning.

Antal could not believe what he was hearing. How could it be that he'd signed a contract regarding a specific job at a specific place with a specific employer and now, after crossing an ocean to honor his family's obligations under that contract, someone else had somehow taken the position?

How could that happen, and what now awaited his family in this strange country? What other slings of fortune would control their destinies before their wanderings would end? They didn't know the ways and laws of the United States and they didn't know how to protect their rights or seek redress in this instance of cruel injustice. There was nothing they could do. They sat in stunned silence as the bearer of the devastating news excused himself and eased his way out of their hotel room, closing the door quietly behind him.

The young priest came again the following morning with a station wagon. He had a place for them, he said. No, it wasn't an estate and there were no thoroughbred riding horses to train. He told her it was a small dairy farm of some 500 acres at a village called Kenbridge near the town of Blackstone, about seventy or eighty miles distant; a simple place where the owner, John Forrester, and a couple of tenant farmers were the only occupants. Apart from the cows, there were two farm horses and two mules. The whole family would be expected to work, but at least there'd be plenty of living space for them. They listened in silence, hoping that the reality would somehow be more encouraging than what they were hearing. "It's the best we can do right now," he told them. He looked at each of their faces in turn. "It won't be so bad," he said. "With a little time you will . . ." His voice trailed off. Then he shrugged his shoulders helplessly. "Perhaps we'd better be going."

Flat lands, tobacco plantations, corn fields, and stretches of unplowed open fields flashed by as the station wagon made its way southwest toward the small town of Blackstone. Dirt road all the way. Red dirt; red everywhere, in the fields and along the banks of the dikes. Red clay walls at the places where the road had been cut through shallow hillsides. And everywhere the people were black. Black faces, some smiling and friendly, some serious and long-suffering. Young faces and old, but always black. When would they see another white face, Erzsébet wondered. It all seemed so alien and she was apprehensive. And when would it end? She couldn't recall any time when she'd traveled so far without seeming to get anywhere. No towns or villages. Nothing but the red clay and the fields—and all those black faces. But she did not speak. She did not wish to trouble her already worried husband. They'd see what they would see and they would somehow cope with whatever circumstances they were called upon to grapple with. They sped on.

Eventually the car slowed and turned into a dirt side road. After about a mile of swaying and bumping their way along, they came upon a group of buildings, most of which appeared in need of more than a coat of paint. Barns for cows and equipment were spread around in random fashion, and a larger, better looking, two-story structure, evidently the main Forrester farmhouse, stood on a rise off to one side.

A weathered face greeted them at the door. Steady clear blue eyes turned their gaze appraisingly on each one of them in turn. The aging man in tan fatigues and a wide-brimmed hat ushered them into a large living room. "I am John Forrester and this is where you'll be living," he told them. The house comprised two sets of living quarters, each with separate upstairs and downstairs accommodations. This was their end of the house, and apart from the living room, they'd have a kitchen, and another two rooms upstairs for sleeping. "When you're settled in, you'll find some hot soup for you," he said. "I'll come and tell you about the rest in the morning." Then he left them.

When John Forrester came in to see them in the morning, they were heating water on the wood-fired stove which, they discovered, was the only means of cooking they'd have at their disposal. They were making tea and they offered him a cup. "Let me tell you about this little spread," he said, accepting the offer. "Besides the main house, there are eight cows, two mules, two farm horses and a few barns." He paused to take a sip of his tea. Then he continued. "I'll have to ask you all to pitch in, even the older children when they're not at school, and I can't afford to pay you more than seventy dollars a month total." He paused again. "Eight dollars a month will be deducted for milk."

Antal didn't yet know what seventy dollars a month would buy or whether it would be adequate or not. He simply nodded and asked the farmer to tell them exactly what they were expected to do. The farmer explained, and soon they were busy with their duties, tending the livestock, sorting out what repair work had to be done on equipment and on the barns. Erzsébet was getting instruction on the cleaning duties she'd have in the farmhouse—both in their own section and in the other half, where the farmer lived.

Within the next few days, they learned that the farmer had a wife and a total of twelve 'children,' the younger ones living with their mother a modest distance away. The older ones, some of whom were married and had children of their own, were scattered around at varying distances. Some of Forrester's children would pay him an occasional visit at the farm. Others were preoccupied with their own lives and were seldom in contact. The bottom line was that John Forrester didn't make a lot of money, and the pay he'd allotted to the Ludányis, though meager, was evidently all he could afford. They learned that the children would go to school in Victoria, a small town about ten miles distant. They'd have to walk a mile to the school bus stop.

Erzsébet wrestled with the cooking and the cleaning. The latter was fairly straightforward but the cooking presented some problems. She had only a wood-burning stove to work with. There was no oven and when she asked John Forrester how people managed to bake bread without an oven, he told her that many farmers did their cooking on a fire made between three stones. Eventually she decided that she would just have to throw the dough in with the burning wood. To her surprise, this method proved quite successful. The finished product had a certain charcoal taste to it, but aside from that, it was very satisfying. She also had to cope with the shortage of cooking oil. The farmer wouldn't let them have much of this, presumably because it was too expensive, so she cooked bacon to get grease from it for cooking other things. She learned to improvise in much the same manner that she'd been forced to do during the desperate days of their flight from Hungary. That had been a hard schooling and she'd learned well.

Antal worked long hours spending most of his time repairing and servicing the farm machinery and rebuilding the barns and sheds. He broke up large stones with a sledgehammer, reducing them to gravel size and mixing them with cement to make concrete walls. The rotting wooden barns and outhouses were gradually replaced by solid weatherproof structures. Though slim and athletic, Antal had never been muscular, but as he gradually accustomed himself to the hard physical labor entailed in his present work, the effect on his physique began to show. He laughed with glee when his wife began to notice his bulging biceps and back muscles. It was exhausting work to be sure, but it was healthy.

Tamás and Nárcissza had their appointed duties, too. Before setting off for school in the mornings, they rode out to bring the cows in for milking. Then, the milking done, they drove them out to pasture again. They worked during the weekends, too, spending some of their time helping their father with his barn-building projects.

Nárcissza learned about segregation on her first school day. Shortly after her one-mile walk and her arrival at the bus stop, the school bus came into view and stopped to pick up the tenant farmer's daughter who had walked with her. When she attempted to follow the girl up the steps and on to the bus, the burly driver waved her off. As she stood there confused, the driver leaned over and barred her way, shooing her off and gently pushing her. Totally puzzled by this strange behavior, she backed down the steps and stood there staring as the children in the departing bus snickered or laughed out loud at her predicament. Her dilemma was solved quite soon when another bus pulled up alongside her. This time she had no difficulty boarding. She saw that the few children already on board were all white. Those on the other bus, she now realized, had all been black.

Her first day at the Victoria high school was equally confusing. She had supposed that at age fifteen she would be assigned to the tenth grade, but when the principal reviewed her curriculum and the reports from the Bavarian gymnasium he told Nárcissza that really she was qualified to go into twelfth grade and graduate that year. The prospect alarmed her. She simply didn't feel confident that she'd be able to adapt to the American system that quickly. After some discussion, she managed to persuade the principal to put her in the eleventh grade.

Later she wondered whether she'd made the right decision. She discovered that she was more qualified than she'd realized—that is, in relation to what was being taught in the eleventh grade. She also realized that conditions in the classroom were different from anything she'd known in the past. She was surprised and disconcerted by the lack of discipline in the school, and by the generally poor behavior tolerated in class every day. She couldn't understand why the students didn't stand up when the teacher entered or left the classroom, and the noise and continuous talking distracted her, making it difficult for her to concentrate.

It was all so different from the polite and structured atmosphere of the Bavarian school. She wished she could be back there trudging her six kilometers to the gymnasium every day, concentrating on real learning challenges in class and chatting with her old friends at recess; in the evening, trudging home again and eagerly reporting the day's events to her parents and siblings. Looking back, she realized that those days had been among the happiest in her young life, and she missed them. But as the weeks and the months passed, she adapted and settled down to farm life and her American schooling.

Summer turned to fall and fall to winter. The Ludányis were sleeping downstairs in the living room now. The upstairs bedrooms had never been designed for anything but storage and they were not heated. Erzsébet was glad that she'd brought her palliasse sacks with her all the way across the ocean. With fresh straw to stuff them they still served well as mattresses. She was glad that somehow they were managing to settle down on the farm. They'd regained their health and strength and they had food and shelter. They also had freedom. Compared with what they would have suffered in their homeland, now occupied by the Russians, it was a lot to be thankful for. And indeed, she was thankful.

But it was not enough. Living on the land in this fashion would keep them alive and healthy, but that is all it would do. It wouldn't provide opportunities for the children to advance themselves, nor would it offer them more than the barest of practical necessities. Erzsébet discussed her concerns with the young priest.

At every opportunity, she urged him to find them a place where they could do a little better, have a chance to buy a few clothes and prepare the children for an eventual move to New York, or some other center where they might make a better life for themselves.

They'd been at the Forrester farm for about nine months when the priest took Erzsébet aside one Sunday at church. He told her of a new place he'd found for her family—another small dairy farm about fifty miles north of their present location near a town called Amelia. Two brothers had inherited the farm from their father and were intent on making it a prosperous venture. These two brothers, Watkins by name, needed help and would pay more generously for people who were hard working, and the priest knew the Ludányis were in that category.

Erzsébet, hopeful though she felt, needed more specific information. "What else can you tell us?" she asked. The young man fumbled in his pockets and pulled out a tattered notebook. Thumbing through the pages, he came upon the required entry.

"The place has about thirty five milking cows and is well organized," he told her. "There are several barns in good repair and there are two tractors, a truck and a variety of other machines."

"Pay for Mr. Ludányi will be a hundred and ten dollars a month and the older children will be paid separately for whatever jobs they do. Tamás, for instance, could mow the big lawn or bring in the hay, and he'll get two dollars a day for that." He paused to let her absorb this information, then he asked her, "How does that sound?"

Erzsébet nodded absently, but didn't answer immediately. Would this move to another small farm really turn out to be beneficial for them, she wondered. Or was the young priest painting a favorable picture of the new place simply to provide an acceptable answer to her many requests for a better opportunity for her family? Had the brothers themselves, in their eagerness to get more help, given the priest an enhanced picture of what they could expect?

In a while, looking directly into his eyes she said, "It sounds too good to be true father . . . is it true?"

"Yes," he replied. "I've told you exactly what the brothers told me. I really think you'll be happy there."

He paused, then added, "Another thing, too. Milk and flour and anything that grows in the garden will be free and you'll have as much as you want."

Erzsébet took a moment to absorb this last piece of information, then her face cleared as indecision left her. "Thank you father," she said. "I think we must go there."

NINE

They had a stove! The three-room tenant farmer's cottage that was their new home had a stove. She couldn't believe it. She could actually bake real bread again. Erzsébet was already in better spirits. She'd found conditions at the Watkins farm even better than the priest had described. Her husband's pay was just as she'd been told and the free food supplies from the farm were generous enough to make a real difference in her budgeting. The stove was a very special bonus. Her family would once again be able to enjoy her fine Hungarian cooking and that was very important to her.

Erzsébet's brightening outlook was contagious. Antal, though working just as hard every day, for hours that were at least as long as they had been on the first farm, nevertheless went about his chores with more enthusiasm. Bringing the cows in at four-thirty in the morning, still an exacting task for a fifty-four-year-old ex-soldier, didn't seem as onerous now. They would all be able to eat well and there'd be enough money left over so that, one by one, they'd be able to buy shoes and simple clothes for their children.

The Watkins brothers Marvyn and Jimmy, and their wives Virginia and Helen, were all young, hard working and fair minded, and they were quick to appreciate that the Ludányis, too, were hard workers. They made conditions as comfortable as they could for them. They knew their concern for the immigrant family's well being would be repaid in full. In the fall, they brought the Ludanyis a mountain of logs for the wood-burning fireplace. A welcome protection against the cold, for the floorboards were thin and the drafts would find their way with ease through the peppering of knotholes that hadn't been filled.

Word about Erzsébet's oven-baked bread got around pretty fast. Soon, the farmers' children came asking for pieces of this wholesome and crusty product of her wizardry. Virginia's two-year old, Nancy, and the older girl Joan, became regular visitors to her kitchen, and Erzsébet, gratified with the opportunity to please the children, watched them eat with relish the wholesome bread she'd baked. Tamás and Nárcissza had their own opportunities to augment the family's income. Nárcissza was paid three dollars for cleaning house for one of the farmers and Tamás got two dollars every time he mowed the large lawn.

Slowly and steadily they were working their way to better times, and opportunities came their way sooner than they'd expected. In the early fall, a few months after their arrival at the Watkins farm, Nárcissza got her first opportunity to go north to the New York area. She'd written to her school teacher in Hungary, and through that teacher, Zsuzsi, one of her school friends, who'd also come to the United States, had learned of her present address. In a letter to Nárcissza, she explained that she and her older sister had been working as servant and cook for a wealthy

American family. This same family now needed someone to care for their small child, and Zsuzsi wondered whether Nárcissza would be interested in the job. The description seemed appealing. It would give her a chance to learn more about urban life in America and it might expose her to better opportunities. She wrote back to say that she would like to have the job. Two weeks later, she took the train to New York.

Her new place of employment dazzled her at first. Crystal chandeliers, fine cut glassware and ornate silver platters; formal dinners with visiting celebrities from many and varied walks of life, Nelson Rockefeller among them. The Websters of Greenwich were indeed upper crust, and for a time Nárcissza enjoyed the luxury of her new surroundings. Mrs. Webster was intrigued with her new helper. One day in Nárcissza's room, discussing the details of a forthcoming dinner party, she noticed a small spoon on the girl's dresser. The top of its shaft was broadened and fashioned into a crest and a coat of arms.

"What is this little trinket—a gift?" she asked.

"It's just one of our teaspoons. I wanted to hang on to some reminder of our home in Hungary, and I couldn't bring anything larger," she replied.

"Well, what does this design signify?" the lady of the house asked her.

"It's our family monogram."

Mrs. Webster picked up the spoon and examined it with growing curiosity. "Why would you have monograms? "

"That's the custom in European countries—Hungary and most other countries that I know of. Titled families have monograms with one sort of crown or another. I don't really know why."

Mrs. Webster was now really fascinated.

"Your family is titled then." Not quite a statement, not quite a question.

"Yes."

On the day of the dinner party, Mrs. Webster asked Nárcissza to help her with the table arrangements. She wanted to know how cutlery would be laid out at a European table and how many and what kind of knives and forks to use. What would be the order of serving? Would salad come first, or was it served with the entrée? What would come last, savories or dessert? Nárcissza, bewildered by her employer's interest in her opinions on such matters, did her best to describe the social practices she had grown up with. Mrs. Webster seemed interested in adopting the European ways, and if that was what she wanted, Nárcissza was glad to help her to do so. Mrs. Webster was also intrigued with the people who picked up Nárcissza on her day off. Who drove that fine looking Cadillac that occasionally pulled up to the Websters front door and waited for Nárcissza? Perhaps the chauffeur of some wealthy family, or some other staff member who'd borrowed his master's car on his day off? She just could not contain her curiosity. One day, while taking little Betty for a ride, she suggested to Nárcissza that they pass by Nárcissza's friend's house just so that she could see where they lived.

Baron Neuman de Végvár and his family lived in a large mansion in an exclusive section of Greenwich. Tininéni, a close friend of the Ludányis, and a school buddy of the Baron's wife, had asked that lady to keep a friendly eye on Nárcissza who was really just a child and lonely. The chauffeur had accordingly been dispatched on several occasions to bring Nárcissza over to the Neumans for lunch and for outings of one sort or another. Now, as they pulled into the Neuman's driveway, the name on the mailbox puzzled Mrs. Webster.

"What is your friend's name?" she asked Nárcissza.

"That's the name on the mailbox," Nárcissza replied.

"You mean the people who own this house are your friends? "

"Yes."

"Oh, they must be quite rich."

"Yes, I think they are. He's a baron."

As the days and weeks went by, Mrs. Webster's preoccupation with social graces and standing began to stifle Nárcissza. She longed to be with ordinary people again, people content with who they were, people who did not look upon others as superior or inferior to themselves. She did her best to keep her unhappiness to herself, but her parents, reading between the lines in her letters, eventually insisted that she return to the farm. In the middle of the February snows, Nárcissza bade the Websters farewell, gave Betty a parting hug, and set out for the train back south.

In the end, it was her cousin Gyongyi who organized the family's move to New York. Gyongyi's family had lived in New York for many years and Gyongyi herself had become a top fashion model in that metropolis. First, she arranged for Nárcissza and Tamás to join her in her Astoria apartment. Then, as they settled in, the rest of the family left the farm to join her, too. Gyongyi's unpretentious two bedroom Astoria apartment now accommodated twelve souls ranging from the very young to the very old. Besides the seven Ludányis, there were Gyongyi, her younger brother Bálint, her mother Frédi, her mother's husband Lorant, and finally Gyongyi's grandmother Fréda. A crowded situation to say the least.

Antal applied for a separate apartment for his family, but the landlord insisted they take a three bedroom unit, a prospect altogether beyond their means.

By this time Nárcissza had almost completed a correspondence course as a means of finishing her primary schooling. The need to work to help support her family had all but disposed of her dream of a college education, but she felt she should at least go through the procedures necessary to obtain a highschool diploma. First, she got herself a job at a Hungarian pastry shop in Dykman Street on the upper West Side. The hours were two in the afternoon until two o'clock in the morning. After her shift she'd take a one-and-a-half hour subway ride back to Astoria, then walk another fourteen blocks home. This schedule coupled with her correspondence course studies left her with very little time to think about the future.

Tamás, not yet sixteen years old, had arrived in Astoria about two weeks after Nárcissza. Despite the strict New York labor laws, he managed to get a job as a messenger boy in the downtown area. He attributed his success to the fact that when he went for his interview, he clicked his heels and bowed at his entrance and departure, a nicety of behavior which prospective employers in his homeland, looked upon as a sign of respect.

Evidently, Tamás's clean-cut features and courtly behavior had so captivated the interviewer that shortly thereafter he found himself hired to ride around Manhattan in a chauffeured limousine delivering messages.

Soon, his father got a job on the line at the Swingline staples and office supplies company. Antal's employers quickly became aware of his mechanical aptitudes and transferred him to the maintenance department, giving him responsibility for the smooth running of all the factory mechanization.

Gyongyi's neighbors were now complaining about the high volume of traffic up and down the stairs in their small apartment building and Gyongyi used this circumstance to support her insistent requests to her landlord for a separate apartment for the Ludányis. The landlord's representative came to investigate. It was a short visit. He simply could not believe that so many people were able to find places to lie down and rest in so small an area of living space. He immediately arranged for the Ludányis to move into a two-bedroom apartment of their own in the same building. They settled in eagerly. For the first time in six years, they had a place they could really call home.

Just when Nárcissza began to dream about a college education again, her father became ill and she recognized that she would have to help out with the family finances. She left her pastry shop job and found a better paying and more convenient position at Abraham and Strauss in Brooklyn. There, for about a year, she worked as a receptionist and Girl Friday until an even better opportunity came her way at the Metropolitan Life Insurance Company. She got into one of the best actuarial departments there and thrived at her work. She was happy. That is, until she found herself involved in a small controversy which challenged her principles. Office girls were supposed to wear stockings. But college girls and high school girls wore bobby socks and Nárcissza wore bobby socks. When her supervisors objected and she remained adamant, the vice president called her into his office, and politely requested that she explain her position.

"No customer ever sees me," she said. "Nobody ever knows that I work here. My take-home pay is about forty five dollars. If I wear stockings I spend at least two dollars a week on that, and that's five percent of my take-home pay. I think that is unreasonable, especially since at the time I joined the company, no one ever told me that I had to wear stockings."

Nárcissza won her case. The compulsory stockings regulation was withdrawn.

With what little time she had left at her disposal, she immersed herself in social life, partying and dancing, singing with the local Hungarian choir—all the while trying to persuade herself that she must abandon her dream of an academic education and be thankful for the progress she was making in other directions.

It was through her choir membership that an unexpected circumstance intervened in her behalf. Her long time friend Eta, also belonged to the choir group, and when she learned of Nárcissza's dream of a college education, she discussed the matter with her mother, who in turn passed the information on to Professor Molnár of Elmhurst College in Illinois. Those two small kindnesses changed Narcissza's life.

TEN

On Tuesday morning, February 15, 1955, the SS United States eased slowly into its berth at pier 86. We were on deck with everybody else, determined not to miss out on our first opportunity to get a glimpse of New York City. To my conservative eyes, it was a garish sight; bright yellow taxicabs everywhere, and large billboards scattered indiscriminately on the sides and tops of buildings. The noise reminded me of that musical masterpiece, 'The Tenement Symphony,' and it seemed to me that its composers must have got their inspiration right there at mid-town on Twelfth Avenue.

Charles Daldorf, an enterprising forwarding agent with whom John had made contact in our behalf, met us at dockside. Charles, in his dapper business suit and gray Homburg hat, welcomed us to the United States and very kindly volunteered to guide us through customs and the disembarking procedures. In a short time, he had cleared our baggage and arranged for its storage until we could pick it up, and we were then whisked into the downtown area for a relaxing lunch. By late afternoon we found ourselves in the quiet of suburban Fleetwood discussing our journey with two of

John's friends, David MacKenzie and his wife, Bonzo. David, a shipping company dispatcher, had booked us into the Gramatan hotel in nearby Bronxville. Bonzo would spend the next few days driving us around the area to help us get our bearings and find a suitable apartment.

On the second day of our rounds, we found a small apartment complex at 781 Palmer Road, just ten minutes walk from the Bronxville commuting station. An available unit on the second floor, comprising two bedrooms, living room, dining area and kitchen, seemed just right. A day or two thereafter, we moved in. Meanwhile, Charles Daldorf had been busy in our behalf. As soon as we were settled in, I called him to arrange introductions for me regarding my need for office space. John had felt that a place in mid-town Manhattan would be more prestigious, but was open to suggestions.

Charles suggested a place he knew of, right in the center of town at 437 Fifth Avenue. Run by an astute and friendly businesswoman, Jacqueline Vicary, the service specialized in providing both office space and pay-by-the-hour secretarial services for small business entities and start-ups. It seemed an attractive and convenient prospect that wouldn't stretch our budget, but I thought it best to avoid making a decision until I had at least looked at one or two other options.

Charles had also suggested that I get in touch with a sales representative friend of his, Adolf Friedman, who he felt might be of some help to me. Adolf owned a small office building and warehouse in the suburb of Mount Vernon, not far from Bronxville. Shortly after my visit to Jacqueline Vicary I went to see him. Adolf was mature and stocky, with fine thinning silver hair. His benign countenance reminded me of my granny George, and his favorite stance, sturdy legs spread far apart, seemed to go with his personality. I liked and trusted him on sight. He puffed on his meerschaum pipe and joshed about my English accent.

"Do you plan to wear a bowler hat and pin stripes to go with that accent when you make your sales calls?" he asked.

"Yes, I knew you Americans were fond of your stereo-types," I replied, "so I bought a bowler and a black umbrella before I left."

He showed me around the attractive brick building and I noted that on the second floor there were one or two large offices that did not appear occupied.

"You could have one of these if you like," he said. "Or I could do a bit of switching and you could have an office on the ground floor. It would probably depend on what sort of stuff you were importing. If you're handling bulky stuff and you want to have any of it in your office, a ground floor office might be a better bet. We've got a warehouse, of course, but you might want samples in your office."

I pondered that; something I hadn't considered before. In the months before sailing, I had negotiated several export agency agreements. They mostly involved reasonably small electrical instrumentation and components, but one agency included Victor Weake's Pamphonic line of high-fidelity loudspeakers and amplifiers, and it wouldn't be easy to move that type of equipment up and down a flight of stairs.

This new consideration put my office requirements in a quite different light. It would make no sense to locate the business in mid-town Manhattan and pay for storage of mer-chandise at high Manhattan rates. We would certainly need some sort of warehousing facility in an area where space was not at a premium, so it seemed more logical to locate both office and warehouse outside the city. An arrangement with

Adolf Friedman suddenly seemed quite practical.

I asked Adolf about rent. He quoted me a very modest figure and said I could start paying after I'd settled in. He expressed concern about my rented car.

"That's an expensive way to get around," he said.

"Well," I assured him, "I shall be looking for a good used car pretty soon, so the renting won't be for long, Adolf."

"Hmm. Better get rid of it now. You can use my other station wagon until you find something." And so it went.

I was glad that Adolf was among the first Americans I encountered. His generosity and concern to help me get started as economically as possible served to give me an appreciation of the innate generosity of Americans in general. I decided I'd find contentment in these United States.

Quite soon I had set up my office, and was already making my rounds to get some idea of the reception I could expect, for the products I had to offer. The electrical test instruments were well received but in every case, some minor modifications were suggested to bring the designs into compliance with standard American practices. I advised John of these requirements and asked that he notify the manufacturers accordingly, but after several weeks of back and forth correspondence, it became clear that our principals had no intention of modifying their products just for the American market. Their order books, they said, were pretty full and since the products were well accepted in many other countries all over the world, they ought to find acceptance in the American market, too. In those days they had not learned to take into account the considerably greater potential in the United States or the long-term payoff that could result from the modest investment required to make a few minor changes. They simply did not want to be bothered with all that.

The high-fidelity sound equipment manufacturer reacted in a similar manner. Its reputation for fine quality performance had preceded my arrival in the United States. Harvey Sampson, Jr., who ran the most popular hi-fi distributorship of the day in New York City, had agreed that he'd be willing to try these units to see whether, as he had been led to believe, they really were superior to the Wharfdale line. The name Wharfdale was in those days synonymous with high quality sound reproduction to a degree I considered a bit extreme. That company's loudspeakers produced very good sound, no doubt about that. But in my view, a couple of old fashioned PX 25 vacuum tubes driving a loudspeaker system that included at least one 'Toward Perfection' Goodman's woofer could do a better job on an organ piece than any Wharfdale combination. For those readers not in the high-fidelity enthusiast category, I should explain that for British music lovers, the PX4 and the PX25 vacuum tubes (valves) were the last great providers of amplified sound before the solid state transistor took over. Indeed, because of their faithful following, these wonderful relics of a bygone era are still in production today.

But for now, we were concerned with loudspeakers rather than the devices that power them, and Wharfdale was the loudspeaker system we had to top. I could hardly wait for the Pamphonic shipment to arrive. I knew it would get a fair shake from Harvey. Somehow, he seemed to be sharing my concern. He was a good-hearted man and he knew that for me, a lot depended on this forthcoming evaluation. Eventually, when I drove up to the curbside in front of his store and wheeled the equipment into his showroom, Harvey was just as excited as I, but when we had pulled the loudspeaker console out of its carton and set it up in a corner, his expression changed. He didn't make any comment. He just looked at the box-like structure and sighed. Then he patted me on the back and said that he would let me know how his evaluation went. Later, over the telephone, he told me that the sound quality had been well received but that he had yet to find anyone who would feel comfortable with the Pamphonic box in his living room.

"Could you get the front recessed?" he had asked. "And what about some short legs so that the thing would not look quite so much like a box?" Yes, I would see to it, I told him. I was sure that the manufacturer would understand. But he didn't. No design changes were made. Harvey eventually sold the unit I had delivered to him, but he did not feel he could sell any more. The twin unit that I had ordered in my optimism remained in the corner of the John Ould office in Mount Vernon.

If the loudspeaker had been the only example of this type of difficulty, one might have considered making modifications after receipt of the merchandise, but the fact that we were experiencing the same problem with most of our other products pointed to the futility of such a course. John, in his understandable concern, decided to try some non-technical products.

Very soon, to my dismay, shipments of various types of tools arrived. The first was a device called an 'Awl-Screw.' As the name implied, it combined the functions of an awl and a screwdriver. It looked to me as if it had been designed for use by yachtsmen to gouge holes in sailcloth while undertaking repairs, but no doubt it had a lot of other uses, too. By pressing a button on the side of the handle, the screwdriver blade would retract to reveal a hefty looking tool that tapered to a point at the end. It was the sort of device that would sell through such outlets as Abercrombe and Fitch, John had written, so that's where I made my first sales pitch.

I did manage to sell a few Awl-Screws to that upscale establishment, but the run of the mill hardware stores would have none of it. Dave Williams at Simm's Hardware, downtown, put it this way: "When a man needs a screwdriver, he will pull one out of his kit, and when he needs an awl, he will fish out an awl. He doesn't need a half-assed gizmo like that combination you've got in your hand. He wouldn't give you a dime for it." That philosophy, with a few variations, summed up the reactions I got from everyone else I talked to, or wrote to, about the Awl-Screw.

Lacking any marketing know-how in the hardware business, I couldn't think of what next to do to find a market for that strange little product of British ingenuity. Since I wasn't having much luck with products I understood, I could see no point in dabbling with things I knew nothing about. Better not spin my wheels.

A little later I began to receive shipments of special types of fishing tackle. I indicated to John that I didn't know how to go about selling things like that, and that it would be best for him to come out and take over the Mount Vernon office. The business clearly wouldn't support us both until the matters of product selection and business direction were solved, and that would take time. I would have to get another job. John agreed, but felt he would like to try one more product before making the switch. The sample shipment arrived a few days later. It was a carton of canned meatless sausages.

I was well aware that while we'd been looking for some way to establish our small enterprise with some salable products,

John's inherited fortune had been dwindling. While I reported failure after failure, John had been financing the venture that paid my salary. It hadn't been lavish but it had been enough to start with, and I was sensitive to my own part in the disappointing results we'd achieved. It wasn't so much my failure to make sales that bothered me, as the fact that I'd been naive in taking on the job without first engaging in a systematic market research program. Much of this could have been done in advance of my emigration, I told myself. I could probably have made a special arrangement with Goff Imhof, under which I would have continued to work for him part time while negotiating product agencies and making periodic trips to New York to investigate the suitability of those products for the U.S. market. I could have, but that was all hindsight. The fact was that I hadn't done it, and now I wanted to relieve John of the burden of my salary as soon as possible so he could come and investigate the situation for himself.

Enter Herb Randall—tall, tanned, and streetwise. We had come to know Herb through the one product in our portfolio that had shown some promise—a special, high-quality recording tape in which Herb had expressed an interest. He had visited me on several occasions to investigate what grades could be made available and how he might work with us to explore the US market for it. When he learned of the impending change in our setup, he promptly invited me to join him as a partner in his export business. Herb was involved in selling sophisticated electronic equipment and components to European government agencies and prime contractors and he needed someone to run his export business for him. He was too busy, he said, with his various other business interests to do justice to the opportunities that the agency afforded. The offer seemed heaven sent. I accepted.

In the course of a gradual transition, I did my best to help John when I could, and I also visited Herb's various principals to familiarize myself with the products I would have to sell. I wanted to get a reasonable understanding of the conditions under which the agency operated. The success I managed to achieve in a fairly short time in this new endeavor did much to restore my confidence in my negotiating abilities, but looking back after nearly two years with Herb, I came to believe that my early good fortune in the partnership had, in a way, been my undoing.

It had worked very well at first. I had made a long and comprehensive tour of our contacts and associates in most of the West European capitals, and our sales of analog computers, resolvers, and inertial guidance components to foreign governments and prime contractors steadily rose. We acquired one or two additional product lines and Hudson Randall International began to enjoy a healthy expansion. Unfortunately, Herb came to believe that with the new partnership, we could afford to broaden both the categories of product lines we would carry and the markets we would serve.

One of our principals, Diehl Electric Motor Company, for whom we were exporting specialized inertial guidance components to Europe, also manufactured an excellent line of electric fans. Herb saw an opportunity to add these products to our portfolio and managed to persuade their export director to give us the Central American and Canadian territories for the line. That meant that we'd have to explore markets in geographical areas that we weren't currently serving, and it was left to me to do the leg work. It proved a stretch to put it mildly. One week I would be making a circuit of Puerto Rico, Cuba, Venezuela, Chichenitza and Mexico City; and the next,

I'd be calling on prospects in Ottawa, Toronto, Montreal, and Quebec City. And, of course, I had time consuming preparation work to attend to as well as post-visit correspondence relating to the business generated by these exercises.

I enjoyed the variety of travel and the new experiences but I wasn't able to switch the focus of my activities back and forth as readily as Herb. Herb called it 'dancing,' and he was very good at it, but I had not yet come to terms with the degree of flexibility which, Herb assured me, was essential for success in these United States. My work with our principal European customers began to suffer, and my head began to spin.

When John Hitch joined us to help with the workload, things began to fall apart. John, an accomplished microwave engineer, had just the right kind of background and experience for our purposes, but he also had the kind of all-American grass-roots personality that likes to call a spade a spade.

It wasn't only that he was outspoken and perhaps somewhat critical of Herb's approach to business matters. It was more that the practical circumstances of the business set-up encouraged concern and, later, distrust on Herb's part. When I say circumstances, I'm referring to the fact that by that time Herb was seldom around. After I had taken over responsibility for the day-to-day running of the agency, Herb traveled less and less frequently from his home in Westerly, Rhode Island, to the New York office. He had other business interests closer to home to attend to, and he preferred to leave the operation of the export agency in my hands. So when I made it known to Herb that I was in agreement with John Hitch concerning which product lines we should concentrate on and specialize in, and which ones we should ditch, Herb, not being party to our discussions, felt that we were ganging up on him. He decided that he didn't trust John, and now he was not at all sure about me.

Herb Randall was larger than life. Tall, swash-buckling, and highly experienced in the wheeler-dealer, three-martini lunch methods of the day, he was, in spite of a less than profound technical knowledge of the products he worked with, usually able to dominate most business meetings in which he took part. Male executives seemed intimidated by his easy assurance and knowledge of world markets. Their female counterparts, I noticed, would sometimes shift uncomfortably in their seats, perhaps adjusting their skirts, as Herb's dark brown eyes would move slowly over the full length of their limbs and torsos, seeming to pause in appraisal of each feature, shapely or otherwise, before moving on.

Herb was accustomed to being in control, and most of the time he was. He revealed his attitude to our relationship when, during lunch at the Plaza Hotel with that celebrated pair, Bill Hewlett and Dave Packard, he stated in his pitch for their export sales agency: "I set things up and Howard handles the details." These were his exact words, and it pained me at the time to hear my contribution to our partnership described in that way. But now, with two trained engineers running his New York office and urging him to limit the company's product lines to highly technical equipment that was becoming more and more sophisticated by the day, it is perhaps not surprising that Herb, in abstentia in Westerly, might have felt some of his control slipping away.

We sat at the bar at Gino's on East 45th Street. Herb, his gray fedora perched on the back of his head, nursing his bourbon and tonic, and I, across from him on the corner stool, just brooding and toying with my scotch and soda. Here and there, wall-mounted fixtures spread cones of amber light across the rich mahogany paneling behind them to penetrate the smoky gloom. The subdued pockets of light, reflecting our moods, enveloped couples and small groups of patrons. The darkness between, isolated them from their neighbors, lending privacy to their conversations.

Herb had chosen this particular venue and this particular Monday for our meeting because the subject matter was going to be serious, and he didn't want to compete with typical weekend barroom decibel levels to make himself understood. Yet neither of us was saying much; there wasn't really much to say. Herb had stated simply, "Howard, I want out," and we had met to determine how our partnership would be dissolved.

It was, after all, Herb's business. The small agency, whose offices were just around the corner at 141 East 41st Street, had been a going concern for years before I came on board, and Herb had built it around his first export activities as agent for the Hudson Wire Company. He had simply given me a nominal partnership to strengthen the technical resources of the enterprise, and to give himself more free-dom to attend to his other business interests, most of which were fairly close to his home in Westerly. When I had joined him, it had been agreed that Herb would continue to furnish working capital for the agency but for the most part he would be a silent partner. Henceforth, I would run the office and do most of the travel.

At any rate, here we were at Gino's, talking about how to handle the termination of our business relationship. Our written agreement had provided that in the event of a split, one of us would offer to pay a certain sum of money to buy out the other, and whoever named the amount would auto-matically forfeit the right to choose between the buy or sell option. This prerogative would then belong to the other part-ner, and he would elect to buy or sell as he chose. Herb said that I should be the one to decide what the partnership was worth, and what I could afford to pay, to buy him out, and that I should think about that for a few days before giving him an answer. He was, of course, aware that I had minimal financial resources, and that as a newcomer to his country I would probably not have much chance of raising enough money to buy him out, much less the means to provide working capital to continue operating the agency. But he made no comment to that effect. He was a good businessman.

We finished our drinks and went our separate ways and I pondered the matter for several days. I reasoned that if I asked for too much, I might find myself stuck with the responsibility for paying out funds which I could see no means of raising, and if I asked for too little, I would be cheating myself and my family. It was a dilemma, for now we had an additional mouth to feed. Leslie, her large brown eyes almost exactly duplicating those of her mother, had appeared on the scene the previous September. Yes indeed, it was a dilemma.

In the end, with an unaccountable conviction that I would quickly succeed at whatever might become my next job or business activity, I told Herb that I would settle for five thousand dollars. He said he thought that was fair, which as you might imagine, convinced me that I had sold myself short. We agreed that the money would be paid out at the rate of $500 per month for ten months, and that would be the end of our relationship. It was. Some months later, toward the end of 1959, we ran across each other at an electronics exhibition at the New York Coliseum. Herb suggested that I meet him at his hotel after the show, to discuss his ideas on a possible new business relationship between us. I said I would be glad to do that, but at the last minute, some sixth sense persuaded me that, although John Hitch was no longer in the picture—he had left of his own accord at the time of my own split with Herb—it would be difficult and time consuming to rebuild the mutual trust we'd once enjoyed. Better leave well enough alone. I did not go to the proposed meeting, and I did not see Herb again.

ELEVEN

Holton Harris, sales manager at Reeves Instrument Corporation, was also a serious and inventive engineer. He was our contact at that company in relation to the analog computing equipment that Hudson Randall International was exporting for them. Holt and I had become friends and when I told him that Herb and I were splitting up, he suggested that I get in touch with the various technical equipment manufacturers I had come to know and make them aware that I was available. For his part, he would check with Reeves' own personnel department to determine whether there might be an opportunity for me in their Sales Engineering Department. Later he learned that there was indeed such an opportunity but, Holt was advised, my alien status would disqualify me. All applicants had to have 'Secret Clearance' and the personnel manager said it would be difficult and time consuming for a non-citizen to obtain such clearance.

Later, in discussion with my contact at the Epsco Company in Massachusetts, I learned that they, too, required that their sales and engineering personnel have secret clearance, and based on the outcome of my previous inquiry at Reeves, I assumed that they, too, would reject my application. It soon became evident that most companies whose products were such as to present a possible employment opportunity for me were currently active in defense-oriented markets or other activities of the kind that would require what I did not have, and would not be able to come by any time soon—secret clearance.

In the train, homeward bound from Grand Central Station to Bronxville, I stared speculatively at my resume. I wondered what types of companies would be suitable targets for the mailing I planned, and what sort of covering letter would persuade the reader to take an interest in the resumé it introduced. My knowledge of European markets for various classes of electrical equipment seemed an asset worth exploiting. I decided to address my application to the marketing directors of companies that appeared large enough to be involved in export, but whose products did not appear defense sensitive. I picked on electrical measuring instruments of one kind or another for my first mailing. I sent out thirty-five applications and got two favorable responses. Yes, they had appropriate vacancies, and my background was definitely of interest to them. They would like to see me and I should call right away for an interview—and by the way, I should understand that secret clearance would be necessary.

Was it just an unlucky coincidence that I seemed unable to find a prospective employer not wrapped up in some sort of defense work? Or was it due to some philosophy of the times that presumed that if present activities were not in this category, they might well become so at some point in the foreseeable future? It seemed evident that the Korean War, not yet five years past, together with the aftermath of McCarthyism and a still flourishing Cold War, had left deep impressions on the American psyche, and security had become the primary concern of the day.

Either way, time was running on and I was getting concerned. What if my next mailing proved to be no more successful than the first? What if I had to start right at the beginning again and take any job I could get? I began in my mind to exaggerate the problem, especially as our best friends were already expressing sympathy with my plight. Dave Wham, a successful advertising executive on Madison Avenue, and his wife Audrey, belonged to the upwardly mobile set of the times. Joyful participants in the American dream, they began offering their help. Dave was sure he could find a good entree for me in public relations, and I was deeply touched by his concern. But pretty soon I began to hear reports of other reputed friends expressing their view that Layton was never going to amount to anything. It was that insidious doctrine that persuaded my wife that we should go back to England.

Not bloody likely. The very mention of giving up the struggle to make it in this land of opportunity strengthened my resolve to somehow find a way. Somewhere out there, was a chance for me, and I was going to find it. Nowhere was it written that the American dream was only for the very young. There had to be room for forty-year-old immigrants too. There had to be room for me. In that ebullient frame of mind I picked up the phone and dialed the home of Charles Daldorf, the friendly forwarding agent and entrepreneur who had met me at Pier 86 on that crisp February morning when I had walked down the gangplank of the S.S. United States to set foot for the first time on American soil.

"Glad to hear from you Howard. It's a welcome surprise. What's going on with you these days?"

"Charles, it's good to hear your cheerful voice again. It's just what I need. Matter of fact, I'm between jobs, as they say." I filled him in about the ups and downs of my times with John, and my subsequent partnership with Herb.

"Since my eventual break-up with Herb, I haven't had much luck in my efforts to get the kind of work I would like, so I've decided to try doing my own thing."

"Well, that's a pretty bold decision, Howard, but I'm sure you've thought it over carefully. Anyhow, I wish you all the luck. I'll be glad to help you in any way I can."

"As a matter of fact, Charles, you could help me quite a bit right now. Remember the day when you went the rounds with me, hunting for office space?"

"I certainly do."

"Well, we visited a place on Fifth Avenue that provides space for people starting their own businesses. I think they had some sort of shared secretarial service, too. Anyhow, I was wondering whether you happen to remember who that was, and if so, whether you'd be good enough to refresh my memory?"

He did and he would. As soon as he mentioned her name I recalled meeting the lady who ran the service. Jacqueline Vicary's enterprise was at 437 Fifth Avenue. The following morning I took a train to Manhattan, met Jacqueline, and rented a small, furnished cubicle on her ninth floor. On that bright summer day of 1958, Mrs. Layton's big son had taken the plunge. With three thousand dollars in the bank and five hundred a month to count on over the next several months, he was going into business for himself.

Fear is an interesting phenomenon. It is said that a coward dies a thousand times and a brave man dies only once. I found that an over-simplification. Certainly, I had knots in my stomach on a daily basis, so I knew which category I belonged to. But nature tends to protect her own and, after a time, the succession of knots began to merge into a single continuous ache. I gradually became accustomed to the condition, and in time, its familiarity bred a degree of acceptance together with what I can only call affection. It seemed in a way to be like a friend who is also a burden. You would dearly like to be relieved of the latter but you put up with it because you would otherwise miss the former.

So it was that the friend in my stomach accompanied me to the New York Coliseum a few days after the signing of my contract with Jacqueline. I was attending the Chemical Engineering Conference and Exhibition to scout for sales agency opportunities. The exhibit hall proved crowded, and exhibitors were understandably more interested in talking to prospective customers than to prospective sales representatives. Those courteous enough to spend time with me were, in general, already adequately represented in the New York area, and those who were not explained that they were looking for established representatives who knew the territory and already had a following. By the end of the day, the friend inside me was grumbling physically and emotionally. I would have to make the rounds again tomorrow—and try harder.

The show was closing for the day when I stopped at a small corner booth to ask for directions to Grand Central Station. The lone occupant of the booth was good natured and forthcoming. It was easy enough, he said, but if I cared to wait a few more minutes, I could accompany him in a taxi and he would drop me off on the way to his hotel. I thanked him and asked about the bulky looking instrument case on display at the front of his booth. "That," he said, "is an industrial particle counter."

"In layman's language, how does it work?" I asked.

"It's really very simple." He pointed to the assembly of glassware that stood at the side of the black box. "You see that column? Well, part of it is a sort of test tube with a very tiny orifice at the bottom, and there are electrodes on either side of that orifice. The electronic counter measures the number and sizes of particles contained in any fluid that passes through it. It does that by recording the changes in electrical resistance across the orifice as the particles go through. Simple, isn't it?"

It didn't strike me as simple at all, but I was able to follow his explanation.

"Anyway," he said, "I'll tell you more about it on the way to the hotel."

Later, in the taxi, we had already dispensed with formalities and were on a first-name basis. Bob was explaining that the black box was a Coulter Counter, originally designed for counting blood cells, and that he, Bob Berg, quite separately from its manufacturer, was developing an industrial market for the instrument. It had been shown to be very successful in such applications as particle size analysis of contaminants in hydraulic fluids or in packaged mashed potatoes, chocolate, sugar and countless other everyday products whose integrity or flavor were influenced by the nature of their particle-size distributions. For the duration of that cab ride, Bob had a captive audience, and he made the most of the opportunity. He was clearly immersed in the scientific and industrial prospects for the instrument, and his enthusiasm and his erudite explanations of its technology began to fire my imagination.

He was still talking, losing me in esoteric descriptions of how all particles, metallic or otherwise, behaved as nonconductors in the instrument's "Electrozone" orifice, when suddenly we were at curbside on 42nd Street. As I got out of the cab and thanked him for the ride and the interesting discussion, I mentioned that I, too, had just recently decided to start my own technical sales business and was on the lookout for products to sell. "Oh, really," he replied quickly, " we should talk about that."

He paid the cabby and joined me on the sidewalk, and soon we were sitting opposite each other at the Oyster Bar, continuing the discussion which, from the moment we entered the Grand Central Complex, had taken a new turn. This time, I was doing the talking and Bob, his noble scientist's head and broad brow cocked a little to one side, was listening—intently. Before we'd left the bar and had gone our separate ways, Bob told me he would give me a call after the show, so we could meet again before his departure for Chicago.

At Gino's a few days later, over a very fine dinner of veal parmigiana, Bob Berg appointed me New York Metropolitan Area Representative for Coulter Industrial Sales. My generous host advised me that a couple of projects for customers in the area were already in the works but not yet shipped, and I would get the benefit of those sales—just to get me off to an enthusiastic start. We shook hands to seal the deal. That's all there was to it. My new enterprise was now truly launched. I had something to sell.

There is a tide, they say, which taken at the flood can really get you going, and suddenly I knew that tide was upon me, and I had better get with the flood. Within days of that memorable dinner at Gino's, a letter from Cedric Benham of the Painton Company in England told me of that company's approval of a retainer for me to act for them in their quest for licensing agreements with American manufacturers. And again, a few weeks later, Godfrey Imhof, my one-time employer in England, wrote to confirm an arrangement under which I would receive a monthly fee for keeping him continually abreast of American developments in his product category. It was not a large amount but at this crucial stage in my venture it was truly welcome. The pain in my stomach began to ease a little.

I met renowned attorney John McGregor through an accountant I had consulted about my desire to register my fledgling business as a corporation. Based on the favorable comments I had heard about this engaging wheelchair-confined personality, I decided I would consult him on the legal matters involved in my incorporation process.

I had originally intended to name the enterprise Layton-Randall Engineers, perhaps involving Herb as a business adviser. Then I had begun to have doubts about the wisdom of maintaining a close business association with so dominant a personality.

I thought about simplifying the name to just Layton Engineering Inc., but I wasn't really satisfied with that either. Better to mull it over for a few days, since the scheduled meeting with John McGregor was still more than a week away. Meanwhile I had work to do.

The appointment book was filling up and I had two or three Coulter Counter prospects to see that week, as well as a meeting at the Waldorf Astoria Hotel to attend. It was a meeting of the ASTM (American Society for Testing Materials), and Bob Berg had recommended that I sit in on it as a means of gaining familiarity with the more common industrial particle measurement and control issues. The prospect of sitting through one of those interminable sessions didn't thrill me at all, but I knew Bob would question me on it afterwards, so it seemed prudent to attend. As things turned out, I found myself increasingly absorbed by the program. The first discussion was about the grading of cashmere fibers by 'microtoming,' that is, by cutting them into extremely short but exactly equal lengths so that by measuring their actual size (volume) you could derive their diameters. Pretty nifty. The Coulter Counter could be used to measure the sizes of those cashmere particles, so it could serve as an important tool in the wool sorting industry. Another sales opportunity for me to look into.

Next, the discussion turned to the measurement of contaminating particles in barrels of ultra-clean solvents and hydraulic fluids. Although this, too, was a Coulter Counter application, what interested me most were the speaker's repeated references to the analyses and tests conducted independently in various widely dispersed parts of the country. Results obtained by these various labs were compared and averaged in the quest for truly representative data. The speaker referred to these as 'inter-lab' tests and I was intrigued by that description. The more I heard the phrase 'inter-lab' repeated as the conference progressed, the more it fascinated me. By the end of the session, I knew I had found the name I wanted for my business.

Early in November, we were gathered in John McGregor's law offices in Mineola. Barbara McKown and Joan Quinn, members of John's staff, joined John as subscribers for the registration of Interlab Incorporated. They in turn elected the directors. When those formalities had been dealt with, and as the paperwork was being completed, John asked finally, "Okay, what shall we write down as the actual incorporation date? Shall it be today or would you prefer to wait until it's all typed up and registered?" I pondered that question for a few minutes, reflecting on the various reasons, superstitious or otherwise, that influenced people when they had occasion to choose numbers, and I decided to go against the popular norm. "Let's make it the thirteenth," I said.

In the months that followed, recognizing that I was involved in a race against time, I worked hard and long. I was under no delusions about my under-capitalized condition. The inquiries I had made in discussions with others renting space on Jacqueline's ninth floor had left me in no doubt about this.

Gary Goodall, in the cubicle next to mine, assured me that to provide for enough time to establish a sales agency, and cover the inevitable waiting period for sales commissions, one would have to count on supporting oneself and one's family and the business overhead for at least twelve to eighteen months. Besides this, it was usual to add a further six months as a safety factor to account for the slings and arrows of business cycles. I knew I didn't have the resources to cover anything like this time span. No question about it, I would have to race.

The days were filled with travel and business appointments and the evenings with drafting correspondence and planning the next day's schedules. Eleanor, who was in charge of Jacqueline's typing-by-the-hour secretarial service, was fast, accurate, and cooperative. With her help I was just able to keep pace with the mounting activity. By the turn of the year I had signed a representation agreement with The Parker Instrument Company to handle their line of ultra-thin panel-meters.

A few weeks later, through an introduction by John McGregor, I was appointed metropolitan area sales representative for Acoustica Inc., a California-based manufacturer of industrial ultrasonic cleaning equipment. Although

Acoustica's New York area sales were currently quite small, they had sold one or two cleaning systems to IBM in Poughkeepsie, and had concluded that there was an opportunity to develop this small foothold into a worthwhile flow of orders. They appointed me to make that happen. I was spread a little thin, but this was America and there was gold out there. It was not, as propaganda has sometimes implied, and as the unwary may have sometimes believed, lying in the streets. Nor was it within easy grasp. One would have to dig for it.

I would dig.

TWELVE

While trying not to appear too unfeminine or indelicate, she had been stuffing herself to the best of her ability for nearly an hour. But there was no way she could swallow another bite of her oversized steakburger without another glass of wine. Nárcissza couldn't tell that to Joska, her date, even though she was beginning to feel more comfortable with him than with any of the other young men she had been dating in the local Hungarian community. She would just have to wait until he noticed that her glass was empty. Trouble was, the last two years of near starvation at Elmhurst College had left her with a diminished capacity for food. No question about it, her stomach had shrunk, so even when she got the chance to stoke up, she was never able to take full advantage of it. To make matters worse, like most Hungarians she had grown up with wine as a routine component of any substantial meal, however unpretentious, and as a result she was not able to digest much food without it.

As she pondered the problem at hand, Joska got up and excused himself to visit the bathroom. When he was out of sight, Nárcissza eyed the remainder of the burger speculatively. What if she just pushed it off the plate into her napkin and stuffed it into her purse when no one was looking? Tomorrow, that healthy morsel would make a very welcome addition to her almost routine potato and soup diet. She pondered that for another minute or so, glancing across at the fast food counters and then at the rows of red Formica tables which at this late hour sat almost deserted. When Joska got back, Nárcissza's plate was clean.

The following morning she got a message to call Professor Pavlokas, head of the Mathematics Department and tutor to those taking advanced math. When she made the call, the professor said he would like her to come by his office after lectures to discuss a possible job opportunity. He seemed insistent about what he was telling her, even though he was aware of her already heavy job schedule.

"But I'm already holding down about eight jobs, Professor," Nárcissza told him, "and that's about forty hours a week on top of my classes. How will I manage another one?"

"This one might give you an opportunity to give up a couple of those house cleaning jobs you've told me about. That is, if you get it." Before she could reply to that, he hung up. She sighed. The weight of her work schedule was beginning to oppress her. She wondered whether she would manage to keep on top of it all until her graduation in eighteen months.

She had come to Elmhurst almost by accident. The Hungarian Department was headed by the Reverend Professor Molnár. Her friend Eta's mother, who knew the Molnárs, had mentioned to them that Nárcissza had long dreamed of getting a college education but had seen no way of raising the money to pay for three or four years of tuition while simultaneously supporting herself. Professor Molnár hadn't known the answer to that one either, but during one of his trips east he'd visited the Ludányis in their New York apartment and discussed the problem with Nárcissza and her family.

"As an encouragement," he'd told her, "I can probably get you a small scholarship, just to start the ball rolling, but the rest would have to come through your sheer determination and hard work." She knew the latter comment was, if anything, an understatement, but he'd given her the incentive she needed. Never mind that the scholarship turned out to be only a hundred and fifty dollars and the annual tuition fees with accommodation would amount to about a thousand a year. That was a lot less money than the Eastern colleges would have cost, and at least she would be among friends. Somehow she would manage.

The deadline date for this year's applications was already long gone, but Nárcissza put hers in the mail anyway. Much to her surprise and delight, she got a letter of acceptance just two days before classes were due to start. Too late to for her to take a bus, but one of the airlines was advertising unusually low fares to Chicago and the travel agent managed to get her a round-trip student's ticket for forty dollars.

On September 9, 1955, wrapped in her checkered winter coat, she lugged her well-worn suitcase up to the airport check-in counter to embark on her very first flight ever. Within the hour she was on her way aboard the morning plane to Chicago—and college.

As soon as she got to Elmhurst she looked for a job. First, she found work in a pastry shop, and soon thereafter, she got jobs cleaning houses. She applied all of her earnings to her college expenses, so with the small scholarship and the little that she'd been able to save, the first semester went fairly well. She soon discovered, however, that for the following semesters, to meet the cost of tuition and accommodation alone, she would need to find more jobs.

Money for eating was quite another story. She hadn't yet figured out how she would cope with that problem. Theoretically, she could have opted for a full-board plan which would have included food, but she knew there was no way she could earn money fast enough to pay for it. Often, when hungry, she'd buy a cup of coffee at the college cafeteria. It only cost a nickel in those days, and if she put four or five spoonfuls of sugar in it, it helped give her enough energy to carry on.

Steadily, she began to expand her job roster. She did baby sitting, worked as an assistant in the chemistry department, tutored physics, chemistry, math, whatever. At one point, her shapely legs got her a leg-modeling job. She did that one summer at a studio where they were photographing shoes. Her cousin Gyongyi got the work for her, and at that job she earned more in one day than the rest of the summer put together.

Eventually, holding a total of eight jobs, which, not counting her schoolwork, added up to about forty hours, she earned enough money to meet her expenses. An exacting schedule to say the least, but at an average pay rate of only seventy-five cents an hour, she just couldn't get by with a lighter workload. Her parents worried about her, but since they couldn't do anything about her financial troubles, she was at pains to keep her family in the dark about them as much as she could.

She couldn't fool her brother Tony, though. Tony had a newspaper route and he made four dollars a week. After the first semester, he sent his sister half of his pay, that is, two dollars a week, every week. For the rest of the time that Nárcissza was at Elmhurst, Tony's contribution reached her every week without fail. She often reminded herself that but for Tony she might never have had a college education. Someday, she hoped, she would be able to repay him for that.

Nárcissza was always happy when a congenial fellow student would invite her out on a dinner date, and since there was a fairly substantial Hungarian contingent at Elmhurst, and newly arrived Hungarians tended to seek out other Hungarians, she never went short of offers. Tibor Halász, an electrical engineer, and Zoltán Cseri, a tool and die maker, were among the students she dated in her freshman year. Then there was Tamás Legeza, a concert pianist, accomplished swordsman and mechanical engineer all in one. Never a dull moment.

During her sophomore year, a lot of Hungarians had come out following the revolution, and the numbers of them at Elmhurst had increased accordingly. That was also the year she met Joska and the dashing Mihály, and they became very good friends for the remainder of her stay at Elmhurst. Nárcissza had more opportunity for dinner dates than at any previous time, but she was limited in the number she could accept. There simply wasn't time. Forty hours of gainful employment and a full class and study curriculum kept her very busy. But between her brother's contribution and the "bonus" nourishment that came her way through whatever dinner engagements she could fit into her schedule, she managed to keep herself well above starvation level. She could not complain.

After classes on the day of the message from Professor Pavlokas, she tidied herself up a bit and went directly to his office. He started right in :

"Nárcissza, I received a call yesterday from someone who needs a student to do some research work for him. He asked that I get my best student to give him a call, and I thought you might be interested."

"Is it a steady job, Professor? "

"Yes, I think so. And I think it would make better and more profitable use of your capabilities than baby sitting and housecleaning. In fact, I think you should apply and ask for four dollars an hour, right at the start."

"I can't possibly do that, Professor. He will want to know what I have been getting at other jobs, and I can't stretch that too much."

"Well, I'm sure he will find he's getting good value for money. Here's his name," he said, handing her a scribbled note. "Robert Berg, and his outfit is called Coulter Industrial Sales." Then he gave her the number to call and indicated with a wave of his hand that the discussion was over. She left with a promise that she would let him know how she got on.

She didn't sleep much that night. Mostly, she was going over the money question, wondering how she would approach the subject and how much she could bring herself to ask for, without jeopardizing her chance of getting the job at all. After classes the following afternoon, she made the call.

"Mr. Berg, Professor Pavlokas said I should give you a call."

"Oh, I take it you are of the female gender."

Those were his exact words, spoken with some surprise and an undeniable touch of disappointment. After asking her one or two questions about her background he suggested that she visit him for an interview without delay. He explained that Coulter Industrial Sales had its headquarters in the basement of his home and told her in a few words how to get there.

The place proved within walking distance—less than a mile and a half away—so she would not have to worry about transportation. A large, sandy-haired man with a twinkle in his keen blue eyes greeted her at the door of the attractive brick ranch-type house on 196 Clinton Avenue. After an initial greeting, he led her to a huge basement, which had been divided into two sections. On one side a finished area served as the company's office. The other side, unfinished and with the wooden studs and framework exposed, served as the 'lab,' where the particle analysis work was done. Nárcissza was ushered to a chair on one side of a cluttered desk, and Robert Berg settled himself into a chair opposite.

When he asked her how much she expected to be paid, she found she was not able to ask for four dollars an hour as the professor had urged. His pep talk had, however, given her an incentive to go part of the way. In the most composed manner that she could muster, she asked for two dollars.

Bob Berg responded, "Do you mind telling me what you were getting at your last job? "

"A dollar fifty," she said.

"And you don't think you want to go back to a dollar fifty?"

"No," she said, but by that time she was sure she had ruined her opportunity and would have gladly accepted a dollar fifty. It was too late now to change course.

Her prospective employer didn't make further comment on the salary matter. He hired her on the spot and began talking about starting arrangements. Then after giving her an explanation of how his particle counter worked, and asking her to run one or two samples for him right then, he departed. He had a university lecturing appointment, he told her, and would be back later. While he was gone, she worked with the instrument and ruined the day by spilling the mercury from the manometer column. She gathered it up as well as she could, then wrote a note of apology and left the lab. It had been a wonderful chance and she'd messed it up the very first day. She resigned herself to the probability that it was all over. In the evening, however, she got a phone call. It was Robert Berg. She dreaded having to talk to him, but when she picked up the phone, he was laughing. "So you spilled the mercury. OK, so tomorrow when you come, I'll show you how to clean it up." Phew!

She didn't know what rate he intended to pay her until three weeks later when he asked,

"How much do I owe you? "

She'd kept a careful record of the hours she'd worked and she handed him a copy. He looked it over and wrote out a check—for a sum which told her that he'd accepted her two-dollars-an-hour 'asking price.' A few weeks later when her new boss hired a draftsman for one-fifty she realized that she had done pretty well.

The new job changed everything. Two dollars an hour gave her, for an hour of work, almost the equivalent pay of three hours of work at any of her other jobs. A godsend, because with her other jobs, apart from the difference in pay, she had to wait to be picked up from here and there at all hours of the day and night. This, on the other hand, was a steady job that did not have those time consuming and exhausting aspects. It was within walking distance and it required a certain fixed number of hours of work per week, in exchange for a steady rate of pay. Steady work with steady pay at a better rate, were not the only advantages of her new job. For starters she wouldn't have to clean houses, which had always taxed her under-fueled energy resources. She found the work tremendously interesting. The particle counter she worked with had not previously been used for anything except blood cell counting and here was an opportunity to explore dozens of other applications for it. She reveled in her good fortune and the fact that for her last year of college she would not go hungry.

Nárcissza, so occupied and fulfilled in her final year of college, almost regretted that it would soon be over. When she handed in her notice to Robert Berg to let him know well in advance that she would be returning to New York, he was visibly upset, and she was gratified that he had been so well pleased with her work. He wanted to know why she had to go and leave such an interesting job. To make it easier on herself, she didn't tell him the truth. She told him that her mother was ill and she wanted to go back to New York to be with her and her family, and find a job there. Berg thought about that for a while, then he said, "Well, there's this Howard Layton over there. He's our sales representative for that area, and I'm sure we could work out something with him."

She didn't respond to that at the time, but she learned later that her boss had called Layton to discuss the idea with him. She didn't know what reaction he got, but in a few days she was told that a letter had arrived from Layton in which he'd written, "The last thing in the world I need is Nárcissza." Undaunted, Robert decided to call Layton again to discuss the matter further, with Nárcissza listening in on the other line. As she listened, she could hear Layton swearing like a trooper, with every other word 'bloody this' and 'bloody that.' She wasn't at all encouraged by what she heard. In the end Robert agreed that after settling herself in again at home, she could go out and find an office for her-self. The decision was made.

Overnight, Nárcissza found herself appointed Eastern Technical Manager for Coulter Industrial Sales.

*Overnight, Nárcissza found
herself appointed
Eastern Technical Manager
for Coulter Industrail sales.*

THIRTEEN

Damn that phone. "Who is it Eleanor?"

"It's Bob Berg. He seems to be in a good mood."

"Put him through."

"Hello Bob, how are things?"

A chuckle at the other end of the line. "Hello Howard, I got your letter."

I can practically hear him grinning like a Japanese general. "So? "

"I guess you don't like the idea of a female coming to show you how to do your selling." More chuckles.

"Bob, I pride myself on my organizing ability and I plan my calls geographically so while I'm in a given area, I can make calls efficiently for several of my product lines on the same day. If I have to take your Nárcissza around with me, she won't want to wait around while I call on other prospects besides yours. And even if she didn't mind, I would feel guilty about it. I would feel I was imposing on her bloody generosity. That's a complication I don't need right now. And as for the idea of her joining me here in this office,

I think that would be crazy. I've got all I can cope with right now, without a woman to complicate things."

"All right Howard, don't panic." Another chuckle, then, "Nárcissza can get an office of her own and simply help you when you need it."

Somewhat mollified, and with a realization that I had been a bit boorish and unchivalrous, I agreed that that would be OK.

By late February I had begun to make some measurable progress with IBM and the Acoustica ultrasonic cleaners. The process engineers at the IBM Poughkeepsie plant had asked whether one or two electrical changes could be made in the interests of operator safety, and Acoustica had agreed to comply. Based on this, several more purchases were planned. Also over these same few weeks, I'd managed to negotiate a technical sales representation agreement with a small power control manufacturer in Stamford, Connecticut. This one, Vectrol Engineering Inc., was an especially welcome find because it brought with it a monthly retainer to cover the engineering and proposal work I would have to do in conjunction with the sales effort. Commission on actual sales was treated separately.

My work on this product line fitted in very well with the visits and demonstrations scheduled for the Coulter Counter, for I would set up my travel arrangements so that appointments with Vectrol prospects could be grouped geographically with the Coulter Counter demonstrations. But then, just as I was fine tuning my schedule for the following month, Nárcissza arrived on the scene. She called to introduce herself and we set up an appointment. And just to further complicate my life, she called again the following day to postpone the date. Bloody good start.

On March 4th at 4 PM, she finally showed up. I went out to meet her in the nicely appointed waiting room that Jacqueline provided for her clients. Several high-backed Jacobean chairs were arranged along each of the opposite walls of this Persian-carpeted room, and Nárcissza was sitting in one facing me as I entered. As I went through the door, she rose and came toward me extending her hand as she spoke:

"Mr. Layton? I've heard a lot about you and I thought I would come and introduce myself as soon as possible."

I ushered her back to her chair. "I've heard a lot about you too, Miss Ludányi, and it's all been very positive," I said.

Then I pulled out a chair and sat facing her, appraising her, I suppose you might say. She sat, quiet and serene, with an expression on her face that signaled her awareness of my inspection.

Hmm. Well . . . Well, I have to say that she was quite different from what I'd expected. No brass, no slick business suit, no high-powered briefcase. She sat there quite composed, her long brown hair drawn up tightly to a bun on the top of her head. A brown tweed skirt and matching blouse. No makeup at all. Just a fresh and healthy looking complexion and a disarming smile. Good legs, yes, very good legs; trim ankles. She was looking at me with cool gray eyes as she waited for me to continue.

"Well, I'm certainly glad to meet you Nárcissza," I said, feeling a little uncomfortable under her steady gaze. "I, ah, well, here we are—and I hope you will let me know if there's anything I can do to help you get settled in."

"I have a few leads and places to see regarding an office, and as soon as I get fixed up I'll be getting in touch with you to see what I can do to help you." She put extra stress on those last words so that there should be no mistake as to who was going to be helpful to whom.

She had a very charming European accent that I couldn't place, and I sat there with my head cocked to one side, listening, and hoping she'd continue. Then, perhaps becoming conscious of the silence and noticing that I was gaping at her foolishly, she said: "I have some shopping to do now, so I think I'd better get going before the stores close—and I still have to talk to another real estate agent about some offices they want me to look at."

She regarded me again with those gray eyes. "We can talk again soon."

"Oh yes, of course," I said, thinking that in this big bad city she really shouldn't have to be office hunting by herself. "Perhaps I can do the rounds with you—for moral support, that is," I added.

"Thank you, I appreciate that, but I think I'll be all right. I'll let you know if I have a problem."

"Well, it's no trouble really. I just have a feeling that, ahh . . . two heads are often better than one . . . in these matters . . ." My voice trailed off.

"I'll call you next week," she said. And with that she rose, and with a brief smile to let me know that the interview was over, she offered her hand. I held it briefly, then she turned and departed. Very composed, very demure.

Damn!

FOURTEEN

I called Nárcissza a few days later to see how her office hunt was progressing. She told me she'd seen a couple of promising places and planned to go for a second look at each of them.

"Why don't I come with you so that in case you like one of them, I can help you with your negotiations."

"That would be nice," she said.

When we did the rounds, the prospective office quarters struck me as pretty crummy places—and in less than desirable locations, but I didn't comment. Instead, I suggested that before making a decision she might perhaps find it worth while to talk with Jacqueline Vicary about some space that had just become vacant on the third floor of her place on Fifth Avenue. In the end, a few days after Jacqueline had shown her around her third floor accommodations, she opted for that choice, thus bringing about the very situation I had been arguing against since Bob Berg had first mentioned her name.

Bob Berg shipped a Coulter Counter together with appropriate supplies from Chicago to Nárcissza's office, to serve for demonstration purposes and to enable her to run parti-cle-size analyses for prospective customers. With that instru-ment on hand, we scheduled a number of trips to the loca-tions of various interested parties. We started with American Sugar Company, American Cyanamid, and General Foods Corporation and added many others in the order that their inquiries had come in. Far from hindering me in my work, Nárcissza, with her quiet competence, seemed to lend a great deal of credibility to our endeavors. I found that technicians and scientists whom we visited were eager to help her with the task of carrying the equipment from our car to the loca-tions where the demonstrations would take place.

We got along well, and as our field work progressed, we were rewarded by a gratifying flow of orders. I also found to my surprise that Nárcissza did not object when I would occa-sionally work in appointments that involved my other product lines. Often, on the way back from trips of this kind, we would stop for an evening meal, and on these relaxed occasions I was able to learn more about her colorful background.

One evening in May, at Gino's on 43rd Street, we were enjoying the house specialty, veal cutlet parmigianna. We were reviewing the day's Coulter Counter demonstrations.

"I have a very good feeling about today's visits," she said, grinning mischievously.

"Yes, the General Foods people seemed very impressed with the way the machine worked. Come to that, so was I. If I hadn't seen it myself, I would never have believed you could use the thing for measuring the smoothness and con-sistency of packaged mashed potatoes, or, for that matter, to predict how milk chocolate would taste! "

"Oh, but there's a special reason why everything went so well today."

"Really? "

"Yes, there is. Today is the thirteenth, and thirteen is my lucky number, so everything had to turn out well."

Noting my amazed expression, she laughed and continued. "Not only that. It's not just the thirteenth, it's *Friday* the thirteenth, and that's the best thirteenth there is."

I stared at her. "But that's my lucky number, too. In fact, I founded Interlab on the thirteenth of the month, just for that reason."

"Oh, but I have a special reason for thirteen being my favorite number. With my family, it's everybody's lucky number. You see, Friday the thirteenth was the date of my parent's first meeting thirty years ago."

The subject of shared superstitions occupied us through the rest of that evening. I was beginning to get to know my new associate. I also found I was looking forward to learning more.

The following week, returning from a Coulter demonstration session at Cyanamid in Boundbrook, New Jersey, we stopped for dinner at the Whaler restaurant in Nyack, just west of the Tappan Zee Bridge. We got ourselves a good corner table and ordered drinks. Nárcissza ordered wine and I asked her whether it was because she was Hungarian, or because she'd acquired the taste for it independently, that she liked wine so much. She replied that it was a bit of both.

"Hungary is a good wine producer to begin with, so Hungarians tend to favor wine more than people from countries that are not prolific wine producers," she said. "But my appreciation for wine may have been sharpened by my childhood experiences. My family had a vineyard and during the war all the men had gone off to the front except for those who were too old or physically disabled in some way. There were only women left, and they were not taught how to siphon a barrel. We did have a man who took care of the vineyard—a sort of supervisor, but he was an alcoholic and his health was not good. The problem was that if you sent him down into the cellar he would siphon so much out of a barrel that you would have to carry him out." She laughed at the memory.

"Nobody except he and I knew how to siphon a barrel. Anyway, before my father, a colonel in the army, had left for the front, he'd taught me how to siphon a barrel— just for fun you see, because it was not an easy thing to do. There's a certain way to do it. You have to avoid getting the dregs. So I knew how to do it and anyway the only man left to do it mostly got drunk in the process, forgetting which wines he was supposed to siphon." She took a sip of her wine and continued. "So I became the official siphoner. When I first learned how to siphon wine I was about eight or nine. My brother Tamás, who was two years younger than I, would always breathe in between siphoning, and he'd lose the wine. I would not breathe while I was siphoning but I suppose it had to do with the fact that I liked wine much more than he did." She looked at me inquiringly to make sure I understood what she was saying.

"You suck, but if you breathe in between, the wine goes back into the barrel. I suppose I did this job for a couple of years anyhow. You see it was more or less casual. If it had to be siphoned, I would do it. When you have wine in the barrel you don't want to mix it up. At the very bottom you have the sludge and you don't want to disturb that, and you don't want the stuff off the top for some other reason. You get this glass, or 'stealer,' which in Hungary we call the Lopoka. You put this into the barrel and suck on it, and when the wine starts flowing, you start filling whatever containers you wanted to fill. When you want to fill a number of bottles, that's how it's done." She paused to take another sip.

"I don't know how they do it nowadays, but in those days barrels would be on their sides and the filler bung would be on the top at one end. The barrels didn't stand on end like beer barrels; they lay on their sides. I didn't do this siphoning commercially," she added. "I just did it for the household use. If you wanted to do it commercially, someone would come in to do it. You'd just do a few for the house, sometimes two or three kinds. Maybe one would be a dessert wine, and there would be some white and some red."

Nárcissza laughed again. "I've been talking too much. Anyway, now you know why I like wine." She looked across at me and grinned.

I could just picture that cellar with stone walls and dim lighting, and Nárcissza as a little kid with pigtails, sitting on a stool in front of a row of barrels, working diligently at her special siphoning art and feeling very accomplished. I began to tell her a bit about my own background and circumstances. Of how my slow progress in making a decent living in America was having its effect on my private life and my marriage. Of how our friends had come to the conclusion that I would never make it in this country at what I was trying to do.

"They explained to my wife, Laura, that it was tough enough for people who were born here and who knew the ropes and had adequate capital to see them through the early ups and downs. But for a foreigner, more or less newly arrived and with minuscule funds behind me, the odds against my eventual success were simply too high."

Nárcissza seemed interested in what I was telling her, so I continued.

"Their kind offers to help me find a decent job tempted me

sorely," I told her. "But they came too late. If, when I was job
hunting myself, our friends had made it known that they were
eager to help me find a good job, and had the necessary connections to enable them to do so, I might have been very glad
to accept their help. But once I'd taken the plunge and had
managed to achieve one or two small early successes; once I'd
tasted the heady wine of independence and freedom of choice
that went along with having my own business, I couldn't bring
myself to turn my back on it. It was probably unfair to Laura
and, perhaps not surprisingly, she's been pressing me to go
back to England. That seems to be occupying her thoughts
more and more these days. Strangely, although she comes
from a well-to-do Jewish-Italian family, she was educated at an
English Mission college, and that gave her an opportunity to
learn a lot about England and the English way of life. So when
I finally brought her home, she enjoyed life in England very
much, and became very socially involved there, too. She says
it's the place where she belongs and I can understand that in
some ways. She's become totally English in her outlook."

Suddenly aware that I was, perhaps, revealing too much
about my personal life, I stopped talking. We finished our dinner and drove on. I was content with the day. All in all, I was
finding that far from being the hindrance to my business that
I'd been expecting through Nárcissza's involvement, I had so
far seen nothing other than quiet cooperation and an increasingly noticeable contribution to my Coulter sales efforts. I
made a mental note to apologize to Bob Berg for the difficult
time I had given him regarding Nárcissza's coming east.

In parallel with the increasingly concentrated business
activity, I needed more secretarial and typing help than I

could yet afford to pay for. As luck would have it my neighbor's daughter, Pat Field, on the lookout for part-time work, came to the rescue. She volunteered to come into the city three half days a week on a temporary basis at a very modest rate. She would stay until she found herself a permanent job to her liking, or until my improving revenues would overtake my present cash-flow crunch so I could employ her on a long-term, mutually satisfactory basis.

The arrangement worked well, and before long we were discussing our need for more generous operating quarters. Jacqueline's accommodations at 437 Fifth Avenue had served my needs very well during the difficult early months of my business activities, but it seemed that we were outgrowing that particular phase. As the Coulter workload expanded, and the need for field demonstrations increased, the disadvantages involved in the time consuming task of loading the demo instrument aboard the car and then getting in and out of Manhattan, were becoming more and more apparent. Clearly, the time had come to ask ourselves whether we needed to be located in Manhattan at all.

Meanwhile the situation on my home front was going in the opposite direction, and Laura's recent announcement of her intention to leave had not really surprised me. She'd talked increasingly of her unhappiness with our present situation and about how much she missed all we'd left behind in England: our friends, our social life, the English environment, and the European way of life in general. Her desire to return to England had first surfaced because of the hard time I was having in making a decent living in the USA, and although I had in recent months begun to make some headway in my latest enterprise, it was already too late.

Laura had had time to think about what a return to

England would imply as far as our marriage was concerned, and it seemed to me that she had, in her mind, dealt with all the difficulties involved. I had booked a flight for her intended departure of June fourth, but now she was intent on leaving sooner. Perhaps if I had not already made two false starts and had not continued to stumble a lot on my third attempt to build a life for us in America, the idea of returning to England might never have occurred to her. Perhaps she would have been perfectly content. Perhaps . . . perhaps . . . It was pointless to conjecture.

One morning at breakfast she said, "Howard, I plan to leave right now. I've told our friends that I shan't be gone for longer than six months, but actually I really don't know when I'll be coming back." Although she didn't actually say the words, I got the message—there would be no return.

On April sixteenth, Laura—exotic, vivacious, restless Laura, my wife of fifteen years—checked out of our apartment and left on BOAC flight 558 for England, taking all her personal possessions and our two-year-old daughter Leslie with her.

Well, I had probably got exactly what I deserved. I had taken a considerable risk in crossing the ocean in the first place and had been totally unwilling to discuss any change of course when things hadn't turned out as well as we'd hoped. And there had been opportunities to recover lost ground. Godfrey Imhof, my former employer in England had invited me to return and run his fast-growing high-fidelity equipment business. Bernard Strong of the Shipton Company had repeated his long-standing offer of a marketing position in his plastics extrusion-machine manufacturing company—which by this time was enjoying good sales growth in the USA. But I had thanked them sincerely and had politely declined. I had not even discussed these alternatives with Laura. I had closed my mind to any thought of turning back. No question, I'd got what I deserved.

At first I wasn't sure how I felt about Laura's departure. I moped around the apartment, conscious of its emptiness. I went out to eat as often as I could afford, and took advantage of the kind offers of hospitality from those who knew of my new circumstances. I went to parties and concerts and local charity functions and when Nárcissza and Pat Field were not around for company, I took my lunches at the nearby Lawrence Hospital coffee shop, which was always good for a little socializing. Then one evening I went home and wrote Laura a long letter telling her that I had come to understand her need for a different lifestyle than I had been able to offer her and that I had faced up to the fact that we'd grown apart. I told her I was intent on continuing to go my own way and that I had come to realize that in doing what she had felt she needed to do for herself, the course she'd taken was perhaps best for both of us. We'd have to deal with the matter of custody of the younger child, of course, but I had come to accept the fact that our marriage was over.

Around ten o'clock, I walked down to the mailbox at the end of Palmer Road and mailed the letter. Then I called my neighbor Ingrid, and we got drunk together.

FIFTEEN

I was becoming obsessed with the matter of moving to larger quarters. What if we were to move to the suburbs, say to my home area in Bronxville? I reasoned that an office in that location would be fairly central to the main highways for travel in all directions within the metropolitan area and New England. It would be somewhat farther for Nárcissza, but by this time she'd bought a car to enable her to give sales support to the other Coulter representatives up and down the East Coast, so it wouldn't be difficult for her to commute to Bronxville. I discussed the idea with Bob Berg and he thought it made sense. Soon we were checking out available office space in that elite dormitory community, and by the end of April we'd moved into a twenty by twenty office on the second floor of 116 Kraft Avenue, just off the main street of Bronxville Village.

Pat Field could now walk to work and she found that very convenient. She switched from temporary to full-time, becoming Interlab's first full-time employee aside from myself. In exchange for the office facilities that I provided for Nárcissza's Coulter work and correspondence, Bob Berg

177

had agreed that Nárcissza would contribute one day a week of her time to Interlab's general activities.

Nárcissza, although content with the new traveling arrangements, was now having a difficult time for other reasons. Her father's illness had worsened and had been diagnosed as stomach cancer, and she was dedicated to the idea that the right nutrition would somehow alleviate the condition and even put it into remission. To that end she prepared a variety of vegetable juices for him every day. She persisted with this treatment, often taking a trip home in the middle of the day to make sure that her father was well supplied with this life-giving nectar, and to see that he drank every drop of the daily quota she'd prescribed for him.

In the mornings, on her arrival at the office, I would try to read her face for signs of some success—some indication that her determined efforts were having a positive effect on her father's condition. But there were no such signs. She went about her work with as much industry as ever, but she didn't smile much. Her preoccupation with her father's illness and with her attempts to help him, seemed to have taken over her conscious mind. Sometimes I had the impression that she was bent on changing the course of events through the application of sheer will power. He was her father, her hero, and she had to find a way to help him. I wanted to comfort her, but her manner seemed remote, and I was unable to find the right words. On occasion, when I was able to utter some sort of expression of concern, the words sounded false and ineffectual to my ears. In the mornings, when her usual arrival time approached, I found myself checking the time, and looking out through the office window, watching for her familiar form, for the hair drawn up in a bun on the top of her head. When the usual time would pass and she had not yet appeared, I found it increasingly difficult to concentrate on my work until the sound of her footsteps along the hall would signal her arrival.

One afternoon, Nárcissza mentioned her need to pick up some new medication for her father from an address further upstate. She would have to leave somewhat earlier than usual to attend to that. When I offered to go with her for company, she did not oppose the suggestion, and by 4:30PM we were on our way. As she sat quietly beside me, I asked whether there was any change for the better in her father's condition. When she did not reply, I glanced across at her face. Her eyes were watering—brimming until the full drops began to spill over and trickle down her cheeks. I glanced at her again a few moments later. She was sobbing quietly. I put my free arm around her shoulder and pulled her close. As I did so, she turned toward me, nestling her head against my chest. Gradually, her sobbing eased, and we drove on in silence.

In a while, I saw that there was a rest area ahead. When we reached it, I pulled in and parked. Then I turned to Nárcissza and wrapped my arms around her. I held her close for several long moments. Then I kissed her tears and her eyes and the softness of her cheeks. I cupped her face between my hands and gently kissed her lips. At last, I held her back from me so that I could look into her glistening gray eyes. I held her like that, casting about in my mind for the words I wanted to say to her, but they just wouldn't come.

At last I heard myself say, "You're a wonderful girl, Nárcissza."

Then I put the car in gear, and pulled out onto the highway.

❖

Her father died—a soldier and patriot to the end. The moments of his passing were well expressed in the writings of his son, Paul, who was with him at the time:

"That day—June 29, 1961—would have been my last day of school, but I had stayed home with my mother who, because of my father's weak condition, did not go to work either. That morning my father asked me to move the fan so it would be more effective. My mother made an attempt to move it but my father scolded us and said that I should do it. Later, when my mother had left the room, my father's last words to me were 'Your mother is a very good person. She deserves that you take good care of her.'

For most of the morning he was resting quietly, falling in and out of sleep. From the room next to his, I heard him say to my mother 'I am so troubled, so troubled—the Homeland.' Those were his last words. When my mother came out of the room, she commented on how at such a time, he was thinking about his duty to his country.

A little later, my father was a bit restless and I went to sit by his bed. My mother stood by his side. I rubbed his shin so that he would feel we were with him. He started breathing slow, heavy breaths. Then they turned to quick shallow breaths that ended abruptly. After that, all was quiet except for the hum and swishing of the oscillating fan. I looked at my mother and we both knew his suffering had ended."

Many months passed before Nárcissza showed signs of coming to terms with her grief. But her composure and good spirits gradually returned. Her distracted and sometimes otherworldly demeanor eventually gave way to a renewed interest in our day-to-day business struggles. She was with us again—immersing herself in her Coulter analysis work and her increasingly valuable one-day-a-week involvement in Interlab's affairs.

Meanwhile, my efforts in behalf of Acoustica were beginning to pay off. I was making pretty good progress with the sale of their products to IBM, and to one or two other large companies in the area. Then it happened. Just as I was congratulating myself on my tenacity and industry in my work with their equipment, I was fired. It was done in the friendliest way. The Acoustica sales manager came east on one of his routine sales support tours and took me out to lunch. When we met outside the restaurant he'd chosen, he pumped my hand heartily. Then at lunch, he thanked me for the spadework I'd done and for the success of my efforts. The easy going manner and casual dress of this large, blond and blue-eyed young man impressed me. He looked like a real go-getter.

"Naturally," he said, as we were working on our main course, "the increasing sales volume justifies appointment of a regional sales manager based in New York, and responsible for all the sales territories up and down the east coast." He paused, clearing his throat. "So we won't be needing your services any longer."

I thought I had not heard him correctly. "I, ah—what was that you said? "

"Well, I was just explaining that with a regional sales manager in the East, we naturally won't need your services any more." Then, perhaps suddenly becoming aware of the expression on my face, he added, "but we want you to know that we greatly appreciate all the good work you've been doing in this territory in so short a time span. Yes, we're very pleased." He coughed, and attacked his liver and onions with renewed zest.

I stared at him, disbelieving. How could it be that I was getting fired for being successful? This was *my* product line, *my* territory, couldn't he see that? Over the months that I'd been working with the Acoustica products I had become emotionally attached to them. I owned them. I was involved with them for better or for worse. Getting those sales at IBM had taken every bit of resource I could bring to bear on the task. It had taken all that I had to give. What this affable stranger was saying to me, just could not be. I sat there, not trusting myself to speak.

I don't remember how I got through the rest of that lunch engagement. I recall my host becoming quite solicitous and asking me whether I was feeling well, and my weak response that the clam chowder had disagreed with me. Then it was over.

The following week, the Parker Instrument Company, whose panel meters I was beginning to sell quite well, also dispensed with my services.

Perhaps I was fortunate in that the temporary nature of sales representation agreements was brought home to me so early in the development of my small enterprise. But at the time it wasn't easy to be philosophical about it. After the loss of those two product lines, I decided that commissioned representation was not for me. I was simply not emotionally equipped to deal with the loss of sales responsibility for products in which I had invested so much of my energies and myself. That kind of flexibility I did not have, and it was important that I recognize that and change course accordingly. I had to do something, and fast. Almost anything would do to help with the cash flow until I could find something to replace the Acoustica product line. Commissions from Coulter and other sales would be arriving in due course, and I still had consulting fees from Painton and Vectrol to count on, but it wouldn't be enough. It didn't take me long to realize that I'd have to get a part-time job to bridge the gap. Better get the papers and start telephoning.

Sometimes the angels look down with compassion—or could it be the devil grinning broadly as he decides to string you along a bit. Whatever or Whoever was responsible for my rescue, I shall be eternally grateful. Almost before I had got into my stride with my job hunting, the phone rang. It was Holton Harris, my old friend from the days of my association with the Reeves Instrument Corporation. Holt's manufacturing business was expanding and the high cost of factory space in Manhattan had persuaded him that a move to some other location would make economic sense. In a way, his reasoning was much like mine had been. He'd eventually asked himself "Why not?" and he'd been unable to come up with any negatives other than the unavoidable but temporary disruption inherent in such a plan. But by contrast with my own overnight transfer from the great metropolis to suburbia, moving a manufacturing business was a very tricky undertaking indeed.

Holt knew he would have to replace most of his workforce with men and women local to his new location, and he couldn't afford a break in production while the hiring and training of new people was under way. It was evident, therefore, that the new manufacturing site would have to be selected and new personnel hired and trained while production in Manhattan went on uninterrupted. He explained that he needed someone to advertise, do some hiring, and get the new place going to minimize the need for his own direct involvement until zero hour on the official relocation date. Then, all operations in the Manhattan site would cease and the move would be completed. Would I care to take on a part-time consulting job to help him with the project, he'd asked. I would indeed.

Holt picked Norwalk, Connecticut, as the new location for Harrel Incorporated, and since that city was less than an hour's drive from my home in Bronxville, I was able to contribute the time and effort Holt needed without seriously disrupting my Interlab work schedules. It wasn't easy but I badly needed the money. In a few months, after Holt had taken over the staffing work I'd started, it was over. The arrangement had served us both well.

Meanwhile, I'd been thinking a great deal about the Acoustica ultrasonic products that I'd become so attached to. What a fascinating and promising field, and what an interesting future lay ahead for that fledgling technology. Yet those generators and transducers that were the heart of the product were not particularly sophisticated. In fact, I reflected, their circuitry was not very different from that of the audio equipment I'd worked with in the past. Without too much difficulty, I reasoned, I could design my own ultra sonic generator and make it myself. Why not? Well, for one thing, I didn't have the money or the manpower to manufacture anything, and even if I had, I would have to find factory space to do it. No, that was out of the question. But what if we did the designs and drawings and got a sub-contractor to manufacture the stuff for us? What if we had our own ultrasonic cleaning line to sell, with our own special logo right on the front of the case? Nobody would be able to take that away from us. Nobody would turn up one day and slap me on the back and say "Thanks very much old son, we hate to ruin your day, but we don't need you any more." No, nobody would be able to do that again—ever.

It was a compelling thought. I snapped out of my reverie and turned to my one-day-a-week mentor, Nárcissza. She was running samples on the Coulter as I walked over to her desk.

"Nárcissza, let's go out to lunch when you've finished that," I said. "I have an idea I'd like to discuss with you."

Sixteen

The compact form of Joe Disbrow greeted me at the door to the long corridor of the Poughkeepsie purchasing department. The sandy-haired IBM veteran was, as usual, smiling broadly as he shook my hand and led the way to the adjacent conference room. Engineers and other IBMers, all of whom I'd met previously in my work in behalf of Acoustica, were arriving in dribs and drabs. There were six of them in all. Some were representatives from the semiconductor processing areas, and others were from Safety and Maintenance. Joe had gathered them together at my request, following my call a few days previously asking for a chance to present my ideas for a new ultrasonic cleaning system which would be designed expressly for semiconductor processing. Joe was always ready to listen to vendors who appeared genuinely interested in helping his company find more cost-effective ways to do things, and I'd been fairly certain that he would lend a sympathetic ear to what I was proposing. He'd lost no time in spreading the word; so here we were, and I had the floor. As soon as we were all seated I started right in:

"Gentlemen, first I want to thank you for your confidence in my services during the time I've been working with you on applications for the Acoustica products. Your confidence has enabled me to achieve a marked increase in sales of Acoustica Ultrasonic equipment, mostly with respect to IBM requirements. Unfortunately that achievement has also resulted in my termination as an Acoustica representative."

There was a murmur of surprise at this revelation, and I waited for a measure of quiet again. I continued:

" Yes, I was surprised and shocked at first, but then I concluded that it was perhaps quite natural that with sales in this general area on the upswing, Acoustica management would decide that the opening of a direct regional sales office was justified. But I've also been wondering how in the future I might find a way to provide you with equipment more precisely tailored to your needs, than Acoustica— or for that matter anyone else—has yet offered."

George Green, the senior of the three process engineers appeared a bit skeptical, but he was good-natured and must have decided to give me a chance to state my case before making negative comments. "It sounds like a good idea. Maybe you'd better tell us how you'd go about it."

I thanked him and continued. "In the course of my discussions with you, I have learned of a number of design areas that you'd like to see modified for your most critical applications. A few examples have to do with sources of contamination that in general industrial applications would be of no concern, but which in semiconductor processing have considerable significance. One of these sources has to do with the outgassing of carbon particles and other contaminants from welded seams. Another is concerned with the leaching of threading compounds from drain connections and other plumbing fittings."

The room was quiet. I felt I had now sparked everyone's interest. "On the question of optimum control capability, you've mentioned at different times that all generators should be provided with power controls so that ultrasonic activity levels can be adjusted as appropriate for processing delicate substrates. These areas are simple enough to address, but because they involve modest price increases, and most industries don't need them, they're not yet incorporated in standard ultrasonic products." I paused to make sure that the interest level wasn't flagging.

"Semiconductor processing has only just got off the ground and many suppliers haven't yet caught on to its enormous potential. I want to put my faith in that potential and serve that field and nothing else."

There were murmurs of approval here and there, but it was not until I was actually saying the words that I realized that that was truly what I wanted to do. I went on— "I've asked for this meeting today to find out what more there are in the way of special characteristics that you'd like to see in an ultrasonic cleaning system designed expressly to meet your special needs. Then I'll build a pair of prototype units for you to evaluate. It goes without saying of course, that there would be no obligation to purchase anything. I would simply ask that you provide me with a written report on your findings." I paused and looked around, then I said, "Thank you, gentlemen," and sat down.

A spirited discussion followed my presentation. Understandably there were those, especially among the maintenance group who, having found the Acoustica units quite satisfactory, were not anxious to introduce another ultrasonic cleaning system at this time. But by the time we all rose to go our separate ways, I had my 'wish-list.' I thanked Joe Disbrow again for calling the meeting for me so quickly. Then I left, stepping lightly as I made my way back to the parking lot.

Back at our Bronxville office we went into high gear. Using what I'd learned from my conference at Poughkeepsie, I made drawings and designs and sent them out to sheet metal fabricators for quotation. Concurrently I got in touch with Gene Belgard of Sonic Systems Incorporated. I'd met Gene in the course of my work with Acoustica and had come to like and respect him and his company. I told him what I was doing and asked him whether he'd be interested in building ultrasonic generator chassis and tanks to my specifications. I explained that we were having generator cases fabricated separately and that we'd do the assembly work in our Bronxville office. Gene said he'd be happy to cooperate, so we went ahead full steam with what was now a quite specific plan of action. Within six weeks of my conference at Poughkeepsie, I was on my way there again to deliver my first prototype of a bench-top cleaning system which I hoped would be judged as meeting most, if not all, of IBM's wish list.

When I placed the generator and tank assembly on the conference room table, George Green expressed his surprise that my prototype was ready so soon. Beyond that, he made no comment except to say that the purchasing department would notify me of the IBM evaluation of the equipment as soon as they'd had an opportunity to try it out and confer on its performance.

I assumed that the test procedures would take a month or two, but to my surprise, three weeks after I delivered the prototype, IBM's evaluation of this first unit came in the form of a call from Joe Disbrow to place a purchase order for two sets of Interlab's new ultrasonic equipment. Two weeks after that, Joe called in another order for two more sets. By the end of 1963, we'd sold and delivered close to thirty units to that IBM location. It was an encouraging start.

Early in the New Year, I began to sell Interlab G4/150 ultrasonic generators and associated cleaning tanks to the IBM Research Laboratories in Yorktown Heights. George Cheroff, one of the scientists at that location, had requested early delivery, and since the labs were only a few miles distant from Bronxville, we arranged to transport the equipment by car to the specific area where it would be installed. When I arrived on the appointed day, George, a fair-haired man whose appearance more resembled a football quarterback than a scientist, explained that he needed the equipment for a new lab now under construction within the existing building.

After a lunch break at the Research Lab cafeteria, he asked me whether I would care to see the location of the new lab. When I indicated my interest and my appreciation of his offer, George led the way to the site of his pet new project. After showing me a small prep area where he planned to install the Interlab bench-top cleaners, he turned and pointed to the far end of an adjacent empty room.

"You see that wall?" he said. "well, that's going to have a cleaning and processing facility occupying its whole length. We'll need a lot of ultrasonic equipment in that set-up too, and it will be designed for use in entirely new applications. He made no mention of the nature of those applications, but he did discuss the type of equipment and chemistry processing hardware he'd require. Much intrigued by this new project, I found myself making suggestions about what components and materials might work well for his purposes. As we talked, the discussion became more and more detailed. Back in his office, George pulled out a drawing of the room we'd just visited, and a layout of the apparatus that it would house. Then he said casually:

"Why don't you quote on the whole thing?"

I laughed. "Don't you remember what I told you at lunch—that we just have a twenty by twenty office in Bronxville?"

He looked at me quizzically across the desk, his blue eyes twinkling. "You don't think I'm serious, do you? "

I laughed again. "How could we possibly build an eighteen-foot processing structure in a medium-sized office—and with no way to get it in and out?"

"Well, you could farm it out in pieces to subcontractors and do the electrical control panels by hanging them around the picture rails in your office, then wiring them like that."

"And how would we put it all together?"

"Oh that wouldn't be so difficult. You could rent a truck and bring all the stuff in here. Then you could come over some weekend and build it right here in the lab."

I stared across at this sandy-haired, easy going scientist, not knowing quite how to reply to his far-fetched suggestions and wondering when this seeming banter would end.

"Just as a matter of interest," I said, "why would you consider a sales rep like me as a source for your equipment when you can readily buy it from any of a number of reputable manufacturers?"

George leaned back in his chair, pondering my question for a moment, then he said, "I have a quotation from Branson Ultrasonics, arguably the biggest and the best in the ultrasonic cleaning equipment business. They're a great supplier and we use a lot of their stuff, but they're not interested in making lots of special purpose equipment, half of which is not in their field. It just doesn't pay them. So they quote the items they do make and anything else in their portfolio of things they've done before. That's a pretty wide range, but they can't do everything." He let that sink in, then he continued "When I was discussing the project with you, you made some practical suggestions; you told me how you would do the job. Most important is that you were telling me how you would go about building exactly what I want, instead of something different."

It finally dawned on me that George Cheroff was serious. He actually meant all those things he had said about how my little company could somehow do the job. I was stunned. For the moment, I didn't know how to reply. But he came to the rescue.

"Go away and figure out how you would do it. Send me a layout and a quotation. Now I've got to get back to the lab."

Nárcissza's brother Tony—great hearted Tony, who, a scant six years before, had pedaled his neighborhood streets delivering papers; Tony, who, every week through most of Nárcissza's college years, had sent her half his earnings, was now a tall, dark, athletic young man of twenty-one years. With two years of electrical engineering training behind him, he'd joined us earlier in the summer. His cheerful manner and eagerness to make a real contribution to our enterprise had already made a big impression on me. I found that whenever I asked him to put in extra hours or change his work schedule at short notice to meet a customer's needs, he never gave me any indication that it would be inconvenient for him. He did what had to be done and he did it with a smile on his face. Today we were all in the office brain-storming the project that had been placed before us, and try-ing to come to grips with the improbable scenario that the IBM scientist had outlined. Tony, his practical mind already sorting out the logistics of the situation, was enthusiastic:

"I can easily rent a truck and do the humping and we can do as Doctor Cheroff said. Just get everything together and deliver and install it over a weekend." Then, with more than a hint of concern in his voice, he added, "But do you think he might be having us on?"

"Well Tony, there's only one way we're going to find out," I replied, "so I think we'd better get busy. What do you think Nárcissza?"

"If you don't take him at his word and put in the best quote you can, you will always be wondering whether you had ignored a good opportunity when it was staring you in the face." I couldn't argue with that one, so with a resolve bolstered by the knowledge that we were all of one mind in the matter, we turned our attention to practical ways and means. We agreed that I would get a proposal together and some preliminary drawings ready within the next couple of days so that we could hand deliver the package by the end of the week—on Friday the thirteenth. That timing appealed to everyone, so we set about making it happen.

George Cheroff was very cordial when I called to make the appointment. Although I assured him that I intended to just stop by to leave the proposal with him for review at his con-venience, he brushed aside the suggestion and said he would have some time and we could go over the drawings and design together when I arrived. When I met him in the IBM lobby on the appointed day, he took me directly to the new laboratory area where the equipment would be installed.

Then his half-bantering easy-going manner disappeared. He interrogated me closely. What were the details of the ultra-sonic equipment design? What would the noise levels be when four ultrasonic tanks were operating simultaneously? Was I familiar with the IBM Research Lab's electrical and safety codes? The grilling went on at length as George pored over the drawings I'd made. From time to time, with tape measure in hand, he made pencil marks here and there on the wall where the equipment would live.

About two hours later, back in his office, George's easy-going manner had returned.

"Well, unless you have any more questions, I think we've covered everything. I can't tell you anything about your pricing—that's up to Purchasing, and they'll be in touch with you shortly."

He had not spoken idly. Before the end of the month, we had our first order ever for a complete multi-stage chemical processing system—to be built right there at the customer's own site. It would incorporate several acid baths, eight ultra-sonic cleaning tanks, and a similar number of ultra-pure water rinsing stages. Controls would include electrically operated feed lines and drain-valves, and independent power-level controls for each ultrasonic stage. The whole system was to be housed in a bench structure fabricated and assembled by IBM staff from special chemically-resistant materials, and the enclosed work area would be equipped with a bank of overhead air filters to maintain a clean working environment. No doubt about it, it would be a learning experience for everyone.

On a Saturday evening some ten weeks later, Tony and I

are working in Dr. Cheroff's new lab. The remaining walls
are in place now, so that the chemistry processing area has
taken on reduced dimensions. It has become a separate
room measuring about eighteen feet square. The processing
benches in which we have installed our equipment, and
which now stretch across the end wall, are more or less complete. Our basic construction and plumbing work has been
done. Electrical wiring has been completed. All tanks and
connections have been leak-tested and all are filled, including those that will accommodate the acid processes. These
latter, for the moment, are filled with water.

Leftovers from hamburgers and soda drinks litter a nearby table. We've made very careful preparations, and have
done a great deal of our assembly work the night before,
completing it quite early on Saturday morning. But Tony, sitting atop a stepladder with a multi-meter in his hand, has a
very worried expression on his perspiring face. The system
does not work.

As soon as we start the electrical testing we find to our hor-
ror that ultrasonic activity is almost nonexistent. It's the same
in every position. With all power controls set at maximum,
we're not able to hear more than a feeble fizz, or see more
than a few bubbles at the liquid surfaces. If there were no
activity at all; not a sound, nor yet a signal light to let us know
that the system is energized, we might be better able to diagnose the problem— probably to discover that a wiring error
of one sort or another is preventing electric current from
reaching the generators. But this is different. This is not a
conventional catastrophic failure. This is a true catastrophe.

We've already spent several hours rechecking our wiring
and comparing every connecting point with the electrical
diagrams we'd so painstakingly prepared, but the reason for

this strange condition has eluded us. From time to time, George Cheroff puts in an appearance to cheer us on, but the salutary influence of his visits is more than off-set by the frowns of the chief of the electrical department when he, too, has stopped in once or twice. He has begun to take an interest in what we we're up to. On his last visit he'd evidently sensed that we were having difficulty, for his frown was deeper and he was shaking his head from side to side as he turned and left the room.

That had been at seven o'clock and it was now approaching nine. We'd reached the conclusion that we' d need to return on another day when we'd be fresh and better able to diagnose the problem. We knew George would be disappointed and perhaps disillusioned about our capabilities, but it seemed that we had run out of options. We were preparing to pack up for the evening.

Tony, making last minute checks, is switching generators back and forth between pairs of tanks, since, in the interests of economy, each pair of tanks is served alternately by a single generator. Pointing to a corner of one of the control panels, he turns to me.

"I don't suppose there could be anything wrong with these switches."

"How do you mean?"

"Well, they're the British Painton switches aren't they, and we never did check to find out whether they're connected in the same way as American switches."

"What could possibly be different?"

"I don't know, maybe we should check."

With that, he climbed down the ladder and went to his toolbox. He pulled out a Painton switch that he'd brought as a spare and began to check which contacts opened and which closed when the switch was actuated. After a minute he began to get excited, checking again all six contacts of the double-throw component. I shall never forget the expression on his face when he looked up from his frantic probing. It was a mixture of triumph and profound relief. He'd found the cause of the problem.

Half an hour later the wiring on all the switches had been changed. Everything worked. Oh how it worked. Like music it worked, like wonderful music; swelling up from the body of water in the process tanks, bursting into exuberant crescendos at its surface, and as Tony turned up the power, filling the room with its strident dissonance.

Tony climbed down the steps, leaving everything running, hissing furiously. We stood there in the middle of the lab, hugging each other as we immersed ourselves in the music of the hiss.

Then we sat down and finished our hamburgers.

George, with his considerable experience in estimating how much equipment should cost, correctly concluded that our quotation had not adequately covered our field installation work. Without mentioning his conclusions to us, he discussed the matter with his purchasing agent.

The check came in ten days later. It was for a significantly larger sum than we had quoted.

SEVENTEEN

J oe Disbrow was on the phone again. More orders for our bench-top ultrasonic cleaners, and an invitation for me to come up to Poughkeepsie again to discuss possible design refinements, broadening the range of potential applications for the products. It proved a productive meeting, for on that occasion I met a pair of visiting engineers from the IBM factory at Corbeil Essonnes in France. They too, were interested in our new cleaning system and asked for a quotation for units suitable for use with the French electric supply sources. The leader of the team, Alain Goutay, assured me that if they found the equipment suitable for their purposes, they would need a significant number of them. Music to my ears. Shortly thereafter, purchase orders were coming in from the Manassas plant and from the IBM factory in Burlington, Vermont. A heady time for us. We hoped it would last forever.

My private life was finally off to a new start, too. By the fall of 1961, Laura and I had reached agreement on all matters relating to our divorce, and the legal loose ends had been tied up. It was agreed that to avoid interference with their education, I would have custody of our two daughters, Peta and Leslie. Laura would be able to see them whenever she wished. In the end, however, the need to be close to her daughters persuaded Laura to return to the United States, and she eventually settled in New York City.

The fast-developing semiconductor industry was moving from the laboratory bench-top phase into the realms of serious production. Bench-top ultrasonic cleaners were not enough. The time had come to move up the processing ladder. Huge new manufacturing facilities were nearing completion and soon a variety of mobile buildings and other temporary structures were sprouting up at the new IBM location at Fishkill, New York. George Green was among those who had moved to the new site, and at one of the earliest meetings in Fishkill, with George, Marvin Pittler and Armin Finger, I was lucky enough to learn something of what lay ahead.

George was speaking: "Howard, the ultrasonic cleaning business is a rat race. New firms are getting into it every day. They're coming out of the woodwork because it's an easy business to get into." He pointed to an Interlab generator on a nearby bench, and continued:

"You know as well as I do that pretty soon others will make cleaners like yours—just as soon as they realize that a big market is ahead in semiconductor processing equipment. But what IBM really needs are comprehensive processing tools; washing and rinsing and even drying equipment, all integrated into a working console with suitable controls. If you want to be among the first to meet these needs, now is the time. All you have to do is to let Purchasing know that you are interested in that approach, and you'll get an opportunity to quote on the next generation of equipment we'll be needing."

He paused. Then in conclusion he said, "From now on, individual pieces of equipment are on their way out. Multistage processing systems are in."

"How do I get to learn more about these other stages you need?" I asked.

"Talk to Pierre Fontaine next time he's here. He's "Mr. Ultra-Pure Water " at the French plant and you'll learn a lot from him. In fact, it wouldn't hurt to visit him at Corbeil Essonnes if you get a chance."

A lot to think about. I began to study the literature and trade papers, following articles on water purification and rinsing; absorbing the current fascinating work by Iverson and others. I studied manufacturers' brochures on the subject and slowly developed an understanding of the technology involved in producing ultra pure water—known in the business as de-ionized, or 'DI', water. Pretty sophisticated stuff. George Green had estimated correctly; when I told Joe Disbrow that Interlab would be very interested in quoting on multistage systems, he added our company's name to IBM's list of vendors in that category and passed the word around.

The first project that came our way in the new category, though simple enough, brought home the need for yet another move. Even a four-foot console with nothing but an ultrasonic wash tank and an associated rinse tank in it was too heavy to move up and down the stairs at 116 Kraft Avenue. And the IBM manufacturing plants were not about to let us build the equipment on site as the Research Labs had done. The rules were quite different. I considered the implications. Certainly, there was no possibility of renting a factory. I just didn't have the money to entertain the idea. There would have to be some other way.

The solution to that problem did not present itself immediately, nor did it arise entirely as the result of business deliberations. But if one had put the question to Pat Field, or to anyone else who might have had the opportunity to observe the steadily developing bond between Nárcissza and me, they might have seen the possibilities ahead. They might have noted the change in my demeanor when Nárcissza arrived in the mornings, and my penchant for detaining her at the end of the day for a drink at the Gramatan bar, or a snack at the nearby Lawrence Hospital coffee shop. They would have concluded that something definitive had to happen between us pretty soon, and with a little extrapolation, they might have 'seen' the most logical answer to my dilemma.

An incident at an upcoming measuring instrument symposium in Philadelphia served to speed things up. Nárcissza had left to spend most of the week looking after the Coulter Counter display which was to be located in a hotel suite. Other Coulter east-coast representatives were also attending, and she planned to use the opportunity to confer with them and help them with any difficulties they might be experiencing in their sales work. I had business to take care of in New York, so I wasn't able to go with her. Within a day or so of her departure, however, having dealt with the matter at hand, I was able to break loose and set off for Philadelphia myself.

I turned up at the show in time to put in a couple of hours of booth duty. Then, after arranging a dinner-date with Nárcissza, I set off to see about a place to spend the night. It didn't take me long to discover that because of an unusually large number of business exhibitions and conferences currently in progress in Philadelphia, every hotel in town was solidly booked. I resigned myself to the prospect of driving to some place out of town at the end of the evening.

When I returned, Nárcissza was busy putting things away for the night and covering the Coulter Counter and other instruments. She filled me in on all that had happened during the two days I'd missed. There'd been some good inquiries, including several in my own territory, and the reps had done a great job, making sure that she didn't get too involved in the heavy work during the set-up of the display, and contributing enthusiastically to booth duty work. All in all, the show had gone very well, she said, but by this third day, she was beginning to feel exhausted.

"You must get a good night's sleep," I told her. "A glass or two of good red wine will help. As soon as you're ready, we'll go see about that nice leisurely dinner."

"That sounds good, I'm looking forward to it, Howard. By the way, where are you staying?"

"Oh, I think I'll stay at the Howard Johnson motel I saw as I was leaving the highway."

"You mean the turnpike?"

"Right."

"But that's at least an hour's drive from here, and an hour back in the morning."

"I don't have much choice. I called the Sheraton. They didn't have any rooms, so they referred me to the Marriott. They were full, too, so they told me to check the downtown Holiday Inn—and so it went. There just isn't a room to be had with all these shows running at the same time."

"There must be somewhere you can get a room in a town the size of Philadelphia."

"Not unless I want to sleep under the stairs. I've called just about every hotel around. Look, Nárcissza, it's really not a big deal. An extra hour of driving won't kill me, and besides, the show doesn't open 'til ten, so it isn't as if I'll have to get up that early."

Nárcissza was quiet for a bit, pondering. Then she said quite matter-of-factly, "Well, there's a spare bed in my room. You can stay there if you like."

I stared at her, not quite believing what I'd heard. I took a deep breath.

"In that case, let's go get some food, and drink a toast to a wonderful evening."

The small Italian restaurant, just two blocks from the hotel, lived up to the standard that the bell captain had promised. Excellent cuisine and friendly and attentive service, combined to enhance the magic of that evening. But somehow, we didn't eat much. My preoccupation with thoughts of the night ahead destroyed my appetite and put knots in my stomach. Looking at Nárcissza across the table, and seeing that she, too, was just toying with her food, I became convinced that she was having second thoughts about the invitation that she'd voiced only an hour before.

I thought of letting her off the hook—thanking her for her considerate offer, telling her that I snored a lot and would keep her awake, or that I was apt to walk in my sleep. But that altruistic notion was short-lived. Just as quickly, I persuaded myself that Nárcissza would be deeply offended by any such talk, and my refusal to accept her kind offer would create a rift between us that would not soon go away. Nature, I decided, would have to take its course.

I will not pretend that that night in Nárcissza's hotel room was the most romantic I'd ever experienced. Nor yet was it very restful. I lay awake for a long time, alternately counting sheep or wrestling with my desire to emulate Clark Gable in the bedroom scene with Claudette Colbert in "It Happened One Night." I wanted to tear down the Walls of Jericho and take Nárcissza in my arms, hold her close and tell her about the love that was welling up inside me. But alas, my better nature persuaded me that this was not the thing to do. Tonight of all nights, I had to show her that I could be trusted. Tonight was my supreme opportunity to show her that I was a man of honor, with nary a thought in my mind of taking advantage of her kindness and her hospitality. By constantly talking to myself, chiding myself for my wicked thoughts, I managed to suppress my desires. In time, I slept. Sorry.

Soon after that fitful (fateful?) night, on the way home from one of our field trips, I poured out my feelings and asked Nárcissza to be my wife. In the spring, in a small Hungarian reform church in Carteret, New Jersey, we stood side by side at the altar, preparing to exchange our vows, as the minister, Reverend Harsányi András, began the ceremony.

Eventually, he posed the question to those before him: "Who gives this woman . . .?"

Without hesitation, Nárcissza's four brothers—Tom, Andrew, Tony and Paul—also standing alongside her, responded in unison with a resounding "We do! "

Bob Berg, standing up for me as my best man, handed me the ring, and soon thereafter, Nárcissza and I were walking up the aisle together as man and wife.

The four of us—Peta, Leslie, Nárcissza and I—moved in together, but the resulting overcrowded 'menáge-a-quatre'

gave impetus to an idea I'd been turning over in my mind for some time. I ran it past Nárcissza.

"What if we could find a house with a really large basement, Nisa? How would that appeal to you?"

"I think it's a good idea. If we can find such a place, it will solve our domestic and business space problems simultaneously, and give the children more breathing space."

We did some figuring and decided that if we could find the right sort of house, we'd be able to improve our living conditions and our manufacturing capabilities simultaneously, without taking on more financial responsibility than we could handle.

The hunt began in earnest, but we soon discovered that to get the kind of house we needed at a price we could afford, we'd have to look in areas farther away from the New York bedroom communities. Would that matter? No it wouldn't. A few miles farther north would take us that much nearer to our best customer, IBM, and we'd never need to be far from a major highway. We scanned The Sunday Times Real Estate section and embarked on a series of weekend expeditions into the wilds of Putnam County, entertaining ourselves with a series of visits to the fascinating and spacious homes of suburbia. Always our first interest concerned the basement and its size and suitability for our purposes, and sometimes it seemed that the nature of the living quarters sitting atop the basement was only of passing concern—necessary but of no special consequence.

Eventually we found it—a four-bedroom split-level with a huge dry basement that had its own ground-level entrance right onto the driveway. Located at Quakerbridge Road in Ossining, the sprawling redwood contemporary sat on a rolling two-acre plot in a small community that had easy access to a major north and south highway. A real find. The modest down payment and the monthly mortgage commitment would not overtax our resources. I told Nárcissza that although both our signatures would be required on the mortgage, I would prefer the house to be in her name alone. Although in practice, mortgage payments would come out of our joint bank account, it would be best that she sign all payment checks herself. That way, in the event of my death, her ownership would be unassailable.

The owner accepted our offer and within a few weeks we were drinking a farewell toast to Bronxville. We thrived in our new home and it was there that children of our own were added to our family. The following year, the imminent arrival of Christine ("Muffin " to us) prompted Nárcissza to take stock of her divided work schedule. The tasks assigned to her by Bob berg were no longer giving her enough to do, and it seemed evident that he was simply doing his best to keep her occupied. Interlab on the other hand, could easily use all the time she could spare. She talked the matter over with her boss and he, albeit reluctantly, accepted her resignation. On that day in June in 1965, Nárcissza joined Interlab as my full-time partner.

Two years later, Alice (Panni)—blond, serene, unhurried and good tempered, yet dogged and determined when it suited her—graced our household with her tiny presence. There were plenty of small children close by in this suburban paradise for ours to play with, and they flourished.

Downstairs in the basement the total area was divided into three sections. A partition separated the equipment assembly area from administration and drafting. At the back, a small cubicle served as an office for Nárcissza and me when we needed some privacy in interviews with customers and sales people. Gradually, as we became involved in more and more processing requirements for the fast developing IBM operations at Fishkill, the process engineers learned of our new location and were glad to visit us to inspect our strange setup and to discuss their specialized needs. Sometimes we'd serve them tea or coffee prepared by newly acquired help in our upstairs living quarters. There, the IBMers could relax with coffee and cake and engage in technical chitchat while sitting at the large bay windows and enjoying an uninterrupted view across the width of the Hudson River to the hills beyond.

But the move was not without its cost. The daily commute between home in Astoria, and Ossining, New York, proved impractical for Tony. He just couldn't cope with the time and the distance every day. His options were to relocate to an address closer to Ossining or get other employment. At this stage we simply could not afford to pay him enough to support the former option so we knew it was just a question of time before Tony would leave us. That time proved less than six months away. Upstairs in the living room we held a farewell party for Tony and congratulated him on the fine new job he'd found. It proved very difficult to replace him, and we didn't really succeed until his older brother Tamás (Tom) joined us two years later.

Meanwhile, IBM's equipment requirements were becoming more and more specialized. Within a few months of our move into the Ossining house we were casting about for the services of a competent draftsman. Ken Yocis—fair-haired, friendly and very young—turned up for an interview in response to one of our ads. According to his references, he was capable and qualified in his field—but he was nervous. In the test that we asked him to do for us, he made mistakes

208

several times in the same section of the drawing. When, eventually, he handed the finished sheet to me for inspection I discovered that he'd done a very good job except that he'd worn a hole in the paper with his eraser. We studied the paper with some puzzlement. We noted the sheer desperation written on his fresh open face. Then we hired him. He turned out to be one of the finest draftsmen we ever had.

In another few months our increasing involvement with the IBM Fishkill processing requirements resulted in yet further expansion of our workforce. Jim Twombly joined us as a production technician. With Amy Rego and Alice Graham in the office, that brought our total employment roster to seven souls. It was at this point that a call came in from IBM Purchasing Department in Poughkeepsie, requesting that I appear for an interview within the next few days. When I made my way to that familiar area and appeared in the purchasing lobby, Joe Disbrow ushered me into the office of the chief purchasing agent.

The chief spoke sternly but not unkindly. "Please sit down—I'm glad you could come so soon."

I mumbled something about it being a pleasure, then he came straight to the point:

"Interlab, we have some serious talking to do. We like your products and we like your service."

He paused, and I sat there wondering why he'd addressed me as Interlab instead of using my name. I also wondered what was coming next. Would it be good or bad?

The chief continued. "But we also know quite a bit about your company and its small size. We know, for instance that right now IBM orders represent more than fifty percent of your sales volume." He paused again to let that bit of information sink in, while I on the other hand was wondering what he would say if he knew that the real figure was near eighty percent.

"This state of affairs is very much against IBM policy and I'm afraid we cannot let it continue." He leaned forward to emphasize his next point and went on.

"We simply cannot accept a situation in which your corporate welfare depends almost entirely on the amount of business you get from IBM."

By this time I was quite nervous. I had a mental impression of a huge door suddenly closing and bringing to an end this wonderful flow of fascinating and profitable business that we had been enjoying all through these recent years. Our little company would be on the rocks again and we would have to start over.

The chief went on. "So here's the bottom line. Our business with Interlab must fall to less than thirty percent of your total sales, and you must help us make that happen. Right now, starting tomorrow, you must go out and get some more customers. That will be the best way to reduce your dependence on IBM." He paused. "We will give you exactly one year to reach the target I've given you. For the duration of that year we will permit the flow of orders to continue unhindered, but after that, if our business with Interlab is not below thirty percent of your total sales, we shall cut back the flow until it is."

I was deeply impressed by the fairness of the program the chief had outlined, and I said so. I assured him that we would lose no time in getting started on the course he had suggested, but on the way home I found myself regretting very much that business had to be done that way. Why couldn't we have just continued happily as we were going, just working for IBM instead of having to please a whole plethora of assorted customers and having to learn all about their separate needs? How was it that something always had to happen to throw a monkey wrench in your way whenever you started to make some real progress? Then, just as quickly, I gave up feeling sorry for myself and began to plan for the sales campaign that we had been ordered to undertake.

Where do you start when you've got to find customers at relatively short notice? If we embarked on a carefully planned advertising program, we could probably expect to get some results in two or three months, but we didn't have the resources to pay for it. We were making good progress, but we weren't yet at a point where we could afford the kind of investment that advertising would entail. We could exhibit in a suitable show—the kind that was held at the Coliseum every year. The IEEE or the Chem. Show for instance. But that, too, apart from being too far ahead time-wise, was more ambitious than we could consider at this stage. There was also something to be said for engaging the services of an independent manufacturer's representative. We'd already been approached by one highly successful rep. whose sprawling territory embraced the Metropolitan area, New York State, New Jersey and New England. Art Evans managed to get around the far flung limits of this area by doing most of his traveling in his own airplane which he piloted himself. That made great sense to me. I gave him a call.

A few days later, we were listening to Art, explaining in his best British north-country brogue, why he felt that our products and capabilities were compatible with his current lines. They were 'front-end' stuff like his present lines, he said, so to sell our products he would call on the same prospects and customers he was now serving. And, of course, he would get around faster than we could manage ourselves. I questioned him about the economics of his method of transportation:

"Art, how do you find flying compares with driving—I mean from an economic standpoint? "

"Well it beats tearing up the highways for at least two good reasons," he said. "For one thing it saves you valuable personal time and often lets you do a round trip on the same day when you might otherwise have to spend money on an overnight stay."

Seeing that I was really intrigued by what he was saying, he continued, "Let's just take a typical example. If I drive to Western Electric at Allentown and put in a few hours of interviews or conferences, and if I then drive back again the same day, I've put in six hours on the road as well as all those hours of productive time with my customers. By the time I get home, I'm bushed."

I nodded that I fully understood.

"But if I fly, it only takes an hour each way, so I save four hours of my time—time which, I might add, I could use far more profitably—like doing some more selling. Just as important, I'm far less exhausted when I get home. I can enjoy my evening and my family. And do you know what?" he said. "Almost all the places I visit have a convenient little airport close by, so all you need is a short taxi-ride to get to your customer—unless, as often happens, he offers to pick you up."

Art really had me hooked. What a great way to sell. And what a great way to avoid those bumper-to-bumper days when you start out in the middle of the rush hour and leave your customer just as everyone else is also leaving their place of work. We signed him on for a mutually agreed trial period, and I made a mental note that some day I would examine the practicality of becoming a flying salesman myself.

But right now, we would have to do more. However successful Art Evans might prove in our behalf, he would need time to determine whether our products were compatible with his other lines and whether he could sell them, and time was what we did not have. Without doubt we would in addition have to help ourselves in a direct and dynamic way. It seemed to me that we would do that best, by piling samples of some of our best products into a van and visiting some of the larger hi-tech factories within a day's travel of Ossining. Show our wares directly, let process engineers see the quality and the features, and maybe organize a talk. Nárcissza, too, seemed to like that idea, so I began to make phone calls, and by some happy stroke of fortune that might be called beginner's luck, I hit the jackpot right away.

Bell Telephone Laboratories at Murray Hill in New Jersey happened to be first on my list. I had seen their imposing campus several times in the past, and had often wondered whether there might be a potential for our products somewhere within that sprawling labyrinth. I called and asked whether there might be an interest in some sort of symposium and display of our products at their headquarters. To my surprise and delight, the response was an immediate "yes" and a date was set. The Laboratories' conference coordinator told me that in addition to any BTL or Western Electric Company (WECo and BTL were affiliated at that time) personnel we might know and wish to invite to the display, he would separately advise appropriate departments of the event to attract an additional audience.

A lucky strike indeed. On the appointed day, we distributed tanks and generators, pumps, filter assemblies and processing consoles around the large room that the BTL conference administration people had set aside for us.

Not much happened for the first couple of hours. One or two scientists from a nearby section came in to see what we had to offer, and toward noon a few students on tour of the labs showed interest in our products. But there were no real 'bites' until the lunch hour arrived. Then several groups from Western Electric Allentown plant suddenly filled the room. They were looking closely at the multi-stage cascade rinsers we were showing, and the vapor degreaser that had seamless rounded corners and no threaded plumbing.

They studied the smooth, electro-polished interiors of the ultrasonic tanks on display and played with the power controls on the generators. They looked at the opened undersides of heated tanks and took note of the manner in which the heating element strips were mounted—spring fasteners instead of nuts and bolts—and they were quick to see that this refinement would accommodate the expansion and contraction of the heaters and dramatically lengthen their working lives.

Heating of the ultrasonic tanks came under scrutiny, too. Since the tank bottom areas of these vessels were occupied by ultrasonic transducers, the heating elements were bonded to the walls instead, and for maximum operating life the required heating power was distributed among elements on all four walls instead of one or two. These small features of design and construction evidently intrigued them as much as they had intrigued the processing experts at IBM. When the groups eventually filed out, one trio remained. Their leader, Ed Mayer, took me aside:

"Would you be interested in quoting a multi-stage cleaning system built into a laminar-flow console?" he asked. "And could you come down to Allentown to a briefing on Friday?" Yes, yes we would, we could, and we did. Within weeks, we had a purchase order to build our first complete cleaning system. We built it in compliance with WECo's processing and performance requirements but to Interlab's design. We coined and registered the trademark 'Micro-Rinse' and perhaps not surprisingly, the model number assigned to this, our first multistage processing system, was MRS-13.

It wasn't until after we'd celebrated the awarding of this magnificent new order that we realized we'd have to contend with the old problem of where we would build it. The smaller consoles we were now accustomed to constructing for IBM were just about within the space limitations of our basement in Ossining, but a multistage system with an air-filtration hood on the top of it was quite another matter. We would have to find a manufacturer for the air-filtration hood itself, then work out an arrangement with that company whereby we'd construct the cleaning system at their location. The name of Dick Bond of Air Control Inc. came to mind. Dick, founder and president of that company, was a bluff, outgoing, can-do, sort of person who we felt would be very receptive to that kind of unconventional arrangement. His location was attractive, too. Just west of Philadelphia, it was only a few hours drive for our construction team to undertake.

Sure enough, Dick Bond's reaction was as we'd expected —positive and cooperative. We made the deal, and that's how MRS-13 came to be a hybrid creation of an Interlab cleaning system and an Air Control 'Microvoid' air filtration hood. I don't know whether MRS-13—that sturdy representative of a most important milestone in Interlab's history—still exists, but some twenty-two years later I had occasion to visit the location where it had been installed. It was still in operation, no longer employed on the project for which it had been purchased—but still very much in use.

That joint effort with Dick Bond's company did, however, bring us face to face with the realization that we'd have to find a bigger place for our growing enterprise. We wouldn't need to move our home, but we had outgrown that wonderful basement. Soon we were casting about for some cheap factory space.

EIGHTEEN

Life as a machinist at the Woodside Screw-Machine Company on Long Island had been pretty good for Tamás (Tom) Ludányi, and he was very good at what he did. He'd developed his skills while serving in the United States Marines and had further refined them through his training in the tool room. Tom enjoyed working with his hands. It was very satisfying, because at the end of the day he could see the results of his labors and skills. So when his big sister asked him whether he'd like to change course and join her in that strange company that built some sort of chemical processing equipment, he wasn't quite sure whether he would like the work described. He also wasn't so sure that he would be good at it.

"What would I be doing?" he asked.

"Well, anything and everything," Nárcissza had told him.

As a machinist, Tom knew where he was and was confident in his skills, but working in a manufacturing plant with complicated scientific equipment was another story. He wondered about the logic of abandoning something he knew how to do to take on a job that he didn't know much about. But the idea of working with his sister in a family business appealed to the adventurous side of him. The future was uncertain, no question about that. But then the possibilities were far more exciting than a future in the tool room was likely to offer. He would be learning other skills, both electrical and mechanical, and there would be more variety. Besides, as the eldest among the siblings, his big sister, bossy though she was, had always known what was best for her four younger brothers. And if things didn't work out at his sister's firm he could always go back to Woodside and his machines.

In the late spring of 1965 Tom took the plunge.

A few months later Interlab moved into its first real factory by leasing the old Post Office in Pleasantville, New York. It didn't add up to the most convenient working space in the world, for if you included the basement, the total space of six thousand square feet was split between three floors. Then too, the absence of a loading dock made loading and unloading of large consoles and equipment something of a challenge. Access was by way of a pair of large doors at the front of the building, so the trucks and moving vans had to back up to these to permit the cargo to be manhandled across the sidewalk. Sometimes the vehicles used would be equipped with mechanized tailgates of their own but more often a pair of wooden planks would serve as a ramp to enable the vehicle to take on or discharge its load. But the rent was reasonable and in comparison with any working space we'd had before, it was enormous. It was not a converted office or a makeshift oversized basement. To us it was a real factory. Now we could really go after projects involving large consoles and heavy and bulky accessories.

We made regular sales calls on the various Western Electric and Bell Telephone Laboratories locations in

Murray Hill, New Jersey, and in Reading and Allentown, Pennsylvania. The timing was right. Bell was expanding its activities in semiconductor development, and Western Electric was gearing up for pre-production of equipment in which these devices were to be used. At the Bell Models Laboratories in Reading we encountered our first opportunity to design a new product from scratch. In that factory, the first 'Picture-phone' device in the world was in pre-production. Thin slices of silicon, commonly referred to as 'wafers,' served as the base upon which the micro-circuitry of the picture-phone system was created. These wafers, produced elsewhere, were made by slicing up three-inch diameter ingots of pure silicon, in much the same way as one might slice up a roll of bologna, except of course, that the machinery used was, you might say, more sophisticated.

The processes being undertaken at Reading involved a series of chemical, mechanical and electrical procedures of which the chemical steps were the most numerous. I had been fortunate enough to see this type of processing several times before but I was glad to have its intricacies re-explained to me. Each process engineer's individual perspective added to my appreciation of the extreme precision required to achieve acceptable 'yields' in this burgeoning industry.

On this occasion I was fortunate in that Harvey Seidel, one of the scientists in charge of the project, was explaining the processing to me. I knew Harvey well through some experimental work we'd been doing for him in ultrasonic cleaning and I had found him to be patient and very willing to spend time making sure that the task at hand was fully understood. But now his interest was in a different part of the process. He explained that in the present application the silicon wafers in use were thinner and more fragile than usual and that the task of drying them after completion of the chemical processing steps, had become a challenge.

The currently popular spin-drying methods were proving too harsh for them so they'd turned to drying with hot nitrogen gas instead. Unfortunately however, heating elements used in the available drying chambers, were generating fine heat-scale and oxidation particles small enough to penetrate any of the filters built into the dryer assemblies. Harvey invited us to think about the problem and see what we could come up with in the way of a solution. We did just that.

I won't burden the reader with a detailed description of the design we developed to overcome the particle shedding problem. In a nutshell it amounted to this: instead of using conventional heating elements, we fed the nitrogen gas through a coil of electro-polished stainless steel tubing, and heated the tube by connecting electrodes at each end and energizing it with a large electric current. The coil was never allowed to get red hot or even to become discolored at all, so it didn't generate heat-scale or oxidation particles. The heating coil was long enough to compensate for its modest operating temperature and the gas was able to reach the desired temperature without difficulty. A simple idea really, but our highly experienced patent attorney, Michael Ebert, insisted that it was a viable invention. In due course, he convinced the United States Patent Office of that fact and a patent was granted. It was our first.

Word spread that Interlab had some talent in the field of wet processing. After a string of projects at Allentown and Reading, we learned of a considerable expansion planned for Western Electric in North Andover, Massachusetts. We were by that time already doing business with that location but so far it had been sporadic. Then Ed Mayer told us that he'd be moving up there in the near future and there would be a need for large quantities of cleaning and etching equipment at that factory, quite soon thereafter. He explained that we would have opportunities to participate in this program but that his colleagues were concerned that our small size and limited square footage would prevent us from producing equipment at the rate it would be required. "Have you thought of getting a larger plant?" he'd asked. No we hadn't. We'd moved to Pleasantville less than five years before and we'd expected to renew our lease when it would expire in another year or so. Besides, financing the current flow of business was taxing enough, and our financial resources, although improving, would hardly allow for additional overhead at this time. For obvious reasons Ed could not comment on that, nor could he attempt to persuade us one way or another concerning the matter of getting more working space, but it was clear that he was trying to give us a message. In the following weeks Marlyn Lewis, Bob Perri and Bruno Falanga, all from North Andover, posed the same question during their visits to check out equipment we were building for them. They talked about the impending expansion program and implied that our small size would limit the extent to which we would be able to participate in it.

No doubt about it, the situation called for a brainstorming session. There were personal circumstances to contend with, too, as well as business requirements. Our family had expanded in both foreseeable and unforeseeable ways during the previous few years. Just after Christmas in 1966, Alice Ann had appeared on the scene and now, four years later, Nárcissza was expecting her third child. Even with live-in help, that alone would have been a sufficient preoccupation to make it difficult for Nárcissza to divide her time effectively;

to take on the demands of the expanding business without robbing her children and herself of the time together that they and she needed.

But that was not all that had taxed our energies and emotional resources during this period. On the Sunday after Memorial Day in 1968, Tony—generous, devil-may-care Tony—ever cheerful, great-hearted Tony—had lost his life. His wife, his mother-in-law and his dog had been killed in the same terrible road accident. His two-year-old son Antal had escaped with a fractured skull, and since he was the same age as our youngest child Panni (Alice), Tony's inlaws agreed with Nárcissza that it would be best for him to join us and be raised as a member of our family. She had her hands full.

NINETEEN

When the delegation from North Andover had gone home, Nárcissza and I spent several evenings taking stock of our situation and debating the prospect of moving yet again. I recalled the advice that had stuck in my mind from a discussion of many years previously when I'd been working at Imhof's in London. Godfrey Imhof, that colorful and successful entrepreneur, had advised a colleague on just such a matter as we were now debating. For Nárcissza's benefit I repeated as accurately as I could, just what he'd said to his listener.

"You expand by bursting at the seams. You don't expand just because business happens to be good and your working space is being squeezed. You expand only when there is no way you can possibly carry on in your existing quarters no matter how creatively you've wrestled with the problem. You expand as the result of bursting at the seams, not before."

"And where do you think we are in relation to that advice?" Nárcissza asked.

"I just don't know. I'm sure the North Andover chaps would say there's no way we'll be able to cope with their needs if we stay in this building, so they'd say that we're bursting at the seams as we are right now." When Nárcissza didn't respond, I asked,. "If we decided that another move would be warranted, do you think we'd be able to find a bank who would finance it?"

"Well, lets play the devil's advocate game. You're the banker and I'm putting the case to you. What's your response?"

"OK, If you're planning this move to cope with this customer's expansion that you talk about, what happens when that expansion phase is over? Will you have other prospects that are promising enough to pick up the slack and justify your increased overhead?"

"Good question." Nárcissza pondered this for a bit, then she said,. "Actually, we're getting a steady increase in business all over the place, but when you get right down to it, aside from IBM, it's mostly all with Western Electric Plants. Various locations of course, but they could all slow down at the same time."

"Then what would we do?"

"We'd anticipate that by going aggressively after new customers while the Western Electric Company's expansion was going on. We'd be expanding our customer base in preparation for the time when WECo's expansion would be over."

By the end of the week, although still undecided, we'd agreed that nothing could be lost by checking out the cost of factory space in the area. We followed ads in local papers and in the New York Sunday Times. We tracked down factory space-to-lease signs here and there just by driving around the neighborhood and keeping our eyes open, but our findings were not encouraging. We'd decided that to justify a move at all, we'd have to find a place about twice the size of our present factory, and all on one floor. Space complying with this requirement proved available, but the rent per square foot in all cases was substantially more than we'd expected or could afford to pay. We put the matter aside for the moment and went about our business. Then, out of the blue, Don Engling, a BTL Allentown scientist, advised us that he was involved in equipping a new laboratory and would require several sophisticated processing systems. Subject to approval by their purchasing department, he'd like Interlab to bid on them.

This particular item of news proved of special significance, for it served to end our period of indecision about moving. We would take the plunge—but we would look farther afield for a better deal.

We learned that industrial space, just over the border in Fairfield County, Connecticut, could be had at much more reasonable rentals than similar space in Westchester County. Moreover, the state was making a special effort to encourage business and industry to move in. Armed with this information we went off in search of an industrial real-estate agent for that region. We found an ad in the Sunday Times, listing a small factory of some eleven thousand square feet for lease in Danbury, Connecticut, and as a starter, we called the listed agent, Pierson and Smith, to make an appointment to view the property. John McManus of that organization became interested in our quest. He went through his files to sort out a variety of additional listings that appeared to him to meet our needs, and one Saturday morning I joined him for a tour of the places he'd selected. Remarkably, on that very first trip, the third place we visited met our stated criteria quite well. It was just off Kenosia Avenue at the back of the small municipal airport, close to the main roads. We found the building in a small complex in which the only other tenant appeared to be a company called Sonics and Materials. The building we saw, offered a mixture of manufacturing and office space all on one floor, and covered a total area of about eleven thousand square feet. Just right—well, almost. It didn't have a loading dock, but that seemed its only shortcoming.

I told John McManus that I would discuss the matter with Nárcissza and perhaps have her join me for a second look at the place. The following week John showed me three other rentals he'd picked out, but none seemed quite as practical, nor as reasonably priced as the one in the Sonics and Materials complex.

"Let's go and have another look at that place," I said to John as we left the last of the places scheduled for the day, and after a break for lunch that's what we did. On our way, as we drove along Kenosia Avenue toward our destination, I pointed to a long white building on our right that occupied most of the length of a small side street.

"Now that's the sort of place I'd really like to have some day," I said.

John laughed and slowed the car for a better look. "That's owned by Simmonds Precision. They have five locations and they're cutting back right now. As a matter of fact I think this one is for sale."

"Well, don't you know?" I asked. "I'm curious."

"I'll make a phone call when I get back to the office, and I'll call you."

"Why can't we stop right now and ask?"

He laughed again. "I don't think I'd feel comfortable doing that—they may not take it too kindly if we burst in just like that."

"Well then, I'm going to bang on the door myself. Hold it

for a minute, John." As the car slowed to a stop, I got out and made my way up the short driveway.

I stopped at the door, suddenly aware of the absurdity of what I was doing. Why on earth was I interested in a factory probably twice as big as we needed and might or might not be up for sale, when all we needed or could afford was a rental? And in any case, why did I have to go barging in right now? Couldn't it wait until McManus made his call in due course?

Somehow it couldn't. Somehow I had to explore this new avenue—and I had to do it right now. I knocked on the door. Then I swung around and beckoned John McManus to join me. With some evident reluctance he got out of the car and trudged across the lawn toward me, all the while shaking his head disapprovingly. When he reached my side I knocked again. Saturday morning or no, there had to be someone there because there were several cars parked in the row of spaces along the front of the building. When it became obvious that my second knock was not going to be answered, I tried the doorknob. It turned easily and the door swung back to admit us into the small entrance hall. On the other side of that, a second door let us into the main office area and as we entered, a large bespectacled man came striding toward us.

"Good afternoon, gentlemen. I'm sorry I didn't answer the door for you. I just couldn't get off the phone. What can I do for you?"

"My colleague here had heard that this property might be for lease, and I was just curious," I said. I glanced at John and saw that he was still uncomfortable, but he backed me up. "Yes, I'm with Pierson and Smith and my client here was admiring your place as we were passing by." He took out a card and passed it to our host.

"Oh, well, no. I'm afraid that's not quite the case. It's not for lease, it's for sale. But anyway, why don't you come and sit down and I'll tell you what I know. I'm Walter English, General Manager, but you'd have to get in touch with the V.P., Doug Coombes, to get the full story."

He ushered us into a small conference room nearby and waved us to sit as he took a chair himself at the end of a polished mahogany-topped table. "You might have heard that even though it says Lowry Engineering on the door, this plant is actually owned by Simmonds Precision. The original owner, Walter Lowry, died in an airplane accident last year and since Simmonds was drawing in its horns anyway, we decided to close this plant and sell the property to ease our cash flow."

A pause, then having started the explanation, Walter English evidently felt he should enlarge on it. He continued. "Everyone knew Walter Lowry as a fine pilot—very skilled—but convinced that he had a charmed life. One night he was flying west in his own small plane to get to some formal dinner engagement he had to attend. He was late, and as I understand it he decided to change into his tuxedo in the airplane to save himself time when he landed. He was flying alone and it seems from all reports that he switched on the autopilot, then squeezed between the seats to the rear cabin and proceeded to change his clothes right there. Evidently the airplane hit some turbulence, a bit more than the autopilot could handle, and when the airplane got into a dive, Walter couldn't get back to the controls to do anything about it. The. "G" forces were evidently too much for him to overcome, so he crashed. A big loss. He was a respected man in the community."

We thanked our host and made motions to depart, but then he said,. "Why don't I show you fellows around while you're here. You might as well have the Cook's tour."

I glanced at John but he seemed content with the suggestion. After all, he was a real-estate broker and while this diversion from our planned program might well be described as a flight of fancy on my part, he undoubtedly had other clients for whom the property might prove very interesting.

As we entered this long narrow manufacturing area, we saw row upon row of lathes, saws, punch presses, all gleaming and immaculate. No filings or swarf or metal turnings on the smooth epoxy painted, concrete floor. No oil drippings, or stains. It was a pleasure to see and I could almost feel the pride that Walter Lowry must have felt when he'd had occasion to show visitors and customers his palace of fabricating excellence, where machine parts of considerable beauty were fashioned with consummate skill. Where, as the potter molds his clay, complex and precisely configured shapes were formed from lumps of raw material.

"What's going to happen to all this?" I inquired.

"We're going to try to sell it all as one package." Walter replied. "And if that doesn't work out, we'll auction off the machinery and sell the factory separately."

"How much do you expect to get for the package?"

"Well, we're asking half a million, but it's been on the market for three months already, and there haven't been any solid offers so far, so maybe we'll have to split the package. I don't know. It's up to Doug Coombes of course, but if it doesn't go at that price, we might have to settle for a bit less."

"How much do you think you'll get for the machinery if you split the package?"

"Oh, I don't know, that lot has to be worth at least a hundred thousand, and if the auctioneer is any good it should be more, even without the furniture."

I fantasized. As we continued our walk down the aisle alongside the rows of machines, they faded from my field of vision, and in their place I could see rows of processing consoles and sub-assemblies. Some were metal frames and some, for use with corrosive chemicals, were of plastic. Technicians were cutting and welding sections of these together. Then, farther on there was a good space where other workers wired and tested smaller sub-assemblies. And at the end of the shop where it widened out, I saw complete systems in final assembly, with technicians in white and beige smocks working on the plumbing. Someday . . . someday. . . I snapped out of my reverie. We were at the loading dock. A loading dock! It was at the right height and it had a ten-foot-wide overhead door, and outside, a convenient ramp for trucks to approach the dock for loading. Oh boy.

John reminded me that if we were to complete our program as planned, we'd better get going. We thanked Walter English for his time and for a most interesting visit, and took our leave.

At the Sonics and Materials complex, we examined the empty building once again to fill in the details I hadn't absorbed in the course of the previous visit. Although closely matching our needs, it somehow didn't feel right any more. I suppose the tour of the Lowry plant had unsettled me and today wasn't a good day for decision making. I explained to John McManus how I felt but he wasn't at all concerned. His lean midwestern face creased into an avuncular grin. "Take your time," he said. "It's a big decision, and you need to be sure."

Afterward, on the way back, as we approached the Lowry factory again, John pulled into the side road and stopped the car in one of the parking spaces near the front door. Then he turned to me, his expression pensive.

"You know Howard, I've been thinking. If you're truly interested in this place, you might be able to get it."

I stared at him, not comprehending. "What do you mean?"

"Well, there are special programs operating in Connecticut right now, to help preserve and support the industrial base. The SBA is offering some very attractive deals and you could probably benefit from one of them."

"What's the SBA?"

"It's an agency of the Federal Government. It's called the Small Business Administration and it works through state and local agencies to make business loans and mortgages available at very low interest rates. I could introduce you to the key people if you wanted to find out more about what's available."

Now he'd truly unsettled me. What was he saying? Was he serious? Knowing my circumstances, did he actually believe I could *buy* a property of this scope. Or buy *any* property for that matter?"

I tried to keep my voice calm and reasonable,. "What sort of down payment do you think it would take?"

"Certainly not more than ten percent. And you might even get away with five."

I shook my head in bewilderment. "I just can't grasp it John; it seems so far-fetched."

He pulled out of the parking lot and we drove back to his agency. We shook hands as I got out of his car, then he said,. "I'll call you on Monday with the information on the SBA and the other groups. By then you'll have had time to think about things."

◆

Nárcissza was talking:

"If you had a hunch and felt you had to investigate the

place, then maybe that means something. Hunches are very strange things. Sometimes you have to act on them and see where they lead you."

We'd discussed the day's happenings over dinner on Saturday evening, and I'd given her a detailed account of my visit to the Lowry building and John McManus' subsequent comments about the SBA programs.

She spoke again: "How do you feel about taking a ride up there again tomorrow so I can have a look at the place, too?"

"Let's do it," I said.

Late Sunday morning we were standing there in the middle of Precision Road, the small side street off Kenosia Avenue that fronted the Lowry property. We were admiring the gray tile and white stucco facade, and the neat grass strip that ran along the whole front of the building. I pointed to the bulky, box-like structures on the flat roof.

"You see those things up there, Nisa. They're heat pumps. The general manager told me this factory was the first in Danbury to use them. The idea was to make it the most efficient all-electric factory in the Danbury area and the manager claims that it's much better than gas or oil. The walls use special high-efficiency thermal insulation too. Each cement block is filled with something called Vermiculite to keep the heating and cooling costs down. They really wanted to make a show piece of the place."

Narcissza looked along the skyline where I was pointing. Then she turned to me with that inscrutable, sphinx-like smile on her face. "You really want this place don't you. I can see that from the gleam in your eyes as you're telling me about it."

I laughed. "Well, I can dream, can't I?"

She didn't reply to that. She stood there lost in thought

for a minute or two. Then she said seriously,. "I think we should make an offer."

Neither of us spoke again for a while. We climbed back into the Toronado and set course for home, each deep in thought about the significance of what Nárcissza had said. Soon, a possible course of action was crystallizing in my mind.

"If John is right about there being some really low interest mortgage programs available, we could just make a low offer, one that we could reasonably hope to finance and carry, even if it's ridiculously low—and see what happens."

"That's right," Nárcissza said. "As soon as we hear from John McManus we should do some figuring and see how much we could afford to offer and how we'd manage the mortgage payments."

I was at peace then. We had a plan of action. For the rest of the journey home, we relaxed and talked of other things.

By the following Thursday we not only had all the information John had promised us; in the interim he'd also made appointments for us to meet the local group who coordinated all the programs he'd spoken of.

We were sitting in conference with Chuck Wrinn of the Housatonic Industrial Development Corp. (HIDC), listening to his explanation of the logistics of the SBA plan.

"Under what's known as the 502 plan, the SBA would fund 45% of the loan at 5.5 % interest, and another 45% would be financed through a participating bank at an interest rate in the region of 9%. Half of the remaining 10% would be picked up by the CDA (Connecticut Development Authority)."

"That leaves us with a down payment of 5% doesn't it?

"Well, if you qualify, the HIDC might pitch in, and leave you with only 2.5 % to cough up."

I was stunned. It seemed just too good to be true. I looked over at Nárcissza and could see that she, the indefatigable mathematician, was already doing calculations in her head, working out the down payment and monthly installments based on her estimate of what offer we might make. She looked as wound up and encouraged by the information as I. Based on those numbers, we could hardly do otherwise than give it a try. Friday morning we called in our offer of two hundred thousand dollars for the factory on two acres, but without the machinery. Then we followed up with a formal letter.

Simmonds didn't receive an acceptable offer for the package deal in the time frame that management had allowed for the divestiture, so they decided to auction off the machinery separately. They then told us that if we could come up with a moderately higher offer, say two hundred and fifty thousand for the real estate alone, that might just tip the scales.

Two hundred and fifty thousand? Could we stretch that much? I doubted it. Besides, as Nárcissza quickly pointed out, our expenses would not end with the purchase of the factory itself. We would have to spend quite a lot of money on additional office furniture, drawing office equipment, air compressors, and a host of other shop essentials to make effective use of the expanded factory and office space we would have available.

After agonizing over the dilemma for most of the following day and night, we decided on a compromise that we considered affordable. We replied to Simmonds with an offer to split the difference at two hundred and twenty five thousand, provided that all the existing office furnishings, administrative equipment and air-compressors were included.

We heard nothing for a day or two. Doug Coombes was in a jam. As we learned later, he was able to get authorization from the Board of Directors to accept our offer, but he'd already promised the auctioneer that he could put the furniture on the block with the machinery. Fortunately, his determination to close the factory sale with us eventually prevailed, and he decided to persuade the auctioneer to release him from that part of the deal. He succeeded. As a Christmas present for that eventful year of 1970, Doug Coombes called to tell us that the all-electric pride of the Connecticut Light and Power Company was ours, —furniture and all.

Jack Burke of the SBA and Chuck Wrinn of the HIDC were as good as their word. They orchestrated the transaction exactly as it had been described to us except that the process took close to six months rather than the estimated sixty days.

◈

One bright Tuesday in July, we find ourselves in the long conference room at the City Trust Bank in Main Street Danbury to close the sale. We are eleven souls in all, gathered around a mahogany conference table that is almost as long as the room itself. We'd assembled at ten o'clock in the morning, and it is now five o'clock in the afternoon. Stacks of legal papers have been making their way around the table all day, for individual review and signature by the various interested parties.

Present are four attorneys: Herb Wanderer for the HIDC, Joseph Beauchemin for the SBA, John Jepson from the Attorney General's office and Bob Wolfe for Interlab. Then there are three bank officers: Edward Kyle, Tom Grant and one other from City Trust Bank; our insurance agent, Charles Dahmen , our daughter Paulette, and finally Nárcissza and me. By this hour everything we own has been signed away as collateral, and we're beginning to wonder whether they'll want our children as well. But by five forty-five it is done.

We make our way back to Precision Road and in the half-furnished front office of our new factory we open a bottle of champagne. We pour the sparkling fluid into two plastic glasses until they overflow. We step outside, glasses in hand, and walk over to the middle of the road. We turn and take a silent moment or two to ponder our new ownership of this magnificent workplace. We let our eyes drift slowly over its long, low facade, its white stucco walls and its close-cropped lawns. I think about the small cubicle at 437 Fifth Avenue in New York City, and Jacqueline Vicary's typing service; of Eleanor and Jane and of the almost overwhelming odds that we battled with in those long ago times, and I begin to see that in the course of a dozen years, with so little to start with, we've come a long way. As well as I am able, I offer my silent thanks, if not to God, then like Abou Ben Adhem, to all our fellow men and women who in their turn along the way, have helped to make this magic moment possible.

In a while, still overwhelmed, still somehow not able to speak, we turn to each other . . . touch our glasses together . . . and drink.

As a Christmas present, Doug Coombs called to tell us that the all-electric pride of the Connecticut Light and Power Company was ours— furniture and all

TWENTY

As expected, we lost several of our experienced staff members as the result of the re-location, including our much loved and respected bookkeeper, Helen Raven. Helen, a mature lady who for more than three years had served as purchasing agent and administrator, was one of our most valued employees. She would have liked very much to commute to Danbury to share a few more years with us, but the prospect was simply not practical for her. We said our tearful good-byes to Helen and to others who wouldn't be able to make the commute.

As an offsetting factor, Nárcissza's brother Paul, had strengthened our ranks by joining us the previous summer. Tall, dark, and taciturn, and with sideburns that later earned him the nickname 'Pablo,' he brought with him technical qualifications and organizing abilities that nicely complemented those of his brother and sister. Soon, he was relieving Nárcissza of the exacting responsibilities involved in the black art of bonding ultrasonic transducers and heating elements to our processing tanks. It was a disciplined contribution to our process control that, in later years, he would apply to the whole of the company's manufacturing procedures.

Planning ahead, and commencing several months prior to our move, we'd begun advertising for help in the local Danbury newspaper. The ads explained our impending move and invited applicants to commute to Pleasantville to work with us for a training period, so that by the time of the actual move, they would have already gained some familiarity with the company and with the roles they would play in it.

Among those who answered our ads, two applicants impressed us most favorably as potential long-term members of our team. Marie Spagnolo, a mature and well qualified lady who we engaged as our future bookkeeper, wasn't able to spend the full three months with us in Pleasantville. Instead, we arranged for her to join the advance crew who would carry out the transition. She would prepare the Danbury factory for the move, setting up the various administrative and operational facilities that we'd need to have in place and functional, before shutting down the Pleasantville plant and transferring the remaining employees.

Bob Sendewicz, our second new member, joined us on January 18, 1971, as an electrical technician. His first few weeks were not easy for him. Sometimes as I watched him on our Pleasantville shop floor, I could see by the frown on his normally cheerful and ruddy face that he was aching to get to work, to make a contribution instead of just standing there and watching. But on certain days Tamás and his technicians were so occupied with getting the job done that they had difficulty in keeping their new colleague fully employed. Fortunately, that period passed quickly. Bob soon became familiar with our technology. He became busier and busier, and visibly more cheerful as the weeks went by. By the time we left Pleasantville behind us and our new factory had become fully operational, both Bob and Marie had graduated as fully effective members of the team.

Our third child Paulette, just a few weeks old, welcomed visitors to our new location at Precision Road in Danbury. Parked in her baby carriage outside the front door of our establishment, she offered visitors an introductory business card. She didn't exactly hold it out in her tiny hand; a small card container bearing the words. "Please take one" was attached to one end of the carriage. Our company name, address and phone number were printed on the lower part of the card. The upper half read. "Paulette Layton, Doorman."

These souvenirs of our move proved popular with customers and vendors alike, and we went through several reprintings before Paulette's baby carriage days were over. Thereafter we welcomed new babies to our factory as a matter of policy, to help mothers-to-be with their newborns during those early critical weeks, so that they wouldn't have to stay away from their jobs any longer than they wished. Ann Kokinchek , an attractive blond draftsman in our engineering department, loved her job. Soon after her first child came into the world, the playpen for her became part of the furnishings of the drawing office where she worked. Others in secretarial positions followed Ann's example, bringing their new sons and daughters in to work with them. This atmosphere, coupled with our free morning and afternoon coffee and tea breaks, eventually earned our company the nickname 'The Country Club.' Ours was a motivated and appreciative crew, and they showed it in their performance and their workmanship.

TWENTY ONE

Ed Mayer, Marlyn Lewis, and others at Western Electric who'd told us of the upcoming expansion of the North Andover factory were accurate in their predictions. As soon as we moved into our new plant, inquiries began to pour in. My visits to North Andover became almost as regular and frequent as the Benghazi Milk Run (the pet name for our daily bombing sorties over Rommel's front lines in WWII). Our workforce expanded as rapidly as we could cope with the training involved. Orders flowed in—first as an almost continuous stream from North Andover, and next in the form of a series of projects with Reading and Allentown, including Don Engling's Model's Lab equipment. A time to celebrate, and celebrate we did. The thirteenth anniversary of our founding was rapidly approaching and that would provide us with an opportunity to celebrate as never before. On this special occasion we'd invite every person who'd ever worked at Interlab in the course of those thirteen years. We would also invite everyone else who had helped us along the way. It would be a formidable list but there would be plenty of room. The party would take place right in the factory.

Sitting with Nárcissza on the porch of our Pound Ridge home one evening late in the summer, I looked over the list of those to be invited, checking the accuracy of our latest information on their addresses. I scanned the names on the first page, calling to mind the faces associated with those names, letting the parade of personalities pass by one after another; reliving the times when they had made their entrances onto the stage that was our company, played their parts in the evolution of the enterprise, and moved on. My eyes found the names of Adolph and Miriam Friedman. When Charles Daldorf had introduced me to Adolph and Miriam just after I had arrived in the United States, I was green and clueless. Adolf had provided me with an office in their Mount Vernon building, asking only a nominal rent. He'd given me free use of one of their station wagons until I could afford a car of my own. Adolph, a successful manufacturer's represen- tative in the high-fidelity equipment field, introduced me to those among his own business friends whom he regarded as potentially useful to me, and gave me a great deal of helpful advice about selling to American industry.

Suddenly I am there in his office complex in Mount Vernon. The year is 1955 and Adolf is standing in his usual way with his sturdy legs far apart, his straw hat on the back of his graying head, and his meerschaum pipe in hand. He is giving me an in-depth evaluation of American business methods as he sees them, and of the pitfalls I must beware of.

"Make no mistake about it, the key to success in this coun- try is merchandising, and if you fall in love with your products you are apt to overlook that. You can have the best products in the world, but if you don't present them properly they will stay in your stockroom." He puffs thoughtfully on his pipe, then continues. "If you're in love with your product, you become mesmerized by its features and you talk to your customers that way when you should be talking about benefits. You should be talking about what it will do for them; about how those features translate into a more cost-effective performance."

I venture a question: "Could you give me a specific example?"

"Well, I'm in the hi-fi wholesale business among other things, and I can give you an example. One of my principals, a loudspeaker manufacturer, failed in his attempt to introduce a great new product by stressing the fact that his new fifteen-inch 'woofer' had a more freely suspended cone than any other loudspeaker on the market. Which would have been OK except that his advertising failed to explain and illustrate what that meant in terms of reproduction of organ music or low notes in general. Certainly, people expected to hear that there would be some degree of improvement in the speaker's performance, but few realized that the difference in quality of music reproduction the manufacturer had achieved in this instance bordered on dramatic." On this last word, his arms spread in emphasis. "Unbelievable . . . but true."

I'm about to ask another question, but Adolph, now carried away with his subject, continues. "I'll give you another example. If you go down to the local Pontiac dealer on the corner of First Street to buy an automobile, the salesman might tell you that his sedans have the widest track on the market, but the advertising doesn't concentrate on that. It emphasizes the resulting safety. It will talk about it being the most difficult car to turn over when cornering at speed. That's what interests the buyer."

The memory fades. My thoughts return to the list before me.

Yes, it will be a great thing to see Adolph and Miriam again—to show them what we've managed to achieve over the years since the times when they were showering me with their warmth and wisdom and generosity. It will be a good time. A time to say "thank you," once more.

I continue to scan the list and under the heading of 'Former Employees' I see the entry for Nárcissza's brother Tony. He will not be among the formally invited guests at our celebration, but he'll be with us in spirit and he'll know how welcome he is. I think of him now and I feel his presence. He is there, over by the back wall, sitting atop a stepladder and holding an ohmmeter in his capable hands. I see from his wide, lopsided grin that he is glad for us in our good fortune.

I drift again. Early June three years ago . . . it's the middle of the night and I'm recalling events as we had pieced them together from the police report:

Ahead, the mist is thick and gray, and the white centerline dividing the two-lane road is barely visible ahead of the blue Chevy sedan Tony Ludányi is driving. He takes it slowly. He cannot see the curb at the right of the car, so he keeps his eyes on the centerline. His wife, Madeleine, is dozing in the front passenger seat with their small dog Beethoven, comfortable on her lap. Their two-year-old child, Antal, in the back behind Tony, is secure in his seat belt, and Madeleine's mother Helen, sitting beside him, is also half asleep. They are relaxing as families do on the way home after a pleasant evening out to dinner. They've been visiting Madeleine's father, Kurt Evers, and her stepmother Jean, and they've had a good time. Tony is glad he's not a drinker and that he has had hardly one glass of wine with his dinner tonight, for now he needs to concentrate. The trip can't be all that long. His in-laws live just over the border in New York State, so the journey back home to Honesdale won't take more than an hour, even in this fog. He holds his speed down and keeps his eyes on the white line, making sure to stay safely to the right of it.

A few miles to the west, Elmer Knight has had a good old time with his friends in Honesdale. Although they've been to a couple of bars they really haven't had much to drink. One way or another he is feeling pretty good tonight as he leaves his buddies and sets off eastbound, to his place in New York.

Boy this fog is a drag. Still, there can't be much traffic late on a Sunday evening.

No need to crawl. Elmer tracks along the center of the highway, nicely straddled across the line. Yes, that's the way to do it. If anyone should happen to be coming the other way he will surely see their lights in time to do a quick little side-step. No sweat. Tum te tum. Yo ho ho and a bottle of rum. God, I like the way this stuff swirls around. Its like you're flying in a cloud. Tum te tum te tum. He drums his fingers on the wheel, getting a bit impatient. His foot presses a little harder on the gas pedal. Yes, it's like flying in the clouds. That's what it is. Tum te tum . . .

The red taillights of the car ahead of him burst into his field of vision too late for him to slow down. Elmer swerves to the left, hits the gas pedal and roars ahead to get past this obstacle to his progress. As he draws abreast, he becomes aware of another burst of light approaching from ahead. Elmer knows there is now no time for him either to fall back behind, or to pull around in front of the sedan on his right. He cuts left instead, but again he is traveling too fast. He is already upon the approaching car, lunging through the beams of its headlights, tearing apart the mass of metal behind; casting it out of his way and forcing ahead . . . until his own vehicle, now also split apart, loses momentum and slides to a grinding stop in the meadow to the left of the road.

The blue Chevy sedan is no longer an automobile. It is a tor-

tured heap of metal, plastic and rubber. Somewhere inside, Tony lies in the twisted framework, moaning. His skull is badly fractured. His wife Madeleine still sits in the front passenger seat. She is dead, and Beethoven on her lap, is cut in half. Madeleine's mother Helen has also had her life snatched from her. The child Antal, still strapped in his seat belt, has a fractured skull—but he lives.

We rush to the hospital at Honesdale, Pennsylvania, where an ambulance has taken Tony and his family. Tony is in a coma from which he does not recover. He dies in hospital three days later. The driver of the other car has escaped without injury. We also learn from the police report of the accident that Tony had jammed on his brakes and had left skid marks for eighteen feet before the impact. The other car, traveling at about sixty miles an hour, had then rammed Tony's car and pushed it back some sixty feet before glancing off into the meadow.

I turn away from the list.

Attendance at the thirteenth anniversary celebration was even better than we'd hoped for. Apart from the list of all those who'd let us know in advance that they would come, at least half of those who'd been with us before our move to Connecticut made the trip to celebrate with us. Since we hadn't yet filled the whole of the factory space with work-benches and production equipment, we were able to clear a large area for the occasion. We had plenty of room for the dining tables and chairs and for the long buffet tables where an abundance of mouth-watering creations whetted the appetite. We set aside a corner for the sound-amplifying equipment and disk jockey, and left a broad area of the polished, epoxied concrete floor clear for dancing. Mostly, for the benefit of the younger guests, the DJ played music in the 'soft' rock category, but we'd agreed in advance that a good number of ballroom dances would be sandwiched into the evening's program. Also, Nárcissza had seen to it that the list would include two or three old-fashioned waltzes.

Soon, food, beer and wine warmed up the evening and raised the general buzz of conversation, thawing out the more reserved of the guests so they were willing to take the floor and join the less inhibited dancers.

Later, when we were satisfied that we'd greeted everyone, including the late-comers, we too—Nárcissza and I—joined in the dancing. Still later, toward the end of the evening when Nárcissza and I were whirling to one of the waltzes she'd ordered, it happened again. I was feeling Tony's presence. He was here with us, come to celebrate the occasion with all the other past members of our crew. He was in the corner behind the sound equipment, perched atop that old ladder with what looked like an ohmmeter in his hand. He seemed to know that I was craning my neck to look at him as I danced, and he was smiling his broad, open, inimitable smile. I decided that when the dance was over I would tell Nárcissza what I had seen and determine whether she might have seen him too, but when I looked again, Tony had gone.

The American dream, now taking shape in our daily lives, embraced us with its heart warming developments. At home, a Hungarian couple, János and Magdi, kept house for us, cooking, cleaning, gardening, grocery shopping and baby sitting. At Interlab the upward trend of our business fortunes pointed to yet more prosperous times ahead. We had some free time at last, time to plan and enjoy an occasional few days off in the sun. In the early spring of 1973, Nárcissza and I packed our bags and took off for Antigua, and for an enchanting ten days, we swam the lagoons, sailed, spread ourselves on the warm white sands and consumed an abundance of exotic culinary creations. In the evenings, to offset our indulgences, we danced away the hours to the beat of tin drums.

In our state of euphoria we didn't pause to reflect on certain other important aspects of the successful flow of business we were enjoying. We didn't concern ourselves with the fact that although business with IBM and others continued to flow, orders from the Western Electric Company, especially those coming from North Andover were, in total, accounting for the majority of our sales volume. They were beginning to monopolize our manufacturing resources. By the end of the year, sales to North Andover alone amounted to nearly $500,000, and the total, inclusive of sales to other Western Electric and Bell Laboratory locations, added up to a total of $650,000 in an overall sales volume slightly more than a million dollars. It didn't occur to us that we were permitting and encouraging the repetition of a dangerous scenario that we'd been warned against once before. We were rejoicing in the here-and-now of our great good fortune. We should have known better.

The flow of orders from the Western Electric/ Bell Telephone Laboratories group didn't gradually taper off. It just stopped. The expansion at North Andover was complete. During the whole of the following year, 1974, total orders from that plant amounted to a little less than $30,000. The bonanza was over.

Our reaction was as prompt and as realistic as we were able to make it. During the first six months of the new year we cut our payroll from its 1973 total of about thirty souls, to less than half that number. We carefully scrutinized and, wherever possible, reduced our expenses on utilities and services—electric power, telephone, factory maintenance, insurance—and we placed strict limits on travel expenses and advertising.

There was also the matter of my flying instruction to consider. I'd raised the subject with Nárcissza one evening during the winter. Her reaction had been negative at first. She had informed me that if I wanted to take up flying, she would take a course in sky diving and risk breaking her slender ankles, her neck, or both. But I persisted:

"Will you at least listen if I explain why this is important to me, Nárcissza?"

"Yes, I'll listen. But I warn you, I'm prejudiced," she said, her arms folded across her chest.

"It'll take a while. Is that OK?"

She nodded. "Yes, that's OK. We're not going anywhere, are we?"

We'd finished eating and were sitting on the settee near the picture window. I went over to the sideboard and poured us both a good measure of Courvoisier. I handed Nisa her goblet, then I paced up and down a bit to get my thoughts in order.

In a minute or so I started talking; sort of thinking out loud.

"Back when World War II had not yet begun, I used to spend some of my Sunday mornings visiting the local airport at Baginton near Coventry. Sometimes I'd go with my friend Doug Phillips, and sometimes I'd go alone. Sitting on the grass at the edge of the field, I'd watch the local flying club doing its stuff. There'd always be takeoffs and landings to see, and sometimes there would be air shows with all sorts of breathtaking maneuvers going on right above the airfield. I got to know some of the pilots and instructors and was able to see how students progressed as the weeks went by. In the first few hours of their training, before they'd learned to advance the throttle smoothly, takeoffs tended to be erratic, and on landing, the little Tiger-Moth biplanes would bounce a few times before settling down on the grass. Now and again they'd bounce along like performing porpoises and the instructor would have to intervene to rescue the landing.

As weeks went by and skill and confidence developed, I'd watch the same student taking off and landing more smoothly. The sudden power bursts on takeoff, replaced by smoothly controlled surges to steady crescendos and, on landing, the point at which the aircraft would touch down becoming more and more predictable. An absorbing way to spend a couple of hours now and then. I promised myself that some day I would be one of those pilots. I would be flying instead of watching."

I paused to see whether she was taking in any of this. I saw that she had not yet touched her cognac. I could have no better indication of her interest in my story. We clinked glasses and savored the warmth of the amber fluid on our palates.

As I continued talking I could hear Neville Chamberlain's voice as he broadcast his historic message on that Sunday morning in September of 1939, the whole of Britain listening with rapt attention to his somber tones as he advised us that our country was now at war with Germany. I'd gone down to the Royal Air Force recruiting office that same day and within a week or two Doug Phillips and I were on our way to the Cardington induction center. We'd applied for pilot training but the recruiting office had warned us that the training centers for pilots were currently quite fully loaded and, if selected, we'd have to wait our turn. Upon arrival at Cardington we would be interviewed by an air commodore for classification. Based on his assessment of our personalities, education and attitudes, he would decide whether we'd qualify for flying duties and, if so, whether or not we'd be trained as pilots, navigator/ bomb-aimers or air gunners. We'd wear civilian clothes for our interviews. Outfitting with uniforms and battledress would come later, after classification.

When we arrived and my turn came for the interview, I strode into the air commodore's office with as much of an air of confidence as I could muster, and marched right up to the front of his desk. He was an impressive person: large, florid, with a shiny bald head and stern eyes that seemed to look through me. Although he was sitting and I was standing, I had the uncomfortable sensation that he was looking down on me from a considerable height.

He came straight to the point:

"So, Layton, you want to be a pilot eh?" he said. "Have you flown before?"

"No sir. I've done a lot of watching at our local airfield and I know that's what I want to do."

"Were you in the Volunteer Reserve?"

"No sir. I applied quite recently but I haven't so far had a reply."

"Well, if you haven't been in the Royal Air Force, what are you doing wearing that tie?"

I was nonplused. "This tie sir?" I picked up the bottom end of my striped silk neckpiece and studied it as if I'd never seen it before.

"Yes. Don't you know you're wearing an RAF sports tie?" He was testy. "That tie is worn only by those who represent the Royal Air Force in a sporting event. How did you get it?"

I was cowed. "I saw it in a shop window. I liked it, so I bought it."

"Hrrumph." He said with some force,. "air gunner."

"What's that sir?"

"I said you're classified as air gunner. That will be all."

Later, I appealed the decision and managed to get myself reclassified, but not for pilot training. I'd be trained as an air navigator/ bomb-aimer. My quest for pilot training would have to wait.

In light bombers I did at least have an opportunity to get some experience at the controls of a flying machine, for it wasn't uncommon for the navigator to serve as co-pilot on the return journey from a mission. It gave the captain a break and broadened the navigator's knowledge of the air-craft so that in the event of the pilot becoming incapacitated, his right-hand man would have at least some chance of get-ting the ship home and on the ground in one piece. I rel-ished these opportunities, but they made me all the more eager to get the formal training myself. Periodically I renewed my application for pilot training and eventually, after two operational tours of flying duty in the Middle East, I learned that my wish would be granted. But there was still a long waiting list and I'd have to be patient.

Long indeed. The war ended. I signed up for a permanent commission. I trained as a signals officer and served for another year in the Eastern Fighter Sector at Horsham St. Faiths. But I didn't settle well to peacetime service life. In a restless frame of mind, I eventually resigned my commis-sion. Only then, a few days before my departure, did I learn that my turn for pilot training had come.

I snapped out of my reverie and looked at Nárcissza. "I

promised myself then that some day I'd get that training, that some day I would fly, and although I haven't mentioned it to you before, the desire to do this—to fly—has stayed with me and has become a sort of smoldering obsession. That's all I can tell you."

She held out her goblet for a refill. When I returned her glass to her, she sat staring straight ahead for a while, almost as if in a trance. Then she looked up, reached over, and clinked her glass against mine., "Let's just agree that you won't go near the New York terminal airports," she said.

We had agreed that I'd start my flying course in the spring and treat it as a much needed diversion from the day-to-day concentration on engineering and sales work, but now it seemed prudent to postpone that program until our finances were in a bit better shape. I raised the matter with Nárcissza on the way to the office one morning, but she dismissed the suggestion.

"Putting off your flying course wouldn't save enough to off-set the good it would do you, and for that matter, the company, too."

"How do you mean?"

"Well, let's just think of it pragmatically. Let's go back to Art Evans's reasoning," she said. "How long does it take you to drive to North Andover?"

"Typically about three and a half hours with average traffic."

"OK, that's seven hours round trip. How long would it take you to fly to the nearby airport at Lawrence?"

"A bit over an hour each way."

"Well, think about it. Right now you drive up in the morn-ing, put in a day of conferences while you're up there, and mostly drive back again the same day. If you were able to fly up instead, that would save you about five hours of valuable executive time as well as all the hassles involved in coping with traffic."

"That's true," I agreed.

"And on those occasions that you'd otherwise have stayed overnight, the saved hours would mostly avoid the need for doing that, so you'd save a hotel bill, too."

The argument was certainly compelling enough for me, and I could see that the same reasoning could be applied to a number of customer locations I visited regularly—Western Electric at Allentown, for example. That was a three-hour drive, but only a one-hour airplane ride, and Allentown, too, had an airport close by. The time saved on a trip to Kodak in Rochester would be even more pronounced, because the flight would take me on a direct course over the mountains and would take only two hours. The dogleg drive via Albany, or the scenic one through the mountains, took us six or seven hours.

We eventually agreed that my training would start in the spring as originally planned, and although by October we knew that the year would show a loss, the plan wasn't changed. The winter passed and on May 3, 1975, I showed up at the Danbury Airport for my first lesson.

Chuck West of Connecticut Air Service, an ex-military pilot, had flown with the Navy on carriers. As an instructor he was a student's dream, invariably cheerful and relaxed in the cockpit and on the ground, yet both persistent and insistent in his teaching methods. I reasoned that with my RAF flying background and with Chuck as my mentor, I would romp ahead faster than most. But I was in for a surprise. I'd completely overlooked the fact that I had never flown in a really small airplane. Until now, I'd considered a twin-engine light bomber small. But everything is relative and I discovered that 'small' is a Cessna 150, which, as my brother Archie observed several years later when I took him up in one, is not a craft that you just climb into. You wear it.

In my first few flights with Chuck I was alarmed by the manner in which this little birdlike machine seemed to bounce around as if it were a row boat set loose on a rough sea. I was reluctant to acknowledge that perhaps my handling of the controls might have something to do with this exuberant behavior, and Chuck had to devote several of our early flying sessions to the task of persuading me that this indeed was the case. But thanks to Chuck's persistence it eventually dawned on me that the Cessna 150 did not, in fact, have a mind of its own. It was nothing more than a small machine that needed small control inputs. As the weeks passed and I became more accustomed to this spritely little craft, takeoffs and landings became smoother, and the outcome more predictable. Chuck's hands no longer hovered over the control wheel when we approached the runway for landing and were close to touchdown. I was making progress.

Early one morning in June we were out there at the misty airfield less than half a mile from our factory. I was doing takeoffs and landings. Chuck seemed a little less laid back on this particular morning. He was reminding me to check my airspeed readings coming down final, and urging me to wait a little longer before flaring for the touchdown. We were practicing 'touch-and-goes,' or as we say in England, 'circuits and bumps'—landings and takeoffs. In these exercises, as soon as the airplane's wheels touch the runway, you pull up the flaps, open the throttle again and begin another take-off roll. Turning left into the traffic pattern, you make your way around the pattern again to repeat the same landing and take-off procedure over and over again. By this means, one could complete ten or more take-offs and landings within a one-hour flying session. Each time around, I was expected to show improvement in some phase of the landing or take-off sequence. On this particular day, as we were in the final stages of one of these approaches, Chuck suddenly instructed me to terminate the landing in a full stop, then taxi off the runway.

"Taxi back to the end of the runway," he commanded as we turned into the taxiway.

I dutifully obeyed. When we stopped to wait for permission from ground control to move on, Chuck opened the door on his side. I thought he wanted to relieve himself and couldn't wait, but then he turned to me and yelled above the engine noise.

"Do three circuits for me and come to a full stop each time you land, so I can comment on your performance," he said. Then he got out and slammed the door.

What was that? I stared wide-eyed at his departing form as he strode over to the grass verge. Was he really letting me loose in this skittish contraption? Did he really know what he was saying? I knew, of course, that eventually I was supposed to fly the thing solo, but somehow I just couldn't believe that that time had now arrived. But there was no doubt about it. There was Chuck, standing outside on the taxiway, waving me on. I glanced at the seat on my right as if he would somehow materialize again to make sure that I didn't make a stupid mistake. But Chuck was not there. I was alone in this airplane. Through all of the years of my wartime flying, through all the hazards and gunfire, I had never been alone in an airplane before. It was a strange, terrifying, exhilarating feeling.

I taxied to the end of the active runway, did my final take-off check and announced to the tower that I was ready to roll.

"Cessna 648 is cleared for take-off,. " The controller announced in matter-of-fact tones.

I suddenly feel like an airline pilot, about to take to the skies for a transcontinental trip. I square my shoulders. "Cessna 648 is rolling," I announce in the deepest voice I can manage.

I open the throttle smoothly, gathering speed as my foot applies increasing pressure on the right pedal to track the centerline. Gently, I raise the nose to put the aircraft in a take-off attitude, and seconds thereafter, the small Cessna becomes a flying machine and separates itself from the runway. We're flying. I almost cannot believe it. The ground falls away behind and below me as I climb to the prescribed pattern altitude of fifteen hundred feet. As I gain altitude, I turn left to work my way around the circuit to return for my first solo landing. Minutes later I find myself on final approach, concentrating on the airplane's attitude and airspeed, maintaining alignment with the centerline.

No time for qualms now. This is the moment of truth. I breathe deeply, consciously loosening my grip on the yoke and setting the flaps a notch lower to their full-down position. I ease the throttle back. We're over the fence now, close to the runway. Time for the flare. Ease back on the yoke. Hold it there—a few inches above the centerline. Pause . . . ease back a little more on the yoke . . . close the throttle now, and ease back some more . . . and more. Don't let it touch yet. Hold it off. The airspeed bleeds off as I ease the yoke farther and farther back. A slight bump as my small craft becomes an earthbound machine once more. We are down. I taxi off the runway and make my way around to the spot where

Chuck, tall, lean, light brown hair riffling in the breeze, is standing. I see that he's grinning broadly. He gives me a 'thumbs up,' and waves me on for another take-off.

Each time I landed and taxied off the runway, Chuck waved me on for my next take-off. After the third landing, he climbed aboard so we could taxi back to the ramp. At the end of the post-flight de-briefing session, he endorsed my logbook, clearing me for solo flight. A day I would never forget.

Although I knew I'd be flying and studying for many more months before the time would come for my written examination and check-ride for a pilot's license, I was at least over that first magic hurdle. From now on, with Chuck's sign-off before each flight, I could drive out to the airport, rent an airplane and fly off to the practice area. Alone.

TWENTY TWO

Whether or not my flying course would eventually prove a justifiable expense, our other planned economies didn't go far enough. Even with the measures we'd adopted, we wouldn't be able to replace our lost sales volume fast enough to cover our overhead, labor force, and expense budget so that we could make a profit. We'd been encouraged early in the year when Kodak had awarded Interlab a large order to provide all the wet chemistry equipment required for their new research labs, but then there followed an extended period of near zero activity. Although we expected to break even for this year, we'd have to reduce a number of salaries, at least temporarily, and the largest reductions would have to apply to my own and Nárcissza's.

Brainstorming the problem at home, we explored all avenues we could think of for saving money. We covered the obvious steps we'd have to take— dispensing with our live-in help, making other arrangements for the care of our children, arranging for our working hours to always coincide with each other's so that we would use one car rather than two to get to the office each day. After a while, Nárcissza lapsed into a thoughtful silence that lasted for several minutes. Then turning to me she said quietly,. "I know what we must do."

"What's that?" I asked.

"We must move into the factory."

"Move into the factory? What do you mean?"

"I mean we must clear the whole of the front office area of the factory, and convert it into an apartment for ourselves and our children," Nárcissza replied.

I looked at her in amazement. "You can't be serious."

"Yes, I am. I've thought about it. There's enough space in the front office area to make two large bedrooms and an attractive living area. One of the ladies' rooms closest to the office complex could have a bathtub and shower added at a modest cost, and the existing kitchen already has a large refrigerator and gas range. The factory ladies' room and kitchen would be the only two factory areas involved in our private needs, and we wouldn't need to use them during business hours, so there wouldn't be any clash. Aside from that, the two solid doors separating the front office area from the factory, will give us all the privacy we need."

I stared at her, trying to take in what she was saying,. "Are you suggesting that we sell the house?"

"No, we'd rent the house to carefully chosen tenants, and in addition to what we'd make from that, we'd save whatever we now spend on the sixty miles of driving we do every day to commute between the two places. Those two ways of saving money may not seem like a lot but when combined with other economies they might just make the difference we need to swim rather than sink."

She paused to give me a moment to absorb this, then continued,. "Besides, there would be tax implications, too. By not living and working in two different states, we would save ourselves the double taxation we're now involved in."

I began to see that she was indeed serious. It certainly was a creative idea and I found myself rather fascinated by it. Boy, what a subject for discussion we would become. I could see the headlines in the Danbury Times—"Local family does a switch on the working-out-of-your-own-home idea. They live-out-of-their-own-workplace instead." I wondered whether anyone had done anything like that before. Certainly no one could object to the idea from a zoning standpoint, for the area already had residential property mixed with light industry. I began to appreciate the financial side of this very creative plan. Yes, yes . . . it would work. It was brilliant. And by golly it might even see us through!

As soon as I had put aside my stuffy British reserve and had persuaded myself that the plan was sound, we lost no time in putting it into effect. We engaged a plumber to transform the ladies' toilet into a full bathroom and made arrangements to move the front office furnishings out into the factory office section. Then, after cleaning up the vacated area and shampooing the wall-to-wall carpeting, we moved in, grand piano and all.

To my surprise and considerable relief, the transformation proved enchanting. We replaced the stark office lighting and decor with the warm glow of shaded, colorful freestanding area lamps, and a mix of rich multi-toned upholstery and accessories. A shaded table lamp sat atop the baby grand, bathing its ivory keys in warm amber light. Other suitably placed fixtures spread their diffuse light patterns across the comfortable settee that occupied the area against the window, and a glass-topped coffee table stood centrally in between. What had been the president's office now served as our bedroom, and the large separate accounting office served very well as a bedroom for our four younger children. Leslie, away at school in Canada, would not be part of the equation.

The three girls and our son adapted readily to this dramatic change in our home life and environment. From their comments over the early weeks of factory living, we learned that their new circumstances were bringing them a kind of closeness and contentment that was different from, and in some ways more consciously felt, than what they'd enjoyed in their earlier, more spacious, surroundings. Christine—'Muffin' to us—was now ten years old. Happy in her new school, when she was not off somewhere else with her friends, they would visit her at our factory and join her in games at home or bicycle riding in our quiet half-residential area. Panni and Antal, both eight years old, seemed to settle quite well in their new schools, too, and the dead end length of Precision Road provided them a safe area for play and for riding their carts and bicycles. There was much to explore and that's what they did. Paulette, now a gregarious three-year-old, never wanted for things to do and people to talk to. And because they were coming to an age of increasing thirst for information on anything and everything, they were intrigued, too, with the workings of the factory. One evening we found ourselves discussing ultrasonic cleaning. They'd all heard the buzzing noises made by the cleaning tanks as they were put through their paces prior to shipment or installation in a multi-stage cleaning system and they wanted to know how they worked.

Muffin, her head tipped to one side in the way that my mother and I have always revealed our puzzlement with a situation or concept, brought up the subject: "If it shakes the water to clean things daddy, why doesn't our dishwasher have it?"

"Perhaps some day, dish washers will use ultrasonics, but right now it would cost too much," I said. "You see, it doesn't just shake the water about. The dish washer already does that."

"Well then, what does it do?" Muffin persisted.

I thought that over for a minute or two, wondering how best I could dream up some sort of analogy that would explain the general principle in a way the children would understand.

"Think of a block of ice, Muffin—a big one. Let's say it's a twelve-inch cube. Now I want you to stretch your imagination, OK?"

"OK, Daddy."

"You suddenly have some magic powers. You place the flat of your hands against two opposite sides of this cube, ready to pick it up. You, too, Panni," I added.

"Yes but it would be too cold and too heavy. Besides, it would slip out of my hands."

"Ah, but remember, you have magic powers. You command your hands to glue themselves to this cube so it won't slip, and you give yourself amazing strength so you can lift it. Have you got it now, up in the air between your hands, just as if it were a concertina?"

"Yes, Daddy."

"Right. Now for some more magic. Heat from your hands melts the ice so it becomes water, but its still a cube and your hands are still glued to its opposite sides. Got that?"

"Yes, Daddy."

"Now, you're going to treat this cube of water as if it were water just lifted out of one of our ultrasonic cleaning tanks, and you're going to treat it as if you were the ultrasonic power. You pull your hands apart a bit and the water stretches a little wider because your hands are glued to it and it has to follow. Then you push your flat hands together a bit and the water compresses slightly between your hands. You keep on doing this back and forth, again as if you were playing a concertina, and the water block stretches and compresses as you do that. Still with me?"

Panni looked puzzled. "Why are we doing this Daddy?" she asked.

"You'll see in a minute, because now your powers are going to get even more magical. You play this concertina faster and faster—in and out, in and out—and the water swells and shrinks faster to keep pace with you. Faster, faster, faster—until your hands are moving in and out so fast, you can't even see them moving. But now the water is no longer able to keep up with you, and a million tiny holes, or bubbles form inside the cube as it splits apart. Before the cube can shatter, you are compressing it again and the holes collapse. And you keep on doing this—in and out faster than the water can follow, and the holes, or bubbles, keep forming and collapsing as you're doing it."

I paused, but they were all rapt with the story now, waiting for the climax.

"It's those bubbles that do the cleaning. Every time they collapse they release energy, just as a balloon does when it bursts, except in reverse. The balloon releases energy because the compressed air escapes from inside, but the cavitation bubbles release energy because of the pressure from the outside. That energy behaves just like a scrubbing brush and scrubs the dirt off the parts in the cleaning tank. That's how ultrasonic cleaning works. D'you get the idea?"

"Daddy." It was Panni again.

"Yes dear."

"My hands are tired. Even a magic persons hands can get tired."

"Well, the magic is over now, so you can put the water back on the table and let it disappear."

I wondered whether my analogy had served my purpose, or at least, whether the children had been entertained by the story. Then I looked at Nárcissza and wondered about the inscrutable smile on her face. Did it mean that I had just been entertaining myself?

No question about it, the reduction we'd achieved in our living expenses and tax liabilities was substantial. But it was still not enough. As we'd predicted, our drastically reduced salaries together with such other economies as we could wring out of our budget, had helped us show a 'break-even' balance sheet at the end of the year. But now, by the early part of 1976, the flow of incoming orders had fallen to a mere trickle. With a diminishing number of projects under negotiation, it was becoming clear that without a near miracle we couldn't keep the company afloat for many more months.

We hoped we'd encounter that miracle at the Semicon East exhibition in the fall. We'd already reserved and paid for our booth earlier in the year, and since the location was close by at the Nassau Coliseum on Long Island, we wouldn't need additional funding to transport heavy equipment across country to make our attendance possible. We'd rent a U-Haul truck and do the humping ourselves.

The only other major business activity that had occupied

our time during the latter part of 1975 and into 1976 concerned our negotiations with the Delco company. They
needed a large wet-chemistry processing system at their
Kokomo, Indiana plant. This project, because of its considerable scope, now seemed to offer our only chance of revers-
ing our downward slide into bankruptcy. The project engineer, Jesse Anderson, was about to visit us for an evaluation
of our facilities and engineering resources. The problem of
course, was that at that time, we had very little work in
progress on the shop floor and very few employees in our
plant. Right now, our factory resembled a deserted railroad
station rather than a place of industry. But we had a plan.
When the day for the inspection arrived, a veritable hive of
activity greeted Jesse.

Our eight employees had brought in a motley crew of family and friends to swell their numbers, and as Jesse walked
down the aisles, they were hammering and banging at imaginary work pieces as if their lives depended on it. Others were
making their way up and down the aisles with important
looking files under their arms, walking the full length of the
building and, after an appropriate interval during which they
shuffled papers at one or the other of the various desks, turning around and walking back again. Veronica Motolo's three
volunteers had joined her in the assembly section and were
busily engaged in wiring and soldering small electrical components. None of them except Veronica herself knew what
they were doing, but they did it very well indeed, maintaining
an intent and industrious demeanor throughout the visit.

We didn't actually tell any lies, neither did we make any
false claims as to our numbers or with regard to the amount
of business we had in house. Nor yet, for that matter, did we
know whether our false front had deceived Jesse at all. Our

sin was simply that we'd tried hard to conceal our true predicament.

Jesse later explained that since his company hadn't done business with Interlab before, his management chiefs were reluctant to place so large a contract with us. He said that he had liked what he'd seen of our products and our workmanship, but he wasn't very hopeful that his recommendations would have sufficient weight to carry the day.

Despite Jesse's comments, we continued to throw all our energies into the negotiations in progress on this one prospect, making regular trips to Delco's plant in Kokomo to answer technical questions and to further our cause in whatever way seemed feasible. In the evenings we scanned our prospect lists, reviewed the few smaller projects we were currently pursuing, and updated our plans concerning where we should be spending our time and applying our resources. In this manner, we coasted, slipping steadily into a financial condition that would soon oblige us to close our doors.

The Semicon East show was well attended and I never could understand the rumors we'd heard about its probable relocation to Boston in future years. Our booth was strategically located in one corner of the great exhibition hall with plenty of space in the wide front aisle for visitors to approach from either side and admire the principal product in our display. This, our newly designed heating system for ultra-pure water, stood proudly beside large signs that we'd prepared to draw attention to its primary features.

Tuesday, the first day of the show. We didn't see him walk up. We suddenly noticed him, standing quite still in the center of the aisle in front of the booth, sturdy legs far apart, large hands on lean hips, keen eyes gazing steadily at our display from below the brim of his white, squarely planted,

ten-gallon hat. Bob Blackwood of FSI International Inc.
seemed intrigued by what he saw. As I took in his stance,
there in the middle of the aisle, I almost expected him to
whip out a pair of silver forty-fives from some concealed hol-
sters and demand that we accompany him to the local jail.
But instead, unsmiling, he took two steps forward and spoke:

"Tell me about it."

"The water heater?"

"Yes, what does it do?"

I explained its operation and the way in which our star
product preserved the purity of the water it heated. He
seemed interested.

"Here's my card. Send me some stuff on it."

Still unsmiling, he nodded and strode away.

There were other less distinctive visitors to our booth, but
it became evident that nothing in the way of important business would happen soon—or at any rate, not soon enough to
help us with our immediate problem. The weeks slipped by.
October now, and we'd not been able to stem the drain on
our dwindling resources. Nárcissza was even more aware of
the seriousness of our plight than I. Her intimate knowledge
of our day-to-day financial condition gave her advance
notice of an end-of-the-road scenario that I wasn't yet able
to see. She knew well enough how best to let me know that
we were in dire trouble. After dinner on the Friday evening
of a particularly stressful week she interrupted my tinkering
on the piano to hand me a liqueur goblet.

The golden fluid sloshing lazily in its bowl was unmistak-
able. Grand Marnier was our consoler. It had become a ritual between us to drink a Grand Marnier toast to each other
when our resources were sorely challenged and when our
problems appeared insurmountable. I took the glass from

her hand, looking at her questioningly as I rose. She led me over to the settee. As we sat, Nárcissza turned to me, her eyes liquid. She spoke in a small uneven voice:, "Things aren't looking good, Howard."

She raised her glass to touch mine and when the clear ringing faded she added:

"Here's to us." Her voice broke on the last word.

"Here's to us," I said.

In the days that followed, we worked feverishly to advance the various smaller sales projects that showed more or less immediate promise of bearing fruit. I occupied my days traveling by car or plane to explore every opportunity to close a sale. Nárcissza, when not occupied on the phone with customers and prospects, attended to the costing and quoting, and helped her brothers with their daily production work. Our supervisors too, whether or not their work now demanded it, continued to apply themselves with feverish intensity, as if reluctant to give credence to the fast approaching end.

At such a time there seemed little purpose in analyzing our business methods and asking ourselves where we'd gone wrong. Any courses of action that might have resulted from a new awareness of our mistakes would be academic. We simply didn't have time for any changes to take sufficient effect to stop our downward slide. But we analyzed just the same.

At home at the dinner table, I philosophized. "I suppose we've been too lucky with our sales efforts, and we've lost sight of the need for marketing and for getting some good sales people into the company. I've been so used to doing the job myself that the idea of somebody else doing it just hasn't occurred to me. Perhaps I've assumed that nobody else could do it."

"So far, we haven't needed any formal marketing," Nárcissza said,. "and there hasn't been enough money to spare to spend on any of that, but I agree that we can't expect to improve on, or even maintain, a more than two million dollar sales volume with just one salesman. If we ever get out of this situation, we'll have to do something about that."

"By this time we should have had the country covered by independent manufacturer's representatives, all spreading the good word about Interlab's capabilities and products."

And so it went.

Then one evening, it happened. Nárcissza, her manner more purposeful, seemed to be concentrating, as if struggling to put an elusive idea into words. No philosophizing, no discussion about what we should have done. I could see she was trying to get a grip on what we should do now. We were sitting at the dinner table hardly into our main course when she placed her knife and fork on the table and just sat still and silent, looking straight ahead, eyes glazed. I was accustomed to this occasional strangeness in her behavior, so I didn't attempt to disturb her. After a while, she said:

"There's someone else we have to convince, Howard. You have to go back to Kokomo again."

I was nonplused. "What do you mean?"

"Tell me who else you've met besides Jesse."

"Well, let me see. There's Dick Dost . . . and of course, Larry Ross."

"No, not those. Tell me about others."

"There are the management people, but I really don't know them, except one I met months ago. That's George Queen, but he's . . ."

Nárcissza shook her head from side to side impatiently—.
" No!"

"Well, there's no need to bite my head off."

She got up from the table and paced the room, her small steps beating out a soft rhythm on the carpet, her clasped hands held against her chin in concentration as she walked, head down, to and fro. In a minute or two she stopped and turned to me.

"It's not management," she said, and continued her pacing.

I was stumped. I just couldn't think of anyone else. There were others in Jesse's department, working in parallel on other projects, but I couldn't see how or why they would influence decisions in the present case. Except perhaps Joe Maieron. Could that be? Yes, perhaps it could.

Joe was an experienced and respected old timer with the company and I had noted in the course of my visits that his colleagues often sought his advice. But Joe was wrapped up in a major project of his own, one that I had hoped to discuss with him in due course. Could Joe be the person that Narcissza had on her mind? Should I be discussing his project with him right now?

I looked up and turned to Nárcissza. "There's Joe Maieron. He's a senior—"

Nárcissza cut me off, really agitated now. "That's it—that's the one. You have to go see him right now."

"But Joe's not involved in this project. He's very much concerned about a totally different area."

"Doesn't matter, he's senior and he's influential. More than you know. If you can persuade him that we have the capability to do this job, it will make a difference. I know it." Nárcissza remained standing a little while longer until the intensity of her mood subsided. Then, her manner calm again, she seated herself, picked up her knife and fork, and reapplied herself to her dinner.

I knew better than to argue. As always, I puzzled over this strange clairvoyance that would sometimes come to her and seem to take over her thinking and her personality. Whenever it happened, all doubts disappeared, and she spoke with an authority that brooked no discussion. Nárcissza had 'seen' the necessary course of action—and I would follow it.

I'd earned my pilot's license the previous year and had thought about flying out in a private plane myself, but it was late November now with snow forecast. No point in getting stuck in Kokomo. The following Monday, I left on a commercial flight. I had not attempted to make an appointment with Joe Maieron. Instead, I called Jesse and explained that I was bringing out some updated flow diagrams for his review. When I arrived, I discussed the drawings with him and left an additional copy with the purchasing agent. Then I asked the department secretary whether Joe Maieron could be reached and whether I could spend a few minutes with him. No, I could not. Joe, in a series of conferences, was not expected to be free until the end of the day. Also, the receptionist added, he would be involved in conferences most of the following day, too.

I sat there, debating the problem in my mind and had almost decided to leave for the day and try again tomorrow, when Joe walked in and saw me. He greeted me and mentioned that his conference had recessed for an early lunch. What was I doing there, he asked. Waiting for him? I explained that I had come over to deliver some drawings to Jesse Anderson, and had thought it would be a good idea while I was there to ask Joe how his own new project was coming along. I added that since he was clearly very busy, I would be glad to come back in the morning.

"No, no," he said. "I'll be up to my neck in other meetings tomorrow. Tell you what, I'm having a box lunch at my desk today, so come on over and we can chat for a few minutes."

I didn't feel it appropriate to discuss Jesse Anderson's project with Joe Maieron, unless he should happen to mention it himself. Instead, I asked him about his own project. Would he care to discuss it yet? Fortunately he would, and we ended up spending almost the whole of his lunch hour reviewing a variety of chemical processing console (wet-bench) sketches and designs.

As we went through the requirements of the job, I offered suggestions about console configuration and exhaust arrangements. I did my best to leave an impression with him that Interlab's knowledge of wet chemistry processing was not superficial; that it had evolved over many years and had provided us with the ability to contribute to our customers' planning of their processing facilities.

Joe, profoundly wise and experienced, seemed appreciative. At the end of our conference he thanked me for my suggestions and indicated that at the appropriate time he'd recommend that Interlab be given an opportunity to bid on his requirement. Then, as he led me to the door and shook my hand, he said "Let's see now, you bid on Jesse Anderson's job didn't you?"

"Yes we did," I replied.

"Hmm. I should think an outfit like yours would do a pretty good job of that one."

"Thank you Joe for saying that—yes, I am sure we would," I said.

On the flight back to New York, the significance of Joe

Maieron's comment registered with me. In his own way, he had let me know that Interlab would get his support. I thought about Nárcissza's prediction and shook my head in wonderment. Then I closed my eyes and offered my silent thanks to Whoever was up there.

A few days later the phone rang. It was Delco's purchasing agent.

"Good morning," he said. "I'm calling to place a purchase order."

Twenty Three

All business, they say, is cyclic. And I suppose that any-thing that varies with the seasons or the whims of fashion and man may be so categorized. At any rate we were glad at this time to subscribe to that philosophy. The tide of our business fortunes had ebbed to new lows over the course of these last years, but now, the arrival of a major con-tract had signaled a reversal in that tide. It was about to rise again and would gather momentum as it did so. At its high-est water, it would bathe us in it its foaming exuberance, washing over our tired and striving limbs and psyches until we would once more relax for a brief and wondrous spell to gird ourselves for yet another turn that would at sometime have to follow.

And so it was. The man with the ten-gallon hat came back into our lives and our fortunes. Soon after we'd received our Delco Christmas present, Bob Blackwood expressed a desire to visit us. He liked what he'd seen at the Semicon East exhi-bition, but as a mid-westerner he was not about to make his next move until he had examined the teeth and the hoofs of our enterprise. When we invited him to dinner at our facto-

ry apartment, he didn't seem surprised at the unusual venue
of our rendezvous. We spent a congenial evening together,
showed him around the factory itself, and explained the elements of our technology, product designs and steadily growing list of patents. Ten Gallon didn't say much. He seemed to
pay close attention to our answers to his occasional questions, but he didn't give us any indication that his inspection
visit had been satisfactory. He thanked us for our hospitality,
tipped the brim of his hat—and departed.

We didn't hear from him again for several weeks. Then,
quite suddenly, his company's purchasing agent called in an
order for one of our sophisticated water heaters. Later that
day, Ten Gallon called to check that we'd received the order.
He told us that in filling this first order a lot would hang on
our performance and on the quality of the equipment we'd
ship. We'd better make it good. His manner was not
unfriendly. Just matter-of-fact.

Several more weeks passed before FSI International telephoned our sales department to place another similar order.
Thereafter, the intervals between placement of orders
became smaller and the orders themselves were no longer
for single units. They were for twos and threes. As more time
passed, the numbers grew yet larger and eventually our business with FSI International, accounted for a significant part
of our overall sales volume.

Time to move our living quarters; to give the children more
space to spread themselves and to breathe fresh country air;
to play among more trees and smell the damp of the woods.
Our house hunting in the area had actually begun many
years previously, even while our negotiations to purchase

the factory were in progress. With faith in the future and in ourselves, we'd routinely scanned the real estate "Homes For Sale" columns of the New York Sunday Times. Occasionally, on a Saturday afternoon or on Sunday, we'd made the rounds with agents to see properties located within an acceptable distance of our future place of work. Remaining in Pound Ridge would have involved us in drawbacks beyond the two half-hour commuting trips we would make each day. We'd have to contend with the double taxation problem again. New York State and Connecticut would both require their share of our earnings and that would make no sense at all.

Eventually, one wintry Sunday afternoon early in 1972, American Country Real-Estate brokers had introduced us to our dream house. True, its price had proved wildly beyond our means, but finding ourselves in the area, our agent had thought we just might like to see this fine French Normandy brick house and its extensive grounds—just so we'd get an idea of the range of properties that were available in this New Fairfield community. She'd become aware that, for us, house hunting also served as a pleasant entertainment, and our visit to this beautiful property had certainly fallen into that category.

We had been truly impressed. Rolling, neatly trimmed lawns in front of the house, were spread over at least two acres of the property. A variety of tall majestic trees, added splendor to the setting. The interior, with its spacious rooms, polished oak floors and cathedral-ceilinged living room, had left us with an impression of another era, of an elegance belonging to the past in which meals would be served by a uniformed staff, on Wedgwood or Dresden china plates. Yet because this five-and-one-half acre property was located in an area where all surrounding zoning was limited to two acres, the price, although beyond our means, had been comparatively reasonable.

Later, on returning to the agency offices, we'd decided that nothing could be lost by doing what we'd done when negotiating the purchase of our factory. We had asked the agent to put in a bid based upon our own budget, rather than the asking price for the property. We settled on $115,000, and duly submitted the bid. I don't know the details of the interview during which our agent had submitted our bid to the mistress of the house but we had later learned that upon hearing it, that good lady had screamed in anguish, and had not otherwise offered a reply.

Now, several years later, another agent was showing us the same property. It had changed hands since we'd last seen it, but the new owner had succumbed to a heart attack soon after moving in. His widow, in her distress, had simply let the property die, too. She had neither the will nor the strength to tend its needs. The once trim lawns were buried under weeds. Errant branches of close-by trees now invaded the back bedroom balcony and spread their limbs across the shallow roof. Here and there, large areas of once-white paint flaked off the once-red brick walls, and outdoor lighting fixtures lay prone and twisted, with wiring exposed. In the living room, broken, wrought-iron chains drooped from the heavy rim of the wagon-wheel chandelier that now hung precariously by a single strand of its frayed electrical cord. A thick oak mantle had detached itself from its anchorage above the fireplace, and elsewhere, sad neglect had left in its wake a trail of broken fixtures and deeply scarred oak floors.

To nurse the property back to some semblance of its former splendor would require prodigious effort and care, but we'd have the time. On this occasion, our very low offer did not provoke distress on the part of its owner. After a modest period of negotiation our bid was accepted. In a matter of weeks our attractive little apartment at Precision Road was history.

TWENTY FOUR

The Cessna Skyhawk bucked and bobbed as Henry Sollman grabbed the yoke and shook it back and forth in his frustration at my thick-headedness.

"For crying out loud get it up there!" he barked.

No doubt about it, that stocky veteran of more than ten thousand hours of flying and instructing was fed up with me today. We were taking off from Danbury Airport to set off for Waterbury-Oxford airport where I was to practice ILS (Instrument Landing System) approaches. Henry was trying to persuade me that since in the real world of 'hard' IFR (Instrument Flight Rules) you would often be in the clouds soon after take-off, climbing as high as possible as soon as possible, was absolutely necessary. The clouds just off the end of the runway might be hiding tall buildings and towers or other man-made obstructions that you couldn't see, and if you didn't remember to climb high into the sky as quickly as possible you stood a good chance of bumping into something. I had no difficulty understanding that line of reasoning, but the trouble was that most of the time, a suitable cloud base was not present on the days that my instruction sessions were scheduled, so I could see any obstructions quite easily.

Like today. There just wasn't a cloud anywhere, and I found it difficult to imagine hitting those trees at the far end of the runway. Besides, until I got the instrument flying bug and started out on this grueling program, my instructors had always tried to impress upon me that smoothness was of the essence in a pilot's approach to all things. Any departure from that principle might result in passengers becoming disenchanted with the idea of flying in general and with the pilot in particular. And now here I was, having to unlearn all that and heave the airplane into the blue as if the devil himself were chasing my tail.

"Go around."

"What?" I turned to look at Henry. His usually pleasant face was stern.

"That's right—go around." he barked. "We're going to keep doing this until I get it through your head. One day your life is going to depend on it."

I did not attempt to argue. This was going to be a tough enough session without any further nudging from me. Dutifully I banked left, climbed again to the fifteen hundred feet pattern altitude, announced my intentions to the tower and made my way back around to final approach again.

"Touch and go?" I asked.

"No. I want you to land and start all over again."

After touchdown I taxied back to the active runway and when the tower cleared me for take-off I went through my pre-take-off checklist meticulously and taxied out to the centerline. As I released the brakes and smoothly advanced the throttle, the eager airplane began its takeoff roll, accelerating quickly. I began talking to myself.

"Okay, Howard, here we go. Hold that centerline . . . watch the airspeed . . . ease that nose up at 55 knots. Then as she comes unstuck, offer up a silent prayer and hold that best angle-of-climb speed . . . 65 knots all the way. Hold it some more . . . and some more."

Pretty soon we were at the minimum safe altitude for the area. I ventured a glance at Henry. He nodded, still unsmiling, and we proceeded on course to Waterbury-Oxford. I breathed again and wondered why at my age I have found this venture so necessary.

I was by this time well aware that the instrument rating course was a difficult enough undertaking even for young persons in their late teens and twenties when their coordination and ability to learn new skills are optimum. But for an over-worked fifty-year-old, it was proving more demanding than I had bargained for.

Copying clearances accurately, learning to make infinitely small corrections and developing the oh-so-delicate touch, essential when making ILS approaches; using the correct entry and exit procedures for holding patterns and handling simulated emergencies under pressure, had taxed to their limit my powers of concentration. There had been times when I had wondered whether I would ever be able to put it all together.

Back on the ground about two hours later, we had a debriefing session:

"How did I do, Henry?"

"Not well."

"Was it that bad?"

Henry sighed. "You're OK when you're wearing the blinkers, but we can't do that yet for take-off or touch down, so we'll just have to wait 'til we get some real weather and then make the most of it." He thought about this for a moment, then he said:

"Imagine that you've flown to a strange airport for a business appointment. There is cloud cover there at about five hundred feet and it stays there all day until you leave. You never do get to see what's hidden in those clouds when you take off again, so you need to get up and out of the way in as short a distance as possible. Don't you see that?"

"Yes, Henry, I do see that. I'll try to remember."

Seeing that I was duly humbled, he relented. "Your approaches are getting better— you broke out right in line with the runway on that last one. That was good, considering the cross-wind."

"Thank you, Henry," I mumbled.

And so we went through a period of last-minute scheduling, waiting for the right sort of cloud cover and making the most of it when it came, even if it meant driving to one of the out-of-town airports that offered the necessary instrument approaches. Little by little I learned how to make my way safely in an airplane when there is nothing to see outside except swirling gray mists or rain drumming relentlessly on the windshield.

Company sales were going through the roof now. The nearly one million dollar volume we achieved for 1978 would be far exceeded in the course of the following year and that meant we were easily able to afford the cost of my concentrated flying instruction schedule. But for me, our business success was in other respects in conflict with my flying interests. Even now, proposals and field sales work were still my sole responsibility, and this intense and time-consuming activity, coupled with the instrument rating course, the most demanding of any instruction that a pilot ever undertakes, was steadily overtaxing my physical and mental resources.

To Henry's mortification I began to make unaccountable mistakes. On one occasion, near the end of my instrument training, we were bound for New Haven Airport to pick up a nav/com radio set that had been sent there for repair. The main runway at New Haven is designated 'Two zero' (200°) at one end, and 'Zero two' (20°) at the other. As the airport came in sight, the tower controller announced that runway 'two zero' was in use and I misread this as 'zero two.' Cleared for a straight-in approach, we were within a half-mile of the runway threshold before I noticed a twin-engined aircraft just then taking off and coming straight at us off the end of the runway. My turn away was one of the steepest I had ever had occasion to make. Henry was beside himself. "What are you trying to do Howard? Are you clowning? Are you trying to make a fool out of me?"

There was nothing I could say. We eventually landed at the correct end of the runway, but although I was lucky enough to make a 'grease-on' landing, it did little to improve Henry's mood. The day was lost.

And yet . . . and yet . . . before that week was out, and despite the bungling and bumbling, Henry signed my recommendation for the instrument rating final test flight with an FAA examiner. I could not believe it.

Within another week I was scheduled to take my check-ride with Richard King, the designated Federal Aviation Examiner. By that time I was stretched to my limit. Early on that June morning, as I was walking up to my favorite Skyhawk, 737RQ, to prepare for my check-ride, I found my vision blurring a little at intervals so that the numbers painted on the tail went in and out of focus. As I reached the aircraft, I stumbled against the sharp trailing edge of the wing flaps. The flaps on a Cessna are just about high enough to scalp a man of average height, and for a moment the blow to the crown of my head stunned me. Then I recovered and carried on with my pre-flight inspection. The slowly developing headache went unheeded. I concentrated. I thought of nothing but the task ahead. This time I must not bungle.

Fortunately, Richard, now in the role of my designated FAA examiner, was in a good mood, but he was nonetheless exacting. Even as we taxied out he applied rubber cover-plates to certain of the instruments to deprive me of their guidance. As we took the active runway, a friendly voice from the tower cleared us: "Cessna Seven Three Seven Romeo Quebec is cleared for take-off. Good luck, Howard."

How did they know?

In some ways I had a reprieve. Richard, aside from his duties as FAA examiner, was also a flying instructor. Before I had started flying with Henry, Richard had given me a lot of instruction on Instrument Landing System (ILS) approaches, so today, already aware of my skills in that area, he concentrated on other maneuvers and approaches which, as it happened, were somewhat less demanding. Nevertheless, when my head began to throb again I misunderstood a couple of his instructions and was sure that I would have to ask for a re-test. But it didn't happen. After another grueling hour of maneuvers, simulated emergencies and other types of instrument landings, Richard congratulated me on my new instrument rating. As we taxied to his office across the field from Connecticut Air Service where 737RQ was based, he was already making the appropriate entry in my log book.

I thanked Richard and dropped him off. Physically and

emotionally spent, I taxied very slowly back to my own base, conscious only of the taxiway before me. A soft voice from the tower penetrated the throbbing in my head,. "Cessna Seven Three Seven Romeo Quebec is cleared to cross the active." A pause, then with concern in her voice,. "How did it go, Howard?"

Oh, what a wonderful sound. Gratitude overwhelmed me. My chest heaved. Right then I wanted to taxi straight over to the tower, rush up the stairs and hug that controller whom I had never met. Hug her breathless.

"I passed," I croaked.

"Congratulations."

"Thank you for asking. You made my day."

I began to sob. Convulsions, slow and shallow at first, then deep and uncontrollable heavings as I continued on my way. Oddly, I found myself alternately sobbing and chuckling at the incongruity of an intrepid airman guiding his plane to its home base, crying like a baby as he taxied along.

The following day the pounding in my head finally triumphed. In the middle of the crowd at Boston's Logan Airport as I was making my way to a conference at North Andover, the great hall began to spin around me. I caught a glimpse of a couple of uniformed first-aid people running toward me as my legs folded. Then oblivion.

Over the years, the wise and the learned have lectured at length about the importance of avoiding hospital stays if at all possible, and a teaching hospital is to be avoided more than others. True, they are usually blessed with almost limitless diagnostic facilities and sophisticated instrumentation, but the medical staff are known to be over zealous on occasion, in putting them to use. Massachusetts General, it seemed to me, was in that category. I wasn't unduly disturbed when their probing and pricking of my limbs revealed a total lack of sensitivity to pain in my right arm and leg. I felt sure that that condition would right itself in a day or two and my faith proved well founded. Even by the morning following my arrival, some improvement was evident. But when, later on that same day, the nurse expressed concern that I had not urinated since arrival, I began to panic.

The nurse told me that if I didn't urinate by the following morning, a catheter would be snaked up my penis to drain my bladder. I'd heard about that procedure before, and it didn't fascinate me at all. Besides, I hadn't had much to drink in the preceding twenty-four hours, so it seemed to me that they were rushing things a bit. Following this dire warning, I made it a point to drink everything I could get my hands on. Mercifully, my plumbing became operational before the day was over. I cannot think of a time since my boyhood days when I was as proud and eager to show anyone how copious a flow I could manage. And yet, as the nurse took the flask, I fancied that I saw a fleeting disappointment in her eyes. I wondered whether she had been brainwashed, too.

When Nárcissza arrived to see how I was doing, she was already convinced that I should be released without undergoing further experimentation by the hospital. On learning of their hurry to get my urine flowing, she had immediately called our cardiologist, Dr. Joe Buchman, and, stalwart that he was, he in turn had made several phone calls to acquaintances of his at the hospital asking that they look into my case.

Within hours, another doctor, a bearded, stern-looking

specialist in head injuries, came to examine me. He conducted a series of tests to determine the significance of the
initial numbness I'd experienced in my right arm and leg,
and the degree to which the blow to my head had affected
my overall sensitivity to pain in various parts of my body. At
length, he began with his questions.

"How did you do this?" he asked

"I slipped as I was walking toward an airplane. It was a
high-wing type and I banged my head on the back of the
wing."

"What made you slip. Was it mud?"

"No, as a matter of fact, I was dizzy."

"Why?"

"I had been working too hard—studying for the instrument rating exam. I was exhausted."

"Ahh, I see."

That was all. With an admonishment that I continue to
monitor my recovery very carefully, and that I should immediately notify my doctor in the event of any new symptoms,
he advised me that I was well enough to be discharged, and
would be released the following day.

TWENTY FIVE

O ur success with the Delco projects together with our rising sales to FSI International, enabled us to achieve a genuine turnaround in our business fortunes. It gave us the time we needed to complete some of the many other sales negotiations we'd been working on since the dramatic drop in our Western Electric business, and bring them to fruition. Our total sales in 1979 had almost tripled that of the previous year. One way or another we were going to make the most of this tide of opportunity and once more take it at the flood. We were confident that we could maintain this wonderful flow of business, but we didn't quite know when and where our next big chance would reveal itself. It came from a surprising quarter, and it wasn't so much great in size as it was prestigious.

For many months, Jack Kurdock and his team at Perkin Elmer in Norwalk had been preparing the great reflector of the Hubble Space Telescope for its final mirror coating. Roughly eight feet in diameter and about a foot thick, its concave surface had to be totally free from even the minutest of contaminants before it could be introduced into the enormous vacuum chamber that would give it its mirror coating. Particles so small that they would be visible only with the aid of the most powerful microscopes would, if they remained on the surface of the reflector, create microscopic faults in the mirror's surface. These in turn would obliterate light from vast areas of the distant cosmos. To prevent this, every square millimeter of its surface had to be as pristine as a semiconductor wafer. Jack Kurdock knew about Interlab and he recalled that when his management had planned a state-of-the-art upgrading of the lens cleaning facilities in their laboratories, Interlab had supplied equipment whose performance had far exceeded the specified requirements. In the early part of 1980, Jack asked whether I'd care to work on the Hubble project as a cleaning consultant. The opportunity delighted me and I accepted his offer. Soon we had a contract and were getting to work.

Lest I find myself turning this story into a textbook rendition, I will include here only a very brief account of the philosophy upon which we based the cleaning equipment design. Simply stated, the mirror was so huge we would not be able to lift it into a series of washing, rinsing and drying tanks, as we did with smaller workloads. In this case, Mohammed would have to go to the mountain. We would have to clean the mirror wherever it happened to be. The design, therefore, used a semi-transportable mechanism, with a rotating arm that sprayed the optical surface with washing, rinsing and drying fluids delivered through an array of specially designed spray-head assemblies.

First, we applied a washing solution for a prescribed cycle time, then flushed hot ultra-pure water through the spray mechanism itself, to clear its component parts of washing solution residues. When no trace of washing solution

remained, we applied the hot rinse water to the optic surface. Following a series of similar rinses, we dried the now
pristine optic with jets of hot dry nitrogen flowing through
the same rotating spray-head assemblies that we had used
for the other cleaning sequences. The application itself was
simple and effective, but the water and gas purification,
heating and control systems were more complex. Before we
had developed a satisfactory design approach, I found myself
burning quite a lot of midnight oil. I was relieved and gratified when later in September, Jack and his colleagues and
other consultants expressed their approval of the resulting
design by contracting Interlab to manufacture and install
the entire system.

The outcome is history. As everyone now knows, curvature
imperfections in the configuration of the optic, necessitated
later application of compensatory measures. Nevertheless, its
flawless mirror surface testified not only to the high integrity
of the coating process itself, but also to the efficacy of the
cleaning system that had prepared the optic for this crucial
and sophisticated procedure.

TWENTY SIX

Nárcissza's part in bringing about the turnaround in our business fortunes was not lost on me. We'd worked our way out of several near-hopeless business predicaments since she'd joined me at Interlab, and it was clear to me that in the most crucial of those instances it had been her creative and fearless thinking that had saved the day. Looking back, I could see well enough that the economies that had resulted from our move into the apartment at the factory, while not alone large enough to enable us to balance our books, had been crucial to our ultimate success in achieving that end. That move had been entirely her brainchild. The idea would never have occurred to me. Even if it had, I would have dismissed it as too far-fetched and radical. Aside from that, I would have felt uncomfortable asking my family to make such an unconventional move. The fact that Nárcissza had dreamed it up herself had enabled me to see the idea in a different light.

The Delco negotiations of a few years previously offered another example of Nárcissza's uncanny aptitude for finding new and productive ways to approach a problem when everything feasible seemed already done. My own strengths in engineering and selling were very well complemented by her abilities in administrative and financial areas, and by her knowledge of chemistry. I felt the time had come when the company would be better served if she were to run it and I were to confine my activities to engineering and selling.

It was in any case almost a fait accompli, for as so often happens, people tend to apply themselves more assiduously in areas where their skills and aptitudes enable them to make the most effective contributions. Nárcissza, already adept at juggling with the company's limited financial resources, somehow managed to stretch them to meet our essential commitments. In the matter of hiring and firing, while I tended to hire people because I liked them rather than because of their skills and employment records, she, with her deeper insight into the strengths and frailties of human nature, was far more objective than I. She judged applicants less on what they said they could do than on what their resumes revealed they'd actually done. In the spring of 1981 I asked Nárcissza to take over as President, and she accepted. It was one of the most enlightened decisions I'd made since founding the company.

We were off and running. Our earlier work with the new Kodak Research Labs had recently come to the attention of the Xerox Company, also based in Rochester. They were sufficiently well impressed with what they'd learned that in May they gave us a similar contract to meet special requirements of their own.

The changes we'd made in the focus of our working relationship were not just nominal adjustments. They affected the way we felt about our jobs. Nárcissza felt more at ease making crucial management and policy decisions in my absences in the field, and I was now able to spend more time traveling on sales engineering missions without feeling that I was neglecting executive responsibilities. Since these missions were accomplished increasingly with the aid of small rented airplanes, I felt it important to involve myself in a continuing training program. In due course, I added spin recovery training to my curriculum, and finally, a commercial pilot's license.

It seemed that the more I honed my flying skills and took every opportunity to fly out to customers' locations—IBM in Endicott, Binghamton, Mannassas and Burlington; Kodak and Xerox in Rochester; GE in Syracuse; and Western Electric in North Andover, Allentown, and Reading—the more our business flourished. Whenever possible I took our engineers and maintenance crew with me to provide a standard of service not commonly offered by our competitors.

The essence of this approach, of being right there on the customer's doorstep when needed, was not lost on those who had occasion to put us to the test. The word spread that Interlab serviced what they sold, and serviced it fast. And that counted.

TWENTY SEVEN

Recognizing that I wouldn't be able to keep up a nearly doubled sales volume unaided, we had begun to engage others to share the responsibility, but they needed training and field support. To transport them efficiently and to support our after-sales services as well, there were limitations to our current practice of renting an airplane as needed. For one thing, there were occasions when the particular aircraft—Cessna 182 Skylanes and occasional 172 Skyhawks—had either been booked by others for that day, or were out of service for repair work. Then, too, there were times when their four-seat capacity proved insufficient for our needs. It was time for Interlab to have an airplane of its own.

I began to take an interest in the availability of aircraft in the six-seater, single engine category, and a Piper Saratoga based at one of the Danbury flying schools attracted me. It wasn't for sale, but I decided to inquire about its features and find out what a good used airplane of that type might cost. It happened that the man I spoke with in the school front lobby was an instructor taking a break between flying missions. He seemed eager to help.

"Tell you what" he said,. "I have the key and I have a bit of time. I'll go out with you and tell you about it. With that, he grabbed a set of keys off the wallboard behind the counter and walked out with me to where the sleek airplane was parked. As I climbed into the cockpit and settled myself behind the yoke, I knew this was my kind of airplane. With the possible exception of the Cessna 182, I had always found single engine airplanes excessively cramped and claustrophobic, but this one was a true exception. Its cabin width, the most generous I had encountered, made me feel right at home. The four rear seats were arranged so that two pairs faced each other to improve legroom. When required, all four seats could be quite easily removed to make room for cargo. In reality, with its powerful three hundred horsepower engine and considerable load-carrying capabilities, the Saratoga was the flying equivalent of a small comfortable truck.

But just as I was telling myself that this was the airplane for me, I noticed the retractable gear handle. No way would I buy a retractable airplane. I knew that pilots with considerably more experience and with far better memories than mine regularly failed to put the wheels down, and I also knew that one day something would distract me during the landing phase and I would overlook that most important ritual. I asked my helpful companion whether these same airplanes were manufactured in non-retractable versions.

"Absolutely," he said. That settled it. The Saratoga was for me.

I scanned the ads in the various trade papers that abound in flying school briefing rooms. I let it be known among my flying acquaintances and instructors that I was looking for a good used Saratoga, but nothing came of it immediately. It wasn't until July of the following year that I learned of a

1980 Saratoga, described as in immaculate condition, for sale at an unusually low price. Based in St. Paul, Minnesota, the airplane belonged to a pair of professional photographers. They'd used the machine for aerial mapping and real estate photography assignments, and were in the process of purchasing a larger plane. To evaluate the condition of the Saratoga for myself, I flew out to St. Paul. If I liked what I saw, I hoped I'd be allowed to take it for a test flight the same day.

I liked what I saw. The partners had taken good care of their airplane. One of them took me up for the evaluation trip, and we flew for an hour and a half, putting the machine through its paces. It was, for me, a euphoric experience. I was hooked. I arranged for an inspection by an independent airplane mechanic. Shortly thereafter, I made an offer and the partners accepted. On August 7th, Ray Harvey, an experienced instructor who'd flown Saratogas before, joined me on my second trip to St. Paul to consummate the deal. Later that same day we were winging our way back home. The Saratoga was mine.

With an airplane at our disposal and with others now participating in our sales work, I was able to spend more time working on updating our technology and developing new products. Which was just as well, because our little company was now deeply involved in coping with a new trend.

When we'd first introduced our 'robotized' processing systems to the marketplace some twelve years previously, it had been necessary to show customers that automation would pay for itself by eliminating or substantially reducing the need for human operators. Despite the reasonable accuracy of our claims, we had not been very successful in selling the concept. Many customers and prospects requested that we offer mechanized transfer as an option, but few actually called for it when the time came to place a purchase order.

As it turned out, we'd used the wrong argument for promoting automation—pressed the wrong buttons, so to speak. The critical devices encountered in the industries we served were so costly to produce that the economies resulting from replacing human operators in cleaning and wet processing operations were not significant in relation to the overall cost of manufacturing the product. Mechanization was just not worth bothering with.

But now, some ten years later, the justification for mechanizing cleaning or etching processes had little to do with economies of that sort. The microcircuit and other industries concerned with further miniaturization of the already small, were now more concerned with the actual predictability and repeatability of processing procedures, than with the cost of employing human operators. Human operators could make mistakes and they might deal with the processing a little differently toward the end of a long workday than when they were fresh and alert in the morning hours. And no matter what precautions one took, human operators were, in themselves, significant sources of contamination. Human hair and skin flakes could readily find their way into the work zones. Modern micro-device processing could no longer tolerate that.

So now here we were, busily refining our mechanizing techniques. So busy, in fact, that in 1984, we were granted three United States patents relating to robotics technology. IBM encouraged us to go even further. They invited us to give some thought to the fact that the robots, moving back and forth over the work area, were themselves a contamination hazard. For one thing, their moving parts, although located at the rear of the work surface and not directly over the processing tanks, nevertheless shed contaminating particles. Some of these could find their way into the fluids and thereby contaminate the devices being processed.

Another matter of concern was the disturbance of the clean airflow caused by the motion of the robot within the work zone. The IBM purchasing agent at Essex Junction in Vermont invited us to devise a mechanized transfer system that wouldn't suffer from these shortcomings.

"Couldn't you somehow streamline the hoist so it doesn't mess up the airflow—and maybe seal it so it doesn't shed particles?" he asked.

I worked on that request and burned a lot of midnight oil sketching all sorts of possible alternatives on my scribble pad. Everything seemed too convoluted and complicated. I decided to bounce a few ideas off Nárcissza. We were sitting opposite each other at a corner table at Fortuna's.

"Maybe we should be shaping it aerodynamically, so it cuts through the air like a jet airplane," I ventured. "It would need a bit more room, sideways, but we could allow for that."

"And what about the particle problem?"

"Well, if we push the hoist back a bit, so that it's behind the laminar air flow pattern directly above the process tanks, that should help quite a bit. The bench would be a bit deeper, front to rear, but everything's a compromise."

"True," Nárcissza answered,. "but if it comes to that, why does the hoist have to be in the work area at all?

I stared at her. "What do you mean? Oh yes, yes! You have it—that's it! We can stick the hoist behind the console—have it run along a track behind and below the work area, and simply let its arm reach into the process area."

Nárcissza was glowing. "See? Here I am, hauling you out of

the mire again, doing your inventing for you. I think I should get a royalty for that."

"Tell you what," I said,. "if we ever get a patent on this, and if Interlab ever gives me a royalty on it, you're welcome to half."

It was a simple idea really. After a couple more weeks on the drawing board, we put together a prototype and tried it out. The new robot rode behind or in front of the console, along tracks bolted to the side fairly low down. The robot's smooth skeletal arm was the only part that reached over into the work zone to carry out the transfer chores. It had one or two teething troubles but it worked, and the contamination hazard and airflow disturbance problems were thereby eliminated. I wrote up a patent application, more to protect our proprietary right to use our design, than to discourage anyone else from copying it. Our sixteenth US patent, describing the new design, was granted in January of 1985. From that time forward, automation became the rule, rather than the exception.

We christened our newest transfer hoist the 'Limpet' because it clung to the side of the processing console. Its design, refined over the years by our creative engineering department, has stood the test of time, and as this account is being written, the Limpet endures as Interlab's standard robot for carrying moderate loads.

But our satisfaction with the progress we were making in our business endeavors was overshadowed by a sudden tragedy within the family. My eldest daughter Peta, whose marriage had ended unhappily, had devoted herself to the task of raising her son Raymond alone, while simultaneously holding down a full-time job. She'd suffered with asthma all her life, and it seemed to us that her changed circumstances were bringing about a significant worsening of that ailment. She'd made plans to move to a climate more favorable for her condition, and talked of going to Arizona where the dry air was said to be beneficial for people with respiratory problems.

A tragic circumstance intervened.

One night early in March, Peta awoke gasping and choking with an unusually severe attack. The inhaler she grabbed from the night table didn't seem to help her. In desperation, she called the local hospital and asked them to send someone quickly to take her to the emergency room. The ambulance arrived very shortly thereafter, but in their eagerness to make the journey as comfortable as possible for her, the attendants who accompanied her made a mistake. They gave her supplementary oxygen while she was actually in the throes of an attack. By the time they arrived at the hospital, Peta was no longer gasping for breath. That most gracious young woman and loving mother had already passed away.

Our private grieving over Peta's death seemed to carry over into our working lives and somehow influence our business decisions and fortunes. Soon, we were on our way down again, slipping toward a catastrophe from which we would not fully recover for almost a decade.

TWENTY EIGHT

When the semiconductor and microcircuit industries went into recession we weren't prepared for
the magnitude of the downswing they suffered. Nor were we
prepared for the request from the Kingsway Bank and Trust,
that we immediately repay the substantial business loan we
were using to augment our working capital. Like many banks
affected by the notorious savings and loan bank failures of
the time, KBT had discovered that they'd over extended
themselves. In an all-out effort to ward off impending disas-
ter, they were calling in loans on any pretext or technicality
they could light on. To compound our difficulties, the timing
of these two alarming events coincided with the completion
at the end of 1984 of our ambitious factory extension project
that had given us an additional ten thousand square feet of
factory space and a four thousand square-foot stockroom.

We carried enough orders into 1985 to ensure that the
year would not be a bad one, but by that time, the flow of
business for everyone in the semiconductor industry had
slowed. With our overhead increasing and our sales decreas-
ing, we were in no position to do what the bank had asked.

To further complicate matters, our chief contact, Jimmy Chambers, left the bank early in the year. Ms. Stanley, the young female account officer who replaced him, paid us a visit to familiarize herself with our activities and to renew our loan agreement. That lady, no doubt intent on demonstrating efficiency in her new position, added a brief clause to the fine print on the back of the agreement. It concerned a minimum asset-to-debt ratio required to maintain compliance with the agreement. When questioned about the change, Ms. Stanley explained with a reassuring smile that the change was just a formality, and that it was very unlikely that we would ever come close to that limiting ratio. The matter was closed and the good lady departed.

The following year, in concert with the slump in the semiconductor industry, the bottom dropped out of our sales. Total volume for the year plunged from around $3,000,000 to $2,100,000, and our year-end statement showed an operating loss of $250,000. Not a happy situation, but we'd expected it and were confident of our ability to ride it through. We duly submitted the report to our bank, which, judging by later events, did not even get around to reading it.

Interlab was one of KBT's favorite little accounts and they were fond of bringing other prospective accounts to visit and tour our facility. By early 1987, we'd built up a good backlog again, and the bank manager visited us with his chief from Hartford to impress him with our bustling success. Surprisingly, however, no questions were asked about our finances. At the door, just as they were on their way out, the manager offered his praises for our performance.

"Nárcissza, you have a fine company here and we could use more customers who perform as well as you do."

"Well, we certainly have a great team, and I'm confident

we'll make up for last year's losses quite soon," Nárcissza replied.

The manager and his boss appeared confused. They looked at each other with puzzled expressions, then questioningly at Nárcissza.

"Well, as you know, we experienced a loss last year, but I am confident that we'll make a nice profit this year," she told them.

The following day, the manager called her. "We need to talk. I'll be bringing my financial analyst over."

Upon arrival, the visitors lost no time in reminding us that according to the fine print on the back of our loan agreement, our asset-to-debt ratio had fallen below their prescribed minimum for borrowers. We were therefore in violation of the agreement. True enough, we hadn't had the greatest year in 1985, but neither had anybody else in our industry. We pointed out that we were still in good financial health. Our balance sheet was good, and aside from our loan with KBT and our mortgage, we didn't owe anybody anything. They were not impressed. The following day they notified us officially that they wanted their money back—in full.

We wrote a protesting letter, but they were adamant.

To crown our misfortunes, we managed to get some very poor legal advice. When the crisis had passed and the dust had settled, we learned that our best reaction to the bank's demands would have been simply to threaten a declaration under Chapter Eleven of the bankruptcy code.

Most companies who take advantage of a Chapter Eleven filing, it is alleged, do not survive. Nevertheless, this particular chapter of the code is supposed to hold creditors at bay to give the filing party an opportunity to reorganize and work out with the creditors, a mutually acceptable way of settling the debts. But the legal advice we received on the matter didn't warn us that money owed to us by our customers at the date of filing wouldn't be included in the protections offered by that filing. Instead, however, on the urgings of a local attorney, we declared a Chapter Eleven bankruptcy.

The bank immediately confiscated our receivables, which at that time were considerable. We were soon left with insufficient working capital to meet our other obligations.

Enter Carl Whitney, our new contact with the bank. Nárcissza was in touch with him daily. After the date of filing, she wasn't allowed to write a single check without calling him for permission. She couldn't pay even the telephone account or the electric bill without his OK. The first payroll had passed without problems. On the Thursday before the second payroll, Nárcissza called him.

"Good morning Mr. Whitney. Since I have payroll tomorrow, I thought I'd better call you."

"How much do you need?"

"About thirty five thousand."

"Have you got that much in the account?"

"Yes, I think there's about fifty-five in there now."

"Hmm. When do you give out the checks?"

"At noon."

"Well, I guess it will be OK."

The following morning at 10:45 AM, Whitney called.

"We're not going to release that money—we've stopped payment."

"Payroll?" she responded, disbelieving. "You mean you're not going to release the payroll money?"

"Yes, that's right."

"I just can't believe it. Do you realize you're going back on your word of yesterday? You told me you'd release it."

"I know, but we've made up our minds that it's not safe."

An hour to go before payroll. My personal account was also at KBT. I rushed out to the local branch to get the funds we needed. They proceeded to issue a bank check.

"No, no," I said,. "I have to have cash."

"But we don't have that much cash on hand."

"Then you'll have to get it."

"Well, it will take time."

"Then call your branches and I'll go pick up the cash myself."

They made their calls and I did my rounds. Frazzled but victorious, I got back in time. Payroll proceeded on schedule. No checks were issued. Everybody got cash.

By the time we turned up at the U.S. Bankruptcy Court in Bridgeport to find out what would happen next, there wasn't much left to save, yet the relentless demand for further immediate payment persisted as the bank presented its case. Until the day of our court appearance, their demand had been for an initial return of $300,000. We'd planned for this and knew we could manage to pay it out of the considerable amount of money due in receivables. On the morning of the court hearing, however, the bank changed its demand. They wanted $500,000—considerably more than the whole of the receivables outstanding. There was no way we could do it without closing our doors.

More pleading and arguing, and finally a 'compromise.' Aside from the $300,000 that the bank had originally agreed to accept as an initial payment, we would have about $62,000 left in our business account. They wanted that, too. We'd have to pay off the balance of the debt by monthly install-ments over a limited period of time. If we didn't think we could live with that arrangement, we would have to file

'Chapter 7' and wait for the sheriff to put a padlock on our doors.

Judge Alan Shiff interrupted. Turning to the bank's attorney, he said: "Tell me, counselor, is it really your client's desire to put this small company out of business?"

As the bank's attorney hesitated, deciding how best to reply to that question, the judge called a recess. He gave us a half-hour to consider our position. We filed out with our bankruptcy attorney, Steven Burke. We piled into his Toronado, smoke from his cigar clouding our vision and our thinking.

Steven started right in: "Well, if you declare Chapter 7, they will have nothing. You'd put all the old inventory in a pile—the stuff that the bank has a lien on—and let them auction it off. Aside from the machinery, that's the only stuff they can claim and it's no use to you any more. They auction off the machinery, and then you start again. You'd just have to change your name slightly. It's possible, of course, that one of your competitors might learn of your filing and want to make a bid, but that's a risk you'd have to take."

The expression on Nárcissza's face was set. "And what if we accept their terms? What do we use for money to keep going?"

"Well, you have to decide whether your private resources, and whatever you might be able to borrow from somebody else, will be enough to see you through."

The half-hour passed. We were back in the courtroom, still undecided. Nárcissza, arms folded across her lap, expression unreadable, was sitting beside me. She was staring straight ahead as if in a trance.

"What do you want, Nárcissza," I asked. "Do you want to hang on, or shall we let it go, and hope we can pick up the pieces somehow?"

She didn't answer.

"Nárcissza, the judge has to know which way we want to go. We've got to decide."

"It's up to you," she said quietly.

Steven, now standing before Judge Shiff, turned to me, his face questioning.

I glanced again at Nárcissza and took her hand. I could feel her tension. It seemed to me that she was steeling herself for whatever my answer might be. I found myself reviewing the roller-coaster existence that had characterized our business lives together. I thought about the early years working with Acoustica and Parker Instruments and the Coulter Counter, when we were losing these agencies as fast as we were achieving any significant sales. I thought about our heady successes when we moved into our Danbury factory —the Space Telescope project, the Kodak Research Labs job, and the Western Electric and IBM contracts; the struggles during the lean times when we didn't know where the next orders would come from, nor how we would manage to meet payroll or pay the factory mortgage and the electric bill. Yes, we'd had a roller coaster ride all right, but coping with those triumphs and disasters was what business was all about. We had chosen it ourselves—it was what we had wanted to do, and it had been rewarding and fulfilling. Giving it all we had to give, and somehow holding it all together, had long been second nature to us. To change now—let it all go? Watch our creation taken apart systematically and distributed to the vultures? Could we do that?

Over the years, before the semiconductor industry recession had taken hold, we'd managed to accumulate close to three hundred thousand dollars in personal savings. I wrestled with the pros and cons of risking the whole of this resource on the chance that we'd somehow work our way out of the crisis. In the end I concluded that it would be more painful for both of us to see our beloved enterprise collapse than to gamble the money that might be the means of saving it.

I heard the judge's gavel, and looked up to see Steven gesturing. Time had run out. We had to answer.

"We'll go with the bank's terms," I said. "We'll stay in business."

◆

The judge ruled on a plan under which we would work our way out of bankruptcy by means of monthly payments to KBT, and we'd look elsewhere for the funds to make up for the loss in working capital we'd suffered. It was done.

Nárcissza, in charge of coping with the company's financial obligations, paid the monthly installments to the bank as they'd demanded. In a few months, our personal loans to the company had used up most of our resources except for our entitlements in the pension trust. Now, after payroll and essential expenses, there simply wasn't enough money available to make any kind of payment to the bank without jeopardizing work-in-progress. If we made another payment right now, we would simply not survive long enough to continue to make payments in the future. On the other hand, if we let things slip for a month or two, our chances of resuming regular payments might improve.

She pondered the matter. What could they do about it anyway? They'd already stripped us of all the funds we had in their account, and after that payroll debacle, Nárcissza had moved Interlab's account to another bank. It was absolutely necessary now, to preserve sufficient funds to finance existing orders—to carry on in business. She thought about the way the bank had broken its own promises to her a few months previously and she decided not to worry. If she couldn't pay, she couldn't pay.

Four months went by before Carl Whitney noticed. Then he called.

"Nárcissza, you haven't been paying."

"That's right, I haven't been paying. I simply don't have the money."

"But you've broken the agreement—you're in violation."

"That's right, Mr. Whitney," Nárcissza replied,. "I broke the agreement in the same way you broke yours. If you recall, it was an hour before payroll."

Mercifully, there were no repercussions. A few months later, the bank was taken over by another firm. Our debt was 'sold' to a collection agency, and eventually Nárcissza, exhibiting yet another example of her shrewd management abilities, negotiated a modest one-shot cash payment as complete settlement of the balance of our debt.

On April 25, 1995, some eight years after our brush with extinction, the court that had heard our original bankruptcy filing declared the case closed.

Through this period, we had somehow kept up with our ongoing sales efforts. Among these, three proposals, having a total potential value of $1,300,000, were under review by IBM in Fishkill, New York. These concerned projects headed by process engineer Ken Kilpatrick, and involved critical and highly specialized processing systems. If we were the successful bidder on the first, similar contracts would, in all probability, follow. Negotiations had reached the stage at which our chances appeared favorable, but a few days before the expected decision, the purchasing manager, Kimberly Caldwell, called to advise us that she'd learned of our financial difficulties and would like a report on them. The following day we submitted a full report to her, and awaited her response. A day or so later, the call came in:

"Please keep me advised of any changes in your financial condition. Here is the purchase order number . . ." That was all. Once again, IBM, aware of our plight, aware of what was at stake for us, had demonstrated their continued faith in our ability to serve them.

Bloodied but not broken, we embarked on the long slow road to recovery. The infusion into the business of all the money we'd been able to save over the years, was not enough to meet our working capital needs, but it gave us time to explore every likely source for additional funding to augment our investment. A number of banks and investment brokers showed interest on initial contact, but it seemed that upon closer examination of our circumstances, they concluded that our chances of recovery were not promising. At any rate, throughout our first year of bankruptcy and through part of the second, we were unsuccessful in obtaining additional funding, a fact that seriously limited our ability to go forward.

Casting about for alternative possibilities, we had on one or two occasions considered approaching Roger Robichaud and Bob Macklin of the Village Bank in Ridgefield, CT. Many years previously, when they were associated with the National Bank of Westchester, they had supported our efforts in countless ways, and had become our fast personal friends and advocates. But the Village Bank in Ridgefield was a small and very conservative institution, hardly likely to look on a small family business such as ours, as a desirable investment vehicle. Nevertheless, we'd kept in touch. In time, as he saw that we were hanging on and still winning valuable contracts from blue-chip companies, Bob Macklin took our case to his board. He was successful. The board eventually gave the matter their blessing. We'd get the help we so desperately needed.

At first the loans were tied to specific contracts that we'd negotiated with our customers. Then gradually this method was augmented by term loans and 'lines of credit.' The amounts were not so substantial that we were able to institute all of the recovery measures we would have liked, but they were large enough that we could now make progress. We could continue paying down our debt to our creditor bank and simultaneously make better headway with our recovery program.

Looking back over the years, names and faces crowded my mind as I recalled the occasions when good, sound-thinking people had put their faith in what we said we could do, rather than only on what we'd actually done. In IBM alone, the list seemed endless—Joe Disbrow and George Green and his associates, who'd given me their time and attention at that long ago conference, and had offered us the chance to show them what we could do to serve their needs; George Cheroff at the Research Labs who'd stunned me with his unshakeable conviction that our small enterprise could design and build what he required for his lab; the purchasing chief at Poughkeepsie, and the eminently fair and constructive way he'd dealt with our excessive dependence on IBM orders. And during the time of our most recent crisis, the IBMers at Fishkill Ken Kilpatrick and Kimberly Caldwell—who, by giving us their support when it was most needed, had provided the foundation on which others, in their turn, had given us theirs. They, and our good friend Bob Macklin at the Village Bank, had been key players in our eventual recovery. We had much to be grateful for.

◈

To make the most of all the help we'd had along the way, however, and to succeed in our long-term recovery plans, we'd have to learn from our disasters. We'd need to analyze the reasons for the predicament that had brought us so close to the point of no return, and we'd also have to work aggressively on ways to avoid a repetition of those same dire circumstances in the future. One evening, shortly after learning that we were finally clear of our Chapter Eleven status, we were in Nárcissza's office discussing marketing plans. Everyone else had left for the day, so we had the place to ourselves. Nárcissza was talking:

"The trouble is, we haven't even learned our first lessons. Way back in the beginning, thanks to IBM, we learned that every business needs a well diversified customer roster. We learned that no single customer should account for more than thirty percent of total sales, so we rushed out and got ourselves some more customers. Then a few years later we made the same mistake again with Western Electric—and came close to going out of business when that bonanza was over."

"Well at least we're more aware of the danger these days, and we do something about it sooner," I said. "Whenever we find the thirty-percent level is being exceeded, or even approached, we take serious note of the danger and work hard balancing it out with business from other sources. We concentrate on that. We don't let it slide. But the real answer is to work harder to develop our markets for standard products and reduce our dependence on custom stuff."

"I grant you—we're making a bit of progress in that direction. But now, through our Chapter Eleven catastrophe, we've got to learn another lesson—that we can't confine our efforts to just one market category either."

"I couldn't agree more," I responded, "but we're doing

something about that right now."

"It's not enough. What it amounts to is that we don't have the financial wherewithal to stay the course when the semi-conductor industry heads south. So we've got to concentrate on selling to alternative markets to the extent that, in the future, semiconductor equipment will never be the biggest part of our business."

"Well, we're doing that now. We've already begun exploring at least two new fields. First there's the Flat-Panel Display industry that's growing like wildfire these days. It's got its place in pretty well all the electronically operated screens you can think of. Secondly, we've had a good look at the p.c. board industry. There's a definite place for us in that area, too. There are plenty of sophisticated 'in line' convey-orized cleaning systems serving that market, and at the other end of the scale, plenty of small, low-capacity units, too, but there's room in the middle ground for us. You have to agree that our first design for that field has shown this to be the case. Our 'Intrax' cleaning unit seems to have got off to a pretty good start."

The discussion continued. Lessons learned from the past were examined and re-examined. We gradually hammered out a course to steer for the future. We already had the beginnings of an entree into the precision optics field, and we'd have to build on that, too. We'd also have to place more emphasis on developing a stronger portfolio of standard products to balance our heavy involvement with sophisticated, one-of-a-kind processing systems.

In the end, our course for the future was determined by a phone call that changed our lives—and introduced us to one of the most fascinating markets we'd encountered in the whole of our corporate history—the Ophthalmic Industry.

Eyeglass manufacturers in the USA were just beginning to get interested in anti-reflective coatings. European countries had long since embraced this technology, but because the ophthalmic markets and distribution methods in the USA were quite different from those in Europe, this feature had thus far made very slow progress in the American market. The eyeglass industry nevertheless conceded that anti-reflective coating would eventually grow to be as important in the US as in Europe, and here and there major players were deciding to take the plunge and promote its growth. If anti-reflective coating was coming to America anyway, they wanted to be among the first to offer it.

So it was that one fine day, Jim Chilcoat of the Coburn Company in Dallas, Texas, decided to give us a call. Jim explained that his company already offered an in-house anti-reflective coating service to retailers in the ophthalmic field, and now, as a new venture, they planned to offer complete coating facilities to eyeglass processing laboratories around the country. To this end, they were importing sophisticated vacuum coating systems from Europe, but they needed critical cleaning systems to prepare lens surfaces for their coatings. "Would you be interested in developing a cleaning system to meet our needs?" Jim had asked.

We would indeed.

Jim guided us through the maze of requirements that we had to take into account to produce a machine suitable for Coburn's application, and in meeting those needs we eventually fashioned a product that excelled in its class. Under the proprietary name of the 'Soniscan' cleaning system, it soon claimed its place as an industry leader and has maintained that position as the anti-reflective coating industry has steadily expanded. But more than this, the Soniscan technology has served as a standard design for use in other industries, too. Jim Chilcoat, upon seeing the final production version of this machine, and noting the ready accessibility of all its components, described it as "user friendly . . . and a maintenance man's dream."

Other companies, both domestic and European, began to notice that Interlab had developed a special niche in the optical and semi-conductor cleaning equipment markets. We began to get suitors. Larger organizations in the cleaning process field were asking about our intentions for the future. Were we planning to go it alone much longer, or might we be interested in becoming part of a larger group? From time to time, we'd explored the possibility and, in one or two instances, had got as far as talking price and terms. We were well aware of the advantages we could enjoy as part of a larger company. It would be a big relief to know there was a big brother in the offing to help out with the periodic cash-flow crunches, and have a world-wide marketing organization out there, giving our products the exposure they deserved. No question, it had its attractions.

But the closer we came to making any sort of merger deal, the more we realized that business is not just design and development, margins and marketing, production and profits. Business is people; people with egos and ambitions, personalities, sensitivities, different kinds of education and different quirks. Attractive as the prospects of financial support and wider market scope appeared, our chief concern with any merger that we might consider, was, we realized, in the human synergies that we could expect to find in the prospective marriage. We'd lose our freedom of action. We'd be responsible, not just to ourselves, but to others, too, for our business performance. And to be content with that situation, we'd need to know that those to whom we would report, would be people we could work with. People who thought as we thought and whose standards and expectations we could understand and view as reasonable. Yes, reasonable people—people like us.

Kerry Ultrasonics, Ltd. in England seemed to us to fall into that category. They were casting about for a means of getting a toehold in the American cleaning equipment market. I'd met their managing director, Gordon Littleford, a few years previously. Gordon, large, bluff, and proud of his man-of-the-people London brogue, had learned of us through Delta Sonics Inc., based in California, and had come over to see what we were all about. That was at the time we were operating out of our basement in Ossining, New York, and I'd been reluctant to let him see our tiny setup. I had arranged to meet him off the train at the Harmon-on-Hudson railroad station parking lot, and we'd conducted our business meeting in the back of our service van. It was an occasion that Gordon ribbed us about for years to come—and it was also the beginning of a fast friendship.

We kept in touch, making periodic visits to each other's factories, picking each other's brains, and bringing our wives to each other's homes. We'd watched each other's progress, Kerry joining the prestigious Halma Group, and Interlab moving out of its Ossining basement; first to the old, three-story post-office building in Pleasantville, New York, and then to our modern factory in Danbury. Aside from compatible business interests, the human synergies between our companies extended from our rapport with Gordon, through the Kerry staff, and on up to the board of the Halma Group, including their most gracious chairman.

With Halma's support, Gordon had the power to talk

about acquiring our little enterprise. We talked about price and terms; we made visits back and forth. But as we learned more about each other's objectives, the business synergies proved not quite as compelling as both parties had first hoped. We didn't make a deal, but we continued with our visits and our friendship. Gordon retired in the nineties. Interlab, the maverick, continued to go it alone.

During this period, pressure from the Environmental Protection Agency was forcing industry to employ water-based processes for their cleaning applications and avoid the use of hydrocarbon solvents. Since components rinsed in water rather than solvents are more difficult to dry, this trend in turn gave rise to increasing interest in more efficient drying methods. Our sales team reminded me of this and also mentioned that the patent on our existing drying system was about to expire. Wouldn't this be a good time to devise something better; something really good.

Their point was well taken. I put all else out of my mind and concentrated on the job of dreaming up a better dryer. Our 'MicroDry' product line resulted from that sharply focussed effort and I subsequently filed a series of applications and was granted patents protecting the new technology embodied in them. Their fast and efficient drying capabilities served to improve the overall performance of the cleaning systems in which we installed them, and in this way made an important contribution to our eventual recovery.

It is a heady time for us now. Customers, intrigued by the current advances in our technology, are beginning to ask what we have in mind for the future—what further enhancements do we have under wraps for the next generation of our product line. This is my favorite subject and I find it difficult not to talk about it. I counter with a promise that a document entitled. "Where shall we go tomorrow, and what shall we do?" is in course of preparation, and they will receive a copy just as soon as our patent attorney gives us his blessing.

TWENTY NINE

W e are in the clear now, flying as it were, straight and level. At long last, clear of the Chapter Eleven debacle, and with exciting new products and an enlightened business policy in place, our star is on the rise again.

It is November. Not any old November, but the occasion of Interlab's thirty-ninth anniversary—the third of the thirteen-year celebrations since our founding. We're at the Elks Lodge with all the Interlab people, past and present, and a number of vendors and customers who we've not seen in countless years. In this spacious hall, we're dancing to a varied sequence of rhythms. Sometimes old-fashioned waltzes, sometimes ballroom dances, and sometimes rock and roll. Everyone seems to be making the most of the occasion; eating, drinking, dancing and sharing memories of our ups and downs—those who've gone before, catching up with those who are with us today.

I make my way to the bar where a number of revelers have gathered. Tamás, Renate, Bill Fenton and Sandy are talking shop—don't they ever take a break? No, it's not shop, it's about Bill's clock. Besides being a very talented development engineer, Bill is an accomplished wood worker, and his grandfather clock which has been a conversation piece in his lab these last two or three years is from start to finish a product of his own labor. I immerse myself in the hubbub and the model-making talk which, with the arrival of Ken Krizan, has now turned to boats and airplanes. These assorted personalities, despite working side by side all through every working week, seem nonetheless glad to be in each other's company, engrossed with the subjects at hand.

In a while I turn again to watch the dancers. Patyi, forever youthful, is doing an elegant tango with Theresa. Married but two years, they move as if they'd grown up dancing together. It is a pleasure to watch them, Theresa with her nimble dancer's footwork, and Paul with his sweeping turns and that unique ankle twist that is his signature. If he had a sack over his head all the way to his knees, I would know him in a crowd of dancers for this feature alone. Perhaps this is the case with most of us, our dancing styles and techniques—like our fingerprints—are like no one else's.

I do my best to follow them with my eyes, but with another graceful sweep they are away again, out of sight. Now I see Tucsi with John Prittie dancing around to where I'm standing. Perhaps the tango is not John's favorite vehicle for demonstrating his dancing prowess, but he is doing well—very well in fact—and I'm sure that Tucsi, a former member of a Hungarian dance group, is bringing out the best of John's repertoire.

I catch Nárcissza's eye and signal my interest in joining the dancers. She indicates her readiness, but by the time I reach her side, it's over. No matter, after another number for the younger set, a waltz is announced, and soon Nárcissza and I are whirling to the strains of. "The Merry Widow." Suddenly my fleeting glance finds him through the haze and the light. There he is . . . over in the corner by the window. Tony is sitting atop that old stepladder. His brow is creased and a lock of his thick dark hair hangs over his left eye. He is holding a multi-meter in his left hand. His other arm is extended toward me and he is waving vigorously.

"Hiya, Howard . . . Hiya!" he calls.

I stop in the middle of the floor and nod my head in Tony's direction as I tell Nárcissza that Tony is here. "Yes, I know,. " she says with that mysterious smile of hers,. "he's been here all evening."

I turn in Tony's direction again and wave back vigorously. "Hiya, Tony."

He smiles that wide and wonderful smile. He seems content now that I've seen him, and soon, as the pitch of the music is at its height, he leaves us. We go back to our dancing. In gatherings of mixed age groups, waltzes are not among the most popular dances these days, so we have the floor almost to ourselves for this one, and we make the most of it. Longer strides, bolder turns, around and around, faster and faster until the room is a blur, and faces and jackets and dresses merge into a kaleidoscopic stream of color in which we are whirling as fast as we can.

Hold the scene in your mind. Revel with us in the dazzling patterns of light reflected from multi-colored mirrors and a myriad of sequined gowns. Delight in the graceful swirling of floor-length skirts. Linger with the music and the gaiety and the clinking of glasses. Hold it a moment longer as the camera, too, begins to take its leave, its lens zooming slowly back and away from us.

The music of the waltz diminishes and dies, and the screen fades slowly to black.

POSTSCRIPT

Our story continues of course, as most true stories do. We simply chose a time to look in on it, and a time to take our leave. The players are still there, about fifty of them, working toward the next thirteenth anniversary. Small children still play in the aisles from time to time, or sit at a table, working on jigsaw puzzles. And even today, in our engineering department, a baby lies serenely in her crib alongside her designer mother. Both are content.

Today, Mike Lee is Director of Engineering, and Bob Sendewicz is in charge of all of our production. Others have taken over my responsibilities in field sales work, so we've sold my beautiful airplane. But with a thousand hours in my logbook, that old craving to fly has been well satisfied, and I am content now, to spend more time on other things—like writing.

The members of what I have chosen to call. "The Thirteen Club"—the solid core of men and women who've served the company for thirteen years or more—are still there, continuing to protect and enhance our reputation for excellence. Others will no doubt join them in the years to come and will contribute to the success of our small enterprise as our present members have done. But that, of course, will be another story.

◉ "THE THIRTEEN CLUB" MEMBERS ◉

PERIOD OF EMPLOYMENT

	FROM	TO
GLEN DAGES	1980	
DONNA DOWNES	1981	
BILL FENTON	1974	
MATT GALLAGHER	1982	1996
LESLIE GEORGE (LAYTON)	1980	1997 *(deceased)*
KEN KRIZAN	1982	
HOWARD LAYTON	1958	
NÁRCISSZA LAYTON		
Part time	1961	1965
Full time	1965	
MIKE LEE	1980	
ERZSÉBET LUDÁNYI	1970	1984 *(retired)*
PAUL LUDÁNYI	1969	
TAMÁS LUDÁNYI	1965	
GYULA MOLNÁR	1972	
JOHN PRITTIE	1983	
BOB SENDEWICZ	1971	
MARIE SPAGNOLA	1971	1997 *(retired)*
BILL TICEHURST	1980	
EVA WESZELY	1967	1984

Order Form

FAX ORDERS: (203) 775-3723

TELEPHONE ORDERS. Call toll free: 1 (877) SPIRES 3
Have your Discover, Visa or MasterCard ready.
On-line orders: threespires@snet.net

POSTAL ORDERS:
THREE SPIRES PUBLISHING,
P.O. Box 5267, Brookfield, CT 06804 USA
Please send the following book(s):

*I understand that I may return any book for a full refund—
for any reason, no questions asked.*

NAME: _____

ADDRESS: _____

CITY   STATE   ZIP

TELEPHONE   STATE   ZIP

Sales Tax:: Please add 6% for books shipped to CT addresses.

SHIPPING:
$4 for the first book. $2 for each additional book.

Payment:: ❑ Check
Credit Card: ❑ Visa ❑ Master Card ❑ Discover
Card Number:_____
Name on card:_____
Exp. Date:_____/ _____

Call toll free to order